in the studio with **joyce piven**

Theatre Games, Story Theatre and Text Work for Actors

in the studio with **joyce piven**

Theatre Games, Story Theatre and Text Work for Actors

JOYCE PIVEN AND SUSAN APPLEBAUM

Methuen Drama

Methuen Drama

1 3 5 7 9 10 8 6 4 2

First published in 2012

Methuen Drama
Bloomsbury Publishing Plc
50 Bedford Square
London WC1B 3DP
www.bloomsbury.com

The authors have asserted their rights under the Copyright, Designs
and Patents Act, 1988, to be identified as the authors of this work

Available in the USA from Bloomsbury Academic & Professional,
175 Fifth Avenue/3rd Floor, New York, NY 10010.

A CIP catalogue record for this book is available from the British Library

ISBN: 978 1 408 17387 9

Typeset by Mark Heslington Ltd, Scarborough, North Yorkshire
Printed and bound in the UK by MPG Books Ltd, Bodmin, Cornwall

Contents

About the authors

Joyce Piven – actress, director, and master teacher

Co-founder with her husband Byrne Piven and Artistic Director Emeritus of The Piven Theatre Workshop, Joyce Piven was one of the founding members and leading actresses at Playwrights Theatre Club, the group led by Paul Sills that spawned Compass Players and Second City. With Playwrights Theatre, Joyce played leading roles in *Midsummer Night's Dream*, *The Seagull*, *Round Dance* and *Caucasian Chalk Circle*. Joyce met her husband, Byrne Piven, while at Playwrights Theatre where he directed her in the critically and financially successful play *The Dybbuk*. In New York, they both studied with Uta Hagen and Mira Rostova while acting professionally and teaching extensively. Returning to Chicago, she and Byrne helped Paul Sills form the Second City Repertory Company (with Bernie Sahlins and Joyce Sloane) and Sills' Story Theater Company. Highlights of her acting career include playing Lady Macbeth opposite her husband, Byrne, in a futuristic *Macbeth*, Bessie in Wisdom Bridge's production of *Awake and Sing*, and Lillian Hellman in *The Julia Project* directed by Shira Piven at New York's Greenwich Theatre. Most recently, she starred in an adaptation of Charles Dickens' *Great Expectations* at Piven Theatre and performed in the Lookinglass Theatre's *Hard Times*.

Joyce and Byrne Piven founded the Piven Theatre Workshop in the early seventies and served as co-artistic directors for thirty years until Byrne's death in 2002. Joyce was the founding director of the Workshop's famed Young People's Company. Today, Joyce spends most of her time directing and teaching in Evanston and Los Angeles. She has directed Lili Taylor in the revival of Maria Irene Fornes' *Mud* at Victory Gardens and the remounting of Sarah Ruhl's *Orlando* at the Actor's Gang in Los Angeles. At Piven Theatre, her directing highlights include: Rochelle Distelheim's *Sadie in Love*, Caryl Churchill's *Top Girls*, Sarah Ruhl's adaptation of *Orlando*, *Brilliant Traces* by Cindy Lou Johnson, *Speed-the-Plow* by David Mamet, *Collected Stories* by Donald Margulies, Sarah Ruhl's translation of Chekhov's *The Three Sisters* as well as an early production of Ruhl's *Eurydice*, and most recently *Two by Pinter*. Her literary story theatre productions include: *Chekhov: The Stories*, *The Emerging Woman*, *What Dreams May Come*, and *American Visions Through Jewish Eyes*. In LA, she recently directed *Suffragette Koan* by Linda Carson. With Emmy Award-winning son Jeremy and director/filmmaker daughter Shira, Joyce is dedicated to keeping the story theatre method and the Piven Theatre Workshop legacy alive and thriving.

Susan Applebaum, PhD – Adjunct Professor of Theatre at Loyola University Chicago and former adaptor/director/teacher at the Piven Theatre Workshop

Susan currently teaches dramatic literature and play analysis for the theatre division of the Department of Fine and Performing Arts at Loyola University Chicago. She has been on the faculty there in both full-time and adjunct capacities since 1975. Susan also has a longtime association with the Piven Theatre Workshop. Starting in the mid-seventies, Susan studied with Joyce Piven, taught classes for children and adults, and directed stories for the Young People's Company. From 1983 to 1985, Susan served as Director of the Junior Company where she developed the story theatre productions *Gaggle of Geese and then some ... , Wishes in the Wings,* and *Birds of a Feather.* In 1987, Joyce Piven went on sabbatical and Susan assumed her responsibilities for the Young People's Company, where she directed the story theatre production *Angels and Wizards.*

Shortly after that period, Susan left the Workshop to pursue doctoral studies in Northwestern University's interdisciplinary PhD program in theatre and drama. Her research on the theatrical representation of mentor mothers and female adolescent protagonists has been published in *Theatre History Studies,* the *Youth Theatre Journal,* and *Encyclopedia of Girlhood.* She has taught courses and seminars at Northwestern University, the University of Missouri–Kansas City, the University of Pittsburgh, and Loyola University Chicago.

Earlier in her career, Susan was a founding member and choreographer for Synthesis Theatre in Fleetwood, Pennsylvania, where she acted in Michael Weller's *Moonchildren* and Jean Giraudoux's *Amphitryon 38* and did choreography for *The Canterbury Tales.* Most recently, Susan understudied and stepped in as Anfisa in *The Three Sisters* at Piven Theatre.

Acknowledgments

The authors want to express their appreciation to all those who lent their voices, their expertise and their encouragement to us over the last ten years. Firstly, we are grateful to all the people at Methuen Drama for their individual contributions to this project. Our thanks go especially to Jenny Ridout, Publishing Editor in Performing Arts, who saw potential in our work and shepherded this book through the publication process. Thanks also to Charlotte Loveridge, Commissioning Editor at Methuen, for giving our manuscript to Jenny. Many thanks to Jen Green, Leslie Brown and Jen Sultz from the Piven Theatre Workshop for helping us access archival files and photos as well as lending their expertise and support throughout this process.

Secondly, we want to express our appreciation to all the colleagues, friends and relatives who took time out of their busy lives to read drafts of the evolving manuscript and give us feedback and support along the way. Thanks to Johanna Rosenbohm, our developmental editor, who played a significant role early on in shaping the work and encouraging us toward more and more descriptive detail for the reader unfamiliar with theatre games. And we owe a debt to early readers and supporters who helped us stay focused and on track – Mike Levine, Stephen Fedo, Cal Pritner, Evamarii Johnson, Nancy Cusack, Sheldon Patinkin, Lesley Delmenico, Michael Bassett, Joyce Gettleman, and Barbara Syverud. Thanks to Robin Hellman for her technical support. Later in the process, Joanne Underwood, Pam Cytrynbaum, and Jen Green lent their considerable insights into the Piven process to readings of the manuscript.

And finally, thanks to all those who lent their rich voices to the text itself – Byrne and Shira Piven, Joan Cusack, Jon Mozes, and Sarah Ruhl – and to all the many colleagues and students who share this language and experience with us and whose work is described in this book.

Each of us has had the love and support of our families through this joy-filled yet challenging writing process. Without them, this project would still be just a dream.

From Susan – I want to express my gratitude to my husband Terry, son Todd and daughter Anne and their families for believing in me and being there when I needed encouragement. I also want to thank Joyce for introducing me to this wonderful work so many years ago. It has enriched my life.

From Joyce – Byrne and my legacy is preserved through the many lives that have been influenced by our work. This book is yet another way to acknowledge this rich legacy. I wish to also acknowledge my writing partner, Susan Applebaum, who was there from the beginning. Without her untiring efforts and talent, this book would not have come into being. Thanks to my children, Shira and Jeremy, who carry the legacy in their presence and whose support and writings made it all possible. Lastly to Lili and Pearl Piven McKay and Adam McKay. I am grateful for their inspiration and patience.

For Byrne, whose vision keeps the work alive.
"But if the while I think on thee, dear friend,
All losses are restored and sorrows end."
(Shakespeare's Sonnet 30)

– Joyce Piven

Introduction

How to navigate this book

We are writing this book to share with you the process of actor training developed by Joyce and Byrne Piven at the Piven Theatre Workshop, the school and theatre they co-founded in the early seventies. In doing so, we hope to communicate the spirit of our creative process and the essence of the unique environment created, one which fostered a community of players with a shared language and a long-term commitment to this work. We do all of this with a healthy respect for the "mystery" at the heart of the theatrical experience. An organic process can never be totally formalized. If all could be communicated in a book, there would be no need for the living experience of the work itself. All we can do here is to offer you a resource for your own exploration into theatrical creativity and presence in performance.

This book is co-authored. It is the product of a collaborative effort over many years. The project began as a series of interviews and conversations, but over time it evolved into a blending of our two voices. The dominant voice belongs to Joyce Piven because this book is an articulation of the method she and her husband Byrne developed at their Workshop. To preserve that spirit, we have chosen to write the body of this book in the first-person singular voice. Our hope is that you will come to understand the basic principles of this work through a sense of participation in the process, that you will feel as though you are "in the room" with a master teacher.

In Part 1, we offer you an overview of the principles that guide the work, the goal we pursue to bring a text to life in performance, and how we use story theatre techniques as a bridge between the games and the performance of play texts. By starting with the thinking that drives the work, we hope to give you the tools to understand why Joyce is making the choices she does as she teaches or coaches in the workshops that comprise Part 2.

In the second section of the book, we focus on the practical application of the concepts and techniques introduced in Part 1. For each principle, we describe in detail two distinct workshops, one training the body and developing community and the other exploring language and sound. The workshops are written in the first-person voice to emphasize that this is the way Joyce is teaching in that moment for a particular group and with a particular point of concentration. Our approach is not meant to be prescriptive. We are not saying that you must do it this way and this way only! Instead, we show you one way to approach each game and the class plan as a whole. We want you to be aware that there are a myriad of ways to teach the same thing and we provide a host of games for you in the alphabetical appendix to that end. By offering these sample workshops, our intention is to give you insight into how the process works and what you might expect to get back from the group during the playing. As you understand why a call is made or what kind of energy is being built by the progression of games chosen, you can apply that knowledge to your own individual style of teaching, using whatever games or exercises serve your purpose. We firmly believe in the old saying "If you know where you are going, there are many ways to get there."

Because this book is meant to serve as a guide and a resource for actors and students of acting, for teachers, for directors – for anyone interested in the creative process of acting, you can approach reading it from many different perspectives and starting points. No matter what you are looking for, however, we recommend that you read Chapter 1, "Introduction to the Central Principles of Game Work," and Chapter 2, "The Goal – Finding the Encounter," before moving on to different chapters.

After grounding yourself in the concepts that guide our work, you might explore the book based on your personal needs. If you are an experienced teacher of game work looking for some new ideas, you might look at the Appendix first. Once you've found a game you like, you might go to the chapter that uses that game in the context of a class. The more detailed and contextual description of how the game is played and what the players do when prompted by calls will give you some insights into the game itself.

If you want to get a sense of curriculum, you might follow the progress of the workshops in Part 2 to see how you first introduce game language and then move into ever more complex and advanced work, from object work into transformation. If you are interested in building ensembles, you might focus on the "Agreement" workshops. If you are curious about story theatre as a teaching technique, we recommend looking at the class based on Round-Robin Storytelling that explores the Greek myth "Arachne" and then turn to the Fairy-Tale Moments exercise. If you are interested primarily in actor coaching through game calls, see the "Encounter" chapter and "The Doings" in the "Specificity" chapter. Take from our work whatever helps you find your own creative voice as an actor or teacher or director. Nothing can replace the sense of empowerment found in making something your own. And, once you do, you become a member of the Piven Theatre Workshop family with a shared language and experience.

Maybe one of the members of that unique community of players that is the Piven Theatre Workshop can speak for all of us. In 2007, Joyce Piven received an award from the Chicago chapter of "Women in Film." Her former student Joan Cusack, now a well-known film actress, gave the introductory speech at the award ceremony in the Ritz-Carlton Hotel in Chicago. Here is some of what she said:

What I learned from Joyce, besides how much I love brisket with Lipton's onion soup mix on it, is the creative process and how you can't be self-conscious if you are playing and participating creatively. Seems like a small thing but it's huge.

Theater games that we learned growing up [that came out of Joyce and Byrne's time at the University of Chicago and their work with Paul Sills and Viola Spolin] are games of transformation, change, working together in unison – all games where participation was based on instinct, spontaneity, and getting out of your head.

There is, as I have come to understand it, another component of the games. You cannot be self-conscious but you must be self-aware. It is the development of your own unique voice in the context of community that solidifies the creative process. That is, you learn not only to be aware of yourself, but at the same time about humanizing and sensitizing yourself to those around you. Fascinatingly, the idea of mirroring one another (one of the games the Pivens have been doing for years, and one which we did over and over and over again), I have learned recently from Merly Lipton at the Rush Neuro-Behavioral Center, is being used for therapeutic purposes to help children with autism learn empathy. This is the work of the Piven Theatre Workshop – empathy!

For me, as a shy kid, these games were so freeing. I was not allowed to be self-conscious when I was playing them and so a burden was lifted and I could be free. And Joyce, I am forever grateful for that. I truly believe I would not be where I am today, with the opportunities I have had, without having had Joyce as my teacher and role model. At the same time, I do sincerely believe it is luck that has given me a chance to work in this field. I know there are so many talented people out there, but when the opportunity struck, I believe it was the Workshop that gave me the tools to take advantage of it. I had developed a creative process and it was my own voice. I had something empowering when I went in to audition. And, well, maybe it helped a little, that when I was trying out for *Working Girl*, it just so happened that Joyce had gone out with Mike Nichols, oh so many years ago … but she married the right guy. And I can't think of Joyce without thinking of Byrne and the Workshop they founded together. In fact, they were the B-OYCE of their generation … at least in Evanston.

I was talking to Joyce the other night at the opening of my brother's film, *Grace Is Gone*, in which Joyce helped work with two of the children that star and give amazing performances. In that story, she was saying that when she talked to Viola Spolin, the creator of the games, Viola said she was in a state of grace when she made them up. Well, I believe Joyce is a state of grace. And we are so fortunate to have her in Chicago.

Obviously, the list of women in film and theater that have come out of the Workshop – Shira Piven, Hope Davis, Sarah Ruhl, Kate Walsh, Lili Taylor, Ann Cusack (and some of the guys – Golden Globe winner Jeremy Piven, Paul Adelstein, Jeff Garlin, Harry Lennix, Aidan Quinn, Eric Simonson plus John Cusack, and many more) are testament to her and the Workshop's influence.

But I believe it is Joyce's real legacy that the Workshop is not about the stars it creates. The children that go to the Workshop are not celebrated as vehicles for stardom or vehicles for their parents' ambition, but they are there to develop their own voice as an end in itself. They are celebrated as individuals to be nurtured and freed. This is the true work of the Workshop.*

---

* Used with permission from Joan Cusack.

Prologue: Values and Influences

Byrne and I developed our passion for the theatre in a post-World War II climate ripe for experimentation. The people we met and the theatre we did at the University of Chicago and in New York in the late forties, fifties and sixties shaped our aesthetic. We are greatly indebted to Viola Spolin and Paul Sills for their work in theatre games and story theatre as the jumping-off point for our own practice. We also drew inspiration from the work of Uta Hagen, Etienne Decroux and Mira Rostova, teaching artists we studied with while in New York. Our approach to acting brings together all these various strains – theatre games, story theatre, mime and the Stanislavski Method.

But from the very beginning, it was the idea of community that guided and shaped the Workshop. In the aesthetic we would develop, in the teaching and mentoring that would be part of it, in the theatre toward which we would be evolving – community would inform and be a part of everything. It would infuse all that we did in creating the theatre we envisioned. We instinctively knew that we wanted to form a safe environment where one could feel secure enough to fail and venture into the territory of exploration, what Byrne referred to always as "explore and heighten." In this environment, one could embrace the "chaos of the unknown." Instead of taking control and "thinking" or manipulating the moment, we

Joyce and Byrne Piven: Founders of the Piven Theatre Workshop

would accept it and rely on intuition to lead the way. No easy task, especially when everyone is watching! So we worked to create a place where one could make mistakes, explore and be supported by the group. Community was our vision and our aesthetic.

Group energy is mysterious. In any game, the sum of the parts is greater than the whole. We worked toward connecting with a theatre audience as the outer community when the time was right – when we had something meaningful to share. Our point of concentration was to find through exploration the myriad ways to create – through game, through story, through text, through presence, through individual and group energy – a living, breathing theatrical performance.

Byrne and I met Paul Sills at the University of Chicago in the late fifties. This was a time of great synergy created by the coming together of post-World War II optimism, the G.I. Bill, and the Hutchins Plan. This fabulous educational experiment in enrollment by examination and study of the Great Books (original texts) was the creation of the University's new chancellor, Robert Maynard Hutchins. It drew young intellectuals, future writers and philosophers, and smart, talented potential theatre artists from all over the country: people like Mike Nichols, Elaine May, Ed Asner, Zohra Lampert, Barbara Harris, Sheldon Patinkin, Susan Sontag and others. Many of these people would work with Paul Sills to set down the roots of improvisational theatre in Chicago through the Compass Players and, later, the Second City Theatre.

Under Paul's direction, we did a groundbreaking production of Jean Cocteau's *The Typewriter* at the Reynolds Club for the University Theatre. It was directed "in-the-round," a revolutionary form at that time, and starred Mike Nichols, who played twins, and Paul, who directed and played the detective. I played the murderer, the forty-year-old Solange. Sheldon Patinkin ran the lights. It was a critical success in the Chicago press. From here Paul and David Shepherd and many of the budding theatre artists mentioned before began the famed Playwrights Theatre Club. We opened with Bertolt Brecht's *The Caucasian Chalk Circle*. It took Chicago by storm and quickly, through the efforts of Bernie Sahlins (later the heir and producer of Second City), Playwrights became a professional Equity theatre. Byrne joined this production and ended up joining the company. It was during our production of *Wozzeck*, with Ed Asner in the title role, when Byrne was helping me apply my old-woman's make-up that we met and fell in love.

Byrne and I spent the next two years in classic repertory doing Shakespeare, Chekhov, O'Casey, Sartre, T. S. Eliot, and Brecht. The Playwrights Theatre Club was new and original in several ways. First of all, it was a "club," a not-for-profit subscription theatre, possibly the first of its kind in Chicago. Secondly, it was an ensemble theatre being schooled in theatre games. It was Paul who introduced us to theatre games. He had his mother, Viola Spolin, conduct workshops with us on Saturdays. She first came when we were rehearsing Chekhov's *The Seagull*. No one in the ensemble had formal theatre training except for Byrne, but that didn't stop us from believing we were all brilliant and adventurous and daring. We were imbued with the optimism of those years. We believed we could do anything.

Those early experiences with the Playwrights Theatre Club played an important role in what Byrne and I eventually wanted the Workshop to be. The sense of empowerment, a place welcoming to talented outsiders, and a technique based on impulse and presence were all things we took from those years and unconsciously or consciously tried to dupli-cate at the Workshop.

In 1954, Byrne and I migrated to New York, where we spent ten years acting, teaching, learning our craft, and starting a family. We studied with Uta Hagen for six of those years and with Mira Rostova, who had been trained by Stanislavski himself. I have returned to Uta's work often to tap into her brilliant use of specificity and personalization. One of Byrne's great talents was the ability to extract a principle from a body of work so that, in doing the games or text work, it was the principle rather than the activity that we preserved. Consequently, many games could be invented and could be applied to script work. In this way, what we learned from Uta Hagen and Mira Rostova became an integral part of our own practice.

We also came to the work with a great love of literature and language. Paul Sills' experi-ments in story theatre deeply influenced our own. Inspired by his work in Germany while on a Fulbright Scholarship, Paul developed the idea for Story Theater. It was a Brechtian idea – no fourth wall, actors in open admission that they were actors transforming into roles, no time or energy spent on illusion, a little bit of lights, a little music – a new theatrical form was born. Paul's Story Theater opened in the summer of 1968 in Chicago. I was a member of this early group.

"The Blue Light" was one of the first stories we did. It is a Grimm fairy tale about an old soldier sent by an evil king into a dark forest where he encounters a witch. I played the witch. I'll never forget the first rehearsal for that story. Paul said, "Okay, read the story." And we sat there and we read it silently and then we looked at him and he said, "Well, just get up and do it, just do it, just *do* it." That was his only direction. I used to kid him about it. Anyway, we were able to do it. With just the direction "Do it, do the story, just do the story," we somehow told the story. We didn't use the text but somebody had a guitar and some-how Paul was able to convey to us how to engender the ambience of the forest, which was a very pure thing.

Byrne and I have spent our entire adult life articulating the process of transformation and improvisation in creating literary story theatre. Byrne's story theatre differed from other people's interpretations of this form at the time in that his placement of narrator put the story in the hands of the individual actor who would narrate his own character into scene. In this way, transformation from actor to character and scene was in open admission, with-out any illusion that character and actor were the same. For Byrne, the actor was the guide for the audience and they could see the wheels in motion with no pretense. What people often don't understand is that the transformation requires as much, if not more art, than is needed to create and play a role. You still rely on great specificity and a fluid emotional instrument. And that's the excitement of story theatre – that discovery in the moment!

Building on Paul's concept, Byrne was more willing to reveal and exercise the emotional instrument in realizing the transformation into scene. The literary story theatre that we do came from the year that Byrne and I spent evolving a number of Chekhov short stories. The first adult show we produced at the Workshop was a collection of stories called *Chekhov: Some Family Portraits*.

My path to fully embracing theatre games came from a frustration with the Method that I began to experience while we were in New York. I had exhausted my teaching or my teaching had exhausted me. I needed a new vision, a way to create a new partnership with those I taught. We both were seeking to have a give-and-take, if you will, where a creative dialogue with our students could bring energy back to us, where a creative motor could be established.

Shortly before we began the Workshop, we moved to Evanston, Illinois with our two young children so Byrne could teach at Northwestern University. During this time, I had a transformative experience as a student of the games. I took a course with Mel Spiegel, a devotee of Viola Spolin. One day, as we were leaving, we played a game – musical chairs, a simple child's game – and I was exhilarated. I experienced play. And once you experience play, then you know, "*Oh, everything I was doing before, it wasn't right because I wasn't there. I wasn't involved. I wasn't creating. I wasn't … my cheeks weren't burning!*"

After this discovery, I began teaching the games in my classes at the Evanston Art Center and we settled down in Evanston to raise our family. Although we always had one foot in the door, ready to return to New York or wherever the work was, the children kept us grounded. After four years, when my students were twelve or thirteen, I honestly didn't know what to do next with them. My solution was to take them out performing. Byrne and I began to take these highly trained young people to venues like the public library and the Amazingrace Coffeehouse to perform stories – folklore and myth. Our experience teaching those early classes and arranging performances turned into a desire to create a workshop for theatre training.

In addition to teaching children and adults at the Evanston Art Center, Byrne and I produced and performed in Harold Pinter's *Landscape* on the lawn with live musical accompaniment. Through these activities, we created a model for the future Workshop: classes for children and teens, ages nine through eighteen; classes for adults; a teen acting company of highly trained and talented young people; and a professional adult theatre – all engaged with our unique combination of theatre games and story theatre performance.

From the very beginning, we made choices that distinguished our work from other programs for young people at that time. The first was our practice of developing our story theatre pieces in collaboration with the company. This communication of trust, belief in and support of the young people we teach shapes the mentoring practices of the Workshop. We try to give young people an opportunity to discover their own particular talents – their own creative voice, whether that voice gravitates toward music, directing, designing, or acting. This kind of collaboration also establishes a communal as opposed to hierarchical atmosphere.

Our second important choice was to consistently combine high-quality literary works with Greek myth, fairy tales and folklore in our programming. We respect beautifully crafted language and believe that concern for language raises the bar on the typical theatre practices for young audiences. Consequently, the adults in the audience as well as the children can enjoy our performances. Early newspaper critics consistently noted the quality of the material, the discipline and naturalness of our young performers and the direct connection to the audience. These qualities set our work apart.

And so the Workshop evolved slowly and organically. We simply let it unfold. In the early seventies we established the Piven Theatre Workshop and moved into the Noyes Cultural Arts Center where we continue to teach and direct plays today. Our goal was to treat theatrical performance as an art form that was beautiful, astonishing, and unexplored.

And that brings me to the importance and prominence of the principles of our work. We rely on them so that greater flexibility and possibilities can be explored in improvisation and scene. And we can hold the principle to the game, sharply and meticulously, no matter what the variation might be. Giving priority to the principles is the core of our work because in opening up possibilities we are able to generate motors of creativity.

Now in 2012, reflecting on this forty-year journey, coming out at the other end and seeing where we were, it's dawned on me in the last ten years that we have fulfilled our vision of creating an artistic community in which young people especially can find a way to express their individual creative voices with the support of others. In a way, Byrne and I have come full circle. We rejected Stanislavski theatre for game work while still drawing on the Method. In the last ten years of his life, I would say, Byrne moved even more actively toward making that translation – finding Method principles and exercises and translating them into games. But, in the end, I think that the work itself, the process, always holds the promise of that moment when our "cheeks are burning," that moment when we feel most alive and connected to others. That is the process we hope to articulate for you in this book.

PART 1:
The Principles of Game Work, the Encounter, and Story Theatre

The creation of something new is not accomplished by the intellect but by the play instinct acting from inner necessity. The creative mind plays with objects it loves.

– Carl Jung

1 Introduction to the Central Principles of Game Work

Improvisation and theatre games are at the core of what we teach at the Piven Theatre Workshop. Our goal for both the player and the actor is to be present and creative in the moment onstage before an audience – to be in a "state of play."

Theatre games are the structures through which we play. Like all types of game, from children's games to sports games, theatre games are based on a set of rules with an objective. Theatre games include running games, tag games, word games, movement games, dance games, story games, verbal games, ensemble-building games. Through this structuring of creative play, we build a supportive environment in which the player can take risks. Byrne captured that critical element of game work, the type of risk-taking that fosters "play" and "creativity," when he wrote:

> A "behind the back" pass in basketball; a "quick kick" in pro football (not done anymore); a "squeeze play" or "pick up throw" to third base in baseball: all of these are designed to catch the opposing team "off balance," to force the players to improvise a response, to make a creative new movement – a new pattern, in fact, from an unaccustomed position. In theatre games, we are constantly trying to set up situations that catch the players "off balance."
>
> This breaking of programmed patterns, we have come to call "creativity." It calls upon the whole being. The experience and stored energy of the past mobilize in the service of the unexpected moment. Something wondrous can emerge. So wondrous, in fact, that others begin to emulate it, to incorporate it into existing patterns and thus, new patterns of

response are generated which must, in turn, yield to the next unexpected moment, the next "off balance" explosion of creativity.

That's why our work is so carefully balanced between freedom and discipline. There must be a viable, organic pattern already in existence for the unexpected response to change, to transform. It is a process of fitting the individual's unique and unexpected response into existing patterns that then become "something rich and strange" (From Ariel's speech in Shakespeare's *The Tempest*).

The structure of theatre games sets up the conditions for the "off-balance" moment, the moment that embraces all those elusive aspects of play – impulse, spontaneity, danger, and risk.

We have identified the underlying principles of improvisation and acting as: Focus on the other person and the task at hand; Play (Impulse and Spontaneity); Agreement; Specificity; and Transformation. In a note to the Workshop faculty in the 1990s, Byrne Piven stressed the importance of the underlying principles to his vision for the Workshop. His objective was "that the games taught, the sequences followed and the language used always be in accord with the principles of the work, that the process to which we have devoted our working lives is being realized." He went on to explain why:

> And it is because we ourselves are in constant reappraisal and, one hopes, constant creative evolvement. We are in constant search for better ways of opening, focusing, breaking through. Better sequences, calls, new games even, to realize the process of freeing the player.

The games we describe in this book are only one way to achieve this freedom. But we believe that, with an understanding of the relationship between the principles and the games, you can find your own path.

"A focus on the other person and the task at hand" is the foundational principle of game work. Viola Spolin first articulated this principle in the sixties through her groundbreaking book *Improvisation for the Theatre*,[1] and it remains the single most important element to master in improvisation and game work.

---

[1] Spolin, Viola, *Improvisation for the Theatre*. Evanston: Northwestern University Press, 1963. Used with permission from Northwestern University Press.

This principle does not sit on the top of a hierarchy but rather forms the core of a circle. It is the necessary first step for realizing all the other principles – play, agreement, specificity, and transformation. Since all the principles have a role in every game, the same game may be used in relation to the other games to provide a point of concentration for a given class. The principles are separate in our discussion only for the purposes of analysis and explanation. In practice, there are no boundaries – all the principles are interdependent.

In our work, play, agreement, specificity, and transformation provide the means for discovering, exploring, and realizing the "encounter" at the heart of a drama, scene, or story. We use the term "encounter" to explain the visceral, emotional experience we seek to bring to life on the stage. The following diagram provides a graphic interpretation of all the principles we discuss and their relationship to one another.

Foundational Principles

PLAY

AGREEMENT   **FOCUS ON THE OTHER & THE TASK**   **SPECIFICITY**

TRANSFORMATION

The foundational principle

The necessary first step toward achieving play lies in the foundational principle of all game work: "A focus on the other person and the task at hand." Most teachers of acting apply this concept in one form or another in their training methods, going all the way back to Stanislavski's use of objectives. Shira Piven talks about the importance of the foundational principle to her work:

> No matter what I am teaching or directing, I always go back to the basic, basic goal and principle, Spolin and Paul Sills' Principle: helping the actor get "out of the head" by focusing on the task and the other person. For

me it's the impulse found in the Hassidic story that goes – if you had to explain the teachings of the Torah standing on one foot, what would it be? And the answer is: "Do unto others as you would do unto yourself."

Like the Hassidic story, if you had to explain the essence of all game work, the answer would be: Focus on the other person and the game. If you can do that, you can get anyone to be present. And then there are all kinds of subtleties to explore.

That's why the highly physical work is great because you just get people into their bodies and working together. It almost doesn't matter what the game is – give someone a game to get them out of that self-conscious ego state. Think about this – the classic children's bad acting is putting a child onstage and having them try to recite their lines correctly. In their heads, they're thinking, Am I doing this right? Am I getting the lines right? As opposed to putting a child onstage and giving them some activity to do or some game or some task to perform and suddenly, they're just being "themselves."

I feel a great reverence for those basic, basic theatre games and principles. If you – in your gut – can learn that basic idea of point of concentration – of how to get out of your head by focusing on the task and the other person, if you know that, then everything else comes from that, like a ripple effect – it radiates out from that. And if you don't get that, you don't get any of it. That principle is at the heart of everything.

In this quote Shira articulates why we have chosen to place this principle at the center of all the other principles. Because whatever the game, that "off-balance" moment, that moment of creativity, that moment of play, cannot happen unless the players are focused outside themselves on the other and the task at hand.

The principle of play

Play informs all the work we do at the Piven Theatre Workshop. "Play" – being present and creative in the moment onstage before an audience – is what we seek. Learning the first principle opens the door to the second.

The word *play* is difficult to manage because it means so many different things in different situations. We play games, we perform plays, we play around.

Someone asks, "What are you playing at?" to find out what your agenda might be. Someone says, "Stop playing around," implying a lack of seriousness. At the Workshop, when you are "in play" we mean you are present in the moment – not thinking about the past or worrying about the future, but fully conscious and focused in the here and now.

To be as specific as I can, in our work *play* refers to:

◆ Experiencing and working "on impulse" with the other players.

◆ Exploring and heightening – words, emotions, characters, situations, ideas.

◆ Finding that creative motor that is capable of endless invention.

◆ Reacting spontaneously – freely and without planning. A reaction that surprises actors and players equally.

◆ Taking risks – the enactment of danger.

◆ Embracing the "anxiety of not knowing," the "off-balance moment," as the source of creativity.

Generally, we all think of play as a lively, free-spirited activity necessary for the health and well-being of the child – a time for fantasy, role-playing, make-believe, and fun. Most of all, it's a time for exploration. A time, too, for perfecting motor skills: running, jumping, skipping, sports, baseball, and so forth. Somehow we're not so sure about the necessity of fun or play for the adult. Play is quickly segregated to sports or physical activity. In school, fun and games are for recess – phased out by the fourth or fifth grade – or as a reward for serious work. Rarely is playing made an integral or organic part of learning.

And yet, we acknowledge the role of play in the artist's so-called "work." (Is he having a good time or what?). The result of the artist's "play" is that we look at the world in a whole new way. For example, Picasso brought all our so-called linear perceptions together simultaneously in one canvas – cubism was born challenging our very definition of reality. Stanislavski coined that powerful "magic if" of imagination. Matisse, in the last phase of his life, wanted only to simplify – to get back to the child's vision, uncluttered, pure, simple. So he pared down everything – threw out the paint and the brushes, leaving himself only scissors and colored construction paper – and he cut out a crude figure of a man, bottom-heavy, and called it "The Myth of Icarus." Matisse thereby captured the human condition of Man, reaching toward the sky (God) while rooted to the earth. Playing allows us to reach beyond ourselves and art illuminates this condition.[2]

But playing is suspect – considered frivolous and an enemy to the serious work at hand. I remember a recent experience where a visual artist told me: "I do not play when I paint. I treat my painting very seriously." Still, the artist generally is acknowledged as one who keeps and preserves that childlike sense of play and wonder and this sets him apart from the rest. But isn't it true that others in society look askance at him, often for that very reason. What is he doing, playing? Having fun when we have to work so hard at the everyday drudgery of running the world?

Through theatre games and improvisation, we are creating a supportive environment in which a person can risk. It is hard to imagine real growth without an exploration that allows for risk. And so, to the artist who says, "I do not play when I paint. I take my painting seriously," I say, "We take our playing very seriously. When we play, we are very serious. We are making connections and maybe even, with the help of the Muse (wonder of wonders), who knows, even art."

The principle of agreement

Agreement is not only an important element of play and improvisation but it is also a central tenet in the unique actor–audience relationship of story theatre and a fundamental aspect of ensemble building. Webster's Dictionary defines *agreement* as "being of one mind, in harmony and united in common purpose." That is an apt definition for this principle. In the game context, when we say that a group is "in agreement," we mean that the players are working together, giving and taking from one another and from the surrounding space in order to play a game, improvise a scene, find a transformation, tell a communal story. For example, when a group is moving in slow motion, they are in agreement only if all are moving at the same speed with the same quality of movement. To do this, each member of the group must be focused on all the others, mirroring the movements and speed that they see and kinesthetically in sync with the actions of those around them.

---

[2] Discussion based on lecture notes from Henry Rago, professor of humanities at the University of Chicago and former editor of *Poetry Magazine*.

Agreement functions similarly in scene work. The players must be in agreement on all of the given circumstances of the imaginary world they are creating. For example, both improvisational scenes and story theatre involve the use of imaginary objects. When creating imaginary objects in a scene, the players must agree on the size, shape, weight, texture, and temperature of the object and maintain that agreement throughout the scene. If one or more players begin to lose their awareness of what the others are doing, the "reality" of the scene will be lost. If an imaginary sofa carried by a group suddenly gets longer and longer or begins to droop as two players let their hands drop and the other two are still holding their hands steady, that group is not in agreement. Remember that, in order for true play and spontaneity to occur, the players must focus on the other and on the task at hand. The task in this case would be maintaining the integrity of the imaginary objects through agreement as to size and shape and weight. In the other aspects of a scene, the players need to build on elements introduced into the space rather than deny something is true. If a player says, "Gee, it's getting hot in here," his fellow player can contribute to the scene by agreeing and building on that reality instead of countering with a denial.

The requirement to be true to the imaginary object or to other elements brought into the scene forces each player to be constantly engaged – seeing, listening, sensing – to what all the others are doing. If the players achieve that state of agreement, if they fulfill that task, they will be present and alive, reacting moment-to-moment, open to creative possibilities. If the players are focused on themselves, they will become self-conscious, they will be in their head, playwriting or trying to be clever. These types of obligations distance players from others and, ultimately, impede their ability to play, to be spontaneous.

The principle of agreement also holds a central role in the concept of ensemble and community that serves as the foundation for our approach to play, transformation, and specificity. Students learn the principles of acting and creating as part of a group of players, an ensemble. An ensemble depends on the support and trust of each of its members. That environment establishes the conditions for the type of risk-taking so necessary to the creative process. It is through ensemble work, playing with others, that the player/actor can enter the "off-balance moment" and get in touch with their intuition. Through group play, the individual can shed the sense of obligation to be "clever," to be solely responsible for making the moment work. By giving and taking from one another, the players become a whole that is greater than its parts, yet each player's unique contribution is an important part of that whole.

Agreement is a principle that operates within the games but it is also central to the actor-audience relationship of story theatre. The audience and the actors participate together in the creation of a story through the connection of direct address, the creation and acceptance of imaginary objects and spaces, and through the process of transformation. Theatre itself becomes a communal dialogue, a sharing.

And finally, the principle of agreement – working as an individual voice within community – sets the conditions for the mentoring process so critical to all the work we do. The acting ensemble and the artistic community provide a safety net, onstage and in life, as each individual player discovers and develops their unique talents and artistic voice.

The principle of agreement is about the accumulation of energy. It is almost as though the players are interacting not only with one another but also with some larger energy that fuels them. It is a spooky thought, but I really believe this. A mystical achievement of cumulative energy comes from the group interaction – from group agreement.

The discipline of agreement and play is such that it requires a point of concentration on the principle itself. The task of the teacher is to guide the students always back to play. They will wander. We will wander until that magical moment where we witness something entirely new, un-thought of, and, in effect, something we couldn't think up – *ever*.

The principle of specificity

Specificity refers to a number of different aspects of the work. On its most basic level, *specificity* means bringing to life on the stage the defining characteristics of fundamental dramatic elements: objects, environments, people, relationships, and emotional experiences. The five senses – seeing, hearing, smelling, tasting, and touching – play a significant role in achieving specificity.

Some people are born with the gift of being in touch with their world through their senses; others have to explore and develop that ability. One aspect of talent has to do with this natural ability. The artist who paints doesn't begin painting when he picks up the brush, he paints when he opens his eyes. He sees things that those of us who don't paint don't see – he sees the world in a different way. Similarly, the gifted actor makes contact with her environment in a different way; she calls on her highly developed sensory apparatus to bring her imaginary world to life on the stage.

Sense memory is based on our ability to observe our environment and the behavior of other people. When Marlon Brando was in New York studying, he would sit at a coffee shop for hours looking out the window, watching various people on the street and making up stories about them. Perfect training for the actor. Even a gifted actor like Brando must hone his skills. We train through observation.

As an actor, you do a lot of standing on the stage, looking out over the audience and imagining by drawing on sense memory. Byrne's and my experiences with both Uta Hagen and Viola Spolin gave us tools for exploring sense memory. Uta Hagen used real objects to work on this skill. For example, she would have students carry a real suitcase and make it appear heavy. But, as this example indicates, even if you use real objects, you must endow them with detail. You are not going to have real gold or silver on the set or real Tiffany glasses, etc. In film, actors often work with very real and very detailed objects. The task for them becomes how to endow the object with the reality of what it's supposed to be in the context of the world being created. And more and more, technology requires film actors to work against a blue screen and imagine whole environments and characters. So the exploration of objects through sense memory and the imagination gives actors the ability to endow objects and environments with specific properties. If we close our eyes, we can try to imagine what ice cream tastes like on our tongue – the temperature, texture, what it does to the whole face in remembering – and going for the further specificity – is it lemon and therefore sour? Or, my favorite, CHOCOLATE – mmmmm!

Sense memory moves us toward specificity. If we stay in the general, the moment means less to us and to the audience. We haven't worked hard enough to imagine our imagined world. The process is demanding. We have to reach into our imagination, our senses, our ability to recall. So much of acting requires that of us because we are creating a world through our imagination.

Object specificity – our work trains young actors to make very specific choices when exploring imaginary objects and environments regarding the qualities of weight, shape, texture, function, and emotional investment. As students mature, the habit of specificity plays an important role in the more complex aspects of character and scene. We believe that learning how to explore an imaginary object is even more demanding than using real objects – because if you can endow the space when there's nothing there, think of how richly you can endow a real object.

Character specificity – as Uta Hagen taught – refers to finding the character's specificity that relates to your own specificity. Making a connection with specific and equivalent sights, smells, sounds, people, images, and emotional experiences locates you in the character and the character in you. But this specificity has to work for you; it has to be personal and meaningful to you.

Relational specificity – the behavior of the actor will cue the audience into the specific nature of a character's relationship to another character. We deal differently with our mother than with a stranger. And we deal differently with our mother from moment to moment. Right now in a particular scene, we might be angry with her or we might relate to her as our best friend with the same comfort and intimacy of that relationship. The actor must always go beyond the general to find the specificity of behavior appropriate to any given moment in a scene or play.

Specificity in story theatre – it is critical for the storyteller to exercise the discipline of detail. The storyteller must be specific in order to enrich the descriptive moment and stimulate the audience's imagination. Contrast these two approaches to narrating the entrance of a character in a story:

1. An elegant lady walked into the room.

2. A tall, statuesque woman wearing ivory lace at her wrists and fur around her delicate neck glided into the elegant drawing room.

In story theatre, the second description gives the teller everything she needs to embody this woman and make the transformation from player to character. At the same time, it stimulates the audience's imagination so they can enter into the moment in collaboration with the storyteller.

Specificity is integral to transformation, a key element in all of our work. It is also "the jumper cable" of the Doings. ("The Doings" refers to the melody of rela-tionships. While not a principle, they play an important role in our work. We discuss "The Doings" in more detail in the chapter on "Specificity.")

All these aspects of specificity provide the link that connects our approach to the-atre games and story theatre with aspects of the Method as taught by Uta Hagen, Mira Rostova of the Moscow Art Theatre, and Stanislavski himself. Sense memory, specificity, the discipline of detail, and the Doings inform and deepen all the other principles — play, agreement, and transformation.

The principle of transformation

Transformation is an essential element of all great theatre and is therefore one of the key principles of our work. Transformation means some kind of change — a change in the physical, vocal, emotional, or spatial dynamics or in the imaginary circumstances.

Sometimes the changes are sudden; sometimes they are gradual. For exam-ple, a player might transform physically from slow to fast or from heavy movement to light, vocally from soft to loud, spatially from high to low, or emotionally from crying to laughter (a very common Chekhovian shift). An imaginary circumstance might transform from a forest to a castle, from a dream to reality. Players discover these changes in the off-balance moments within a game or scene. In story thea-tre, players must transform from the real world to the imaginative world of the story and then continue to transform from storyteller to character and back to the storyteller, from locale to locale, from character to character, as the telling progresses. In a play, the actor draws the audience into the imaginary circum-stances in a different way, but a transformation into character and scene must take place nonetheless.

The principle of transformation and the principle of play function together. Organic transformations are discovered during the process of playing. We are sep-arating transformation from play and the other principles here only to emphasize its centrality to our work.

Transformation goes to the heart of the nature of theatre. In exercising transfor-mation, the actor has to submit to the "chaos of not knowing," a very scary place to be because it asks the actor to be vulnerable. It is very difficult to remain vulnerable while performing with a group of other people. In fact, being vulnerable is never an easy thing to do, onstage or off. But over and over and over, the player must be encouraged to take a chance, to submit to the moment of not knowing, the moment of "what the hell am I doing here? I don't know what comes next." The moment of not knowing is the crucial moment; it is the moment when the instinctual part of the brain steps in and makes a choice for us. It is the moment of creativity, the moment of surprise. We are not planning what will happen, we are not "in our head," playwriting, controlling. We have submitted to the unknown and are open to the possibilities. Here is where true creativity resides. Sometimes we can fool people and get away with it, but ultimately there's no "fooling" in art. That's the essence of keeping our point of concentration on transformation – *the moment of change!*

There are born actors who are open to this state of being because of their DNA. Robin Williams is one performer who can achieve this state. He is a one-man band of transformation. For the rest of us, it takes work and play and discipline – the discipline of not taking over and being clever or showing off. I once saw a documentary on Orson Welles. He was backstage putting on his make-up and preparing himself for the role of Macbeth. It was thrilling to see a consummate actor talk about the character, put on his make-up as he was talking and getting into costume, and slowly transforming into Macbeth. It was seamless. It was Welles who started – the actor talking – and it ended with the "man who would be king," eventually, at any cost!

Such a transformation is much like the transformation required by story theatre. In story theatre, we, the audience, are meant to be in the hands of the actor/story-teller. The actor is the guide able to transform into the moment and into character. This process is the essence of story theatre, but the irony is that the actor has to do the same thing in a play. Ultimately, the best exercise for the actor is the transformation necessary to accomplish story theatre.

Critical to the achievement of transformation is the concept of focus on the other person or task – a focus driven by need, motivation, want, objective, and point of concentration, whether in a scene or in a game structure. If players are focused on taking from the other and building on what they see and hear and experience, the energy for transformation is generated – a motor if you will, that allows each one to emerge as a unique contributor to the whole.

At many other points in this book, we describe the process of transformation in games like Circle-Object Transformations and Mirror Scene Transformations. That's the gorgeous part of our work. If two people focus on the task at hand and are not each driving the car alone and are not in their heads, but are taking inspiration from the other person, then the accumulation of energy between these two people takes on a character all its own. You've surrendered to the other and you are both going on a journey together. In the back and forth, there is a fusion – you are unified in the transformation.

Once you are in contact with that energy, that *motor*, you can go on transforming and creating forever, stopped only by exhaustion or the physical need for food and drink. You might exhaust yourself, but never the work, once you are in touch with that motor. For the teacher, the point of concentration is on getting that motor going, helping the players consent to be on a journey of transforming together.

All aspects of our work – character, object, activity, location, sound – are springboards to change. The fundamental requirements for making a transformation bear repeating: one must be in the space, connected to the other players, connected to the audience, and open to creative possibilities. You cannot force a transformation. It cannot be mechanical. It is something that occurs right before our eyes, an unexpected event.

These principles – a focus on the other person and the task at hand, play, agreement, specificity, and transformation – are the means for freeing the player/actor to be improvisational, present, and creative in the moment while playing before an audience. These five principles provide the fundamental points of concentration for us in our teaching and directing. They are where we are going – they provide the path to freeing the player to his or her potential. This is our work.

2 The Goal: Finding the Encounter

The concept of "encounter" refers to the emotional experience or "encounter" at the heart of a set of given circumstances. Finding the encounter is the overarching goal of our work. The encounter of a moment in a story, in a scene, or in an entire text is a combination of the deepest theatrical metaphor of human experience contained in the given circumstances and the personal, emotional investment given to it by the actor, ensemble, or director. The encounter has "to draw blood" in some way; otherwise you are just giving a representation of a scene or story – something that may be good but is not really alive. "Encounter" is the best term I have found to express a process that gets one to think and create on the deepest level.

Finding the encounter is a dynamic process involving play, active exploration, experimentation, and trial and error. The objective is to discover the most visceral expression of the encounter, the one that breathes life into the key moments of the text on the stage.

Whether you are working as an actor, a director, or a scene coach, finding the encounter of each moment is a journey of exploration that leads you deeper and deeper into a text. Finding the encounter is a way of opening a door. In rehearsal, game work becomes the means for finding the encounter. **But it is important to note that you must find the emotional experience through the game, not substitute the game for the emotional experience at the core of the moment.**

All moments or "beats," to use a term associated with Stanislavski, are not equal. In rehearsal, it is important to focus on key moments and to work on these moments with tremendous focus until the core emotional experience is realized to the best of the actor's ability. To realize the encounter of the whole story or play, it is critical to give such moments their due. Glossing over them often makes the story or scene pedestrian. And, conversely, when key moments are fully realized, the rest of the piece falls into place because the actors have come to understand their underlying emotional journey – the central encounter of the entire text.

Finding the encounter with analysis of the Greek myth "Persephone"

In order to explain how to find the encounter, I offer a series of questions meant to guide the actor, director, or teacher progressively deeper into the text. For this example, I will be citing a key moment from the Greek myth "Persephone," the moment the goddess/mother Demeter realizes that her daughter Persephone is missing and its aftermath.

"Persephone" is a myth about how the seasons came to be. In the story, the god Hades kidnaps Persephone from a field where she is playing with her mother. Hades takes her to the Underworld where he makes her his queen. Demeter finds Persephone in the Underworld and bargains with Zeus for her life. But Persephone has eaten the food of the Underworld, five pomegranate seeds, so Zeus must craft a compromise between the demands of Hades and those of Demeter. He rules that Persephone can spend five months of the year with Hades (winter) and seven months with Demeter (spring).

The most basic question to ask of any moment or beat is one that addresses the literal circumstances – *What is literally happening in this moment?* So, what is happening in this key moment in "Persephone"? The goddess Demeter and her daughter Persephone are playing hide-and-seek in a meadow. Suddenly Demeter realizes that her daughter isn't playing anymore, but appears to be missing. Demeter is compelled by her love and attachment to find Persephone. At this moment, Demeter does not know that the king of the Underworld has kidnapped Persephone; she knows only that Persephone is nowhere to be found. The encounter on the literal level is "a missing child."

At this point, it is important to inquire into the human essence of the moment by addressing the universal human emotion at its core. *What is the emotion common to us all in this particular experience – the core emotional experience of this moment for the parent?* This component of the encounter deals in the extremes of emotion – terror/fear, profound grief/sadness, joy, hatred, jealousy, despair – because it is here that we can get in touch with the visceral. For Demeter, this moment is one of panic and intense desperation. Almost everyone can relate to the feeling of panic at the sudden disappearance of a child, a loved one, or even a cherished, irreplaceable possession.

Another way to think about and articulate the encounter at this level is to ask the question this way: *What is the metaphor that embodies this emotional experience in these particular circumstances?* In this instance, our task is to express the metaphor in evocative words that will stimulate the imagination and provoke an active response to the emotion of desperation. For this example, I chose the metaphor STORMING THE UNIVERSE. This metaphor vividly expresses how the goddess-parent Demeter responds to the literal circumstance of her missing child given her emotional state of desperation. As a goddess, everything Demeter does will be larger than life; she will take on the other gods, she will leave no stone unturned – no city, no house, no person, no danger, no element of nature will escape her wrath. She will descend into hell and *demand* her child back from Hades and not leave without her child even if Zeus commands it.

The best choice of metaphor is one that provokes a visceral response in the actor. The choice of active verbs as a way to stimulate the actor has its roots in Stanislavski's method but the metaphoric concept, as I've conceived it here, remains more open to many possibilities and stays fluid during the exploration and rehearsal process in order to stay vigilant and keep the moment alive.

In searching for encounter through the literal circumstances, core emotional experience, and metaphor, we tap into our understanding of human behavior – one human to another. But to bring the encounter to life on the stage, we need to explore the specifics that inform or give life to the circumstances, the core emotional experience, and the metaphor. Here I again draw on Stanislavski and Uta Hagen by addressing the given circumstances of the situation. I explore place, atmosphere, time of day, weather, relationship of mother to daughter, identity, and so on. Finding the specific expression of these elements in the Persephone story will give life to the moment by supplying a contrast between the initial perfect harmony (their mother–daughter relationship as expressed in the game in the meadow) and the breaking of this vessel into chaos (the kidnapping of Persephone).

In developing the myth of "Persephone" for performance by the Young People's

Company, I directed the actress playing Demeter to "storm the universe" by looking everywhere for her daughter as if on a rampage, harshly confronting people she saw about things that looked like possessions belonging to Persephone. In one short improvised scene, the actress playing Demeter grabbed the arm of a young girl shopping with her mother and demanded to know where she got a particular belt. In another, Demeter made all the crops wither and die. In rehearsal, the actors found many different actions that Demeter could take in her desperate search for any sign, any clue to where her daughter might be. The most specific and expressive were chosen for the performance. Finding these specificities is connected to the use of game as a tool of exploration.

Theatre games and calls provide the means for finding the encounter and bringing it to life. All the questions asked so far are only preparation for the active exploration of the moment in rehearsal. This preparation helps the director determine, initially at least, what games will aid the players in bringing the encounter to life. To continue our example from "Persephone", *What games would help the players find the most effective moments of action to express the metaphor "storming the universe"? What game exploration would express the anarchy, the chaos of this loss and this desperate search?* Scene Tag was the first game that came to mind. It seemed particularly suited to the encounter identified in my preparation.

Basically, Scene Tag is a tag game where two players improvise a short scene or beat *on impulse* at the moment of tagging. In this circumstance, the actress playing Demeter is always "It" and she would pursue the other players in particular places called by the director – town to town, mountaintop to valley, etc. The moment of scene explores the different people Demeter encounters and her verbal and physical exchange with them. Playing Scene Tag using slow motion/ double time provides one way for us to find those moments of specificity through improvisation. (In rehearsal for this piece, the "Where did you get that belt?" moment mentioned earlier was found through Scene Tag and became part of the final performance.)

In the same way, Scene Transformation, To Gets, and Constructs were played to find improvisational moments or structures to fulfill the encounter. For example, Adjective Constructs (a mime game where players design the space with their bodies and respond to adjectives through movement and sound) was played to explore the *withering* fields, *parched* crops, and *earthly devastation* wrought by a distraught and desperate goddess-mother. The task for both the actors and the director is to explore through circumstances, poetry, observation, and empathy what will express the encounter of this wrenching loss. The game Adjective Constructs provided a means for showing the impact of Demeter's emotional state upon the world.

You can get some idea of how the games were integrated into the final performance of "Persephone" by looking at the working script that follows. The games are indicated in italics. The story is done in constant transformation between scene and third-person narrative, between the chorus creating moments and ambience and the main characters taking stage.

Greek myth: "Persephone"
Script adapted and directed by Joyce Piven
YPC 1987 Spring Story Theatre Festival: "Medicine for Melancholy"

Opening Game: Streets and Alleys, with the actresses playing Demeter and Persephone running in and out of the streets and alleys created by the chorus in a game of Hide and Seek.

Chorus

Once there were two goddesses that reigned over
The earth and held nature in an eternal balance
Between Spring and Summer.

Demeter

Demeter, the mother – warm and golden as ripened corn.

Persephone

Persephone, the daughter – cool and pale as the Spring.

Demeter

More like friends

Persephone

Like sisters

Demeter

Than mother and child.

Persephone

They played together: (*ball toss*)

Demeter

They worked together.

(Improvised scene: Demeter teaching Persephone how to plant and Persephone asking questions like a young child)
And Demeter taught Persephone everything she knew
About nature and the earth.
(Improv, changing constructs as Demeter lists – hoeing, sowing seed, etc.)

Chorus

And they were happy, in a harmony that was fluid, perfect.
(Chorus begins to circle them in a Greek folk dance, adding people as they exit with Demeter and Persephone last to leave the stage. On the following line, everyone is offstage except for Demeter and Persephone who give the line directly to the audience.)

Demeter and Persephone

Perfection! *(They exit.)*
(Male Chorus members re-enter, one at a time, on the following lines.)

Chorus

Now one day, something happened to change all this.
It happened one day in a secluded cove where
A wood surrounds a pool
And the green leaves keep off sunlight
And the ground is cool
And the ground is moist with lovely flowers growing
And the season is always spring.
(The following dialogue is spoken in counterpoint – give and take – between the characters and the chorus members)

Persephone	**/Chorus**
And into this wonderful cove	And it happened that
Persephone came running	Hades and his magnificent
With a basket of flowers	chariot was passing
Cupid	**/Chorus**
When up sprang Cupid who drew	
from his arrows the sharpest shaft of all	And struck Hades in his heart!
Persephone	**/Chorus**
Here it is! A whole field of purple	Hades, not killed, smitten instead
Narcissus. And as she reached *(freeze)*	with love

Persephone

And as she reached for the purple

Narcissus . . . "I win! I win!"

(Chorus member grabs Persephone's hand and a chaotic scramble ensues)

Hades

And suddenly the whole earth opened up

Chorus

(Each line shouted by player running to edge of stage)

And a golden fiery chariot

Drawn by four black horses

Lifted Persephone

And everyone – horses, chariot, Persephone –

All vanished!!

Demeter *(from offstage/laughing)*

Persephone, where are you? I know you're there.

Come out. Stop teasing. Persephone?

(Game: Cat's Corner. Two people exchange places per line)

(scurrying exchange)

Birds rose, startled

From their nests

Animals

Ran for cover

Flowers

Rolled from the abandoned basket.

(Now Persephone and Hades group re-enter and go into counterpoint with Demeter.)

Hades group

Down into the earth the chariot sped

Through dark caverns and underground tunnels.

Persephone

Who are you? Where are you taking me?

Take me back to my mother. Take me back.

Mother!!

Demeter *(slow motion)*

Where are you? Persephone?

Persephone

Moth--er!

Hades group (*In scene transformation*)

And the chariot flew over the river Styx where

Charon the boatman was ferrying ghostly souls

Across the water (*realize scene in action*)

Till they came to the gates of Hell (*realize*) where Cerberus

The three-headed dog guards (*realize*) the gate so that

No live mortals may enter and no souls of the

Dead escape. *Nobody escapes from the Underworld.*

Demeter

Where are you? Persephoneeeeeeeee ...

Persephone

Mother!!

(*Slow motion*) And the beautiful Persephone who loved the sunshine

Became Hades' queen and sat on a cold throne in

His cold palace.

Hades

And Hades gave her his gold crown and bright

Jewels but her heart was like ice and

Persephone

She neither talked nor ate nor drank.

Demeter

At last Demeter realized that Persephone was really gone. Her fury
turned to stone and, disguised as an old woman, she descended
Mount Olympus and came down to earth to look for her daughter.
(*Transformation to Market Place – sellers of carpets, fruit, vegetables,
jewelry, fish.*

*The following dialogue is spoken contrapuntally between Demeter and
members of the ensemble.*)

Chorus

She wandered the world in search of Persephone but no one
recognized her as a goddess now.

Demeter

Have you seen my daughter?

S1

No, lady, we've seen no one. Fresh fruit – the finest in Greece!

Demeter

Red hair like the sun?

S2

Carpets: Bocar, Persian – finest weave in the land.

Chorus

Men treated her as a beggar woman, well or ill.

Demeter

Blue eyes?

S3

No, lady. No, I don't think so.

Demeter

Pale, as beautiful Spring. This piece of ribbon, where did you find it?

S4

Try the next town.

Demeter

This locket – it's one I gave Persephone.

S5

Velvets, silk all colors.

S6

Trinkets for sale! Lace! Earrings for sale!

Demeter

This belt of pearls!!

Chorus

Once even, by a well, she thought she saw Persephone.
(*Scene*)

Demeter

Persephone!!

Woman

No, her name is Cressid and she is my daughter.
Leave her alone. We never heard of your daughter.

Demeter (*threatening*)

Where did you get this belt?

Girl

Ow! You're hurting me!

Demeter

Tell me or I'll turn you into a lizard.

Woman

Leave her alone ... I'll tell you ... I didn't see her being
Taken away but a farmer saw it all.
A chariot carried her off. The earth just
Swallowed her up. Ow! You're breaking my arm!
It was Hades!

Chorus

Struck to the core, Demeter's fury began to

Demeter

Rise. She cursed the land.

(Quick constructs)

Chorus

What is the light and green to me now?

Demeter

Breaking the ploughs that turned
The earth.

Chorus

Dark to me is the earth

Demeter

And killing the cattle and men in anger.

Chorus

Dark to me are the heavens

Demeter

Making the fields wither, blighting seed and crop.

Chorus

Where is she that I loved?
(drum roll) The child with the blue agate eyes?

Demeter

May the earth be in perpetual darkness until
Persephone is returned to me. No distance is too
Great for me to stride. I will storm the universe!

(Quick portraits)

Chorus

She went to Poseidon, the Sea God.

To the Messenger of the Heavens, Hermes.

To Hephaestus, the smith god, who plundered the earth for metals.

But in sky and earth, no one had seen Persephone (*drums*).

Demeter

She stormed the heavens and the Universe until she came to Zeus himself.

(*Transformation into palace – quiet marble space*)

Zeus

Yes, I saw Hades steal Persephone. Scream as she might

He snatched her from the earth and took her down into the

Underworld. She rules there as his Queen.

Demeter

Then the earth will never bear fruit again. No spring or

Summer or life again. Eternal winter.

Zeus

Wait. Let's continue talking. Summon Hades.

(*Hades construct*)

(*Hades on one side of stage; Demeter on the other*)

Contain your grief, Demeter. If Persephone has not

Eaten the food of the dead, you, Hades, must restore her

To her mother.

Hades

And so Hades led Demeter to his kingdom – across the

River Styx, rowed by Charon, the ferryman. Through the

Gate guarded by Cerberus and there sat …

Persephone

Persephone.

Demeter

Persephone! Your hands are as cold as ice.

You're coming with me! Quickly … let's go.

Hades

Wait! Not so fast. Has any food in the Underworld passed

Persephone's lips?

(*Silence*)

Demeter

No answer. Now, Hades, I shall take my daughter.

(*Grabs Persephone's hand and starts to leave*)

Child (*Blocking their way*)

I did. I saw Queen Persephone

Eat some pomegranate seeds. She thought she was

Alone in the orchard and she reached for a pomegranate,

Hungrily, greedily and ate the juice and seeds and all.

I saw her.

Hades

Here (*Holding up the pomegranate*), one side is open.

Five seeds are gone. (*Holds it for all to see*)

(*The Hades group and Child – construct people – hold on to one of Persephone's hands. Then in the following, slowly, others come to pull the weight through Demeter's hand, which holds Persephone, building to a tug-of-war with Persephone being pulled both ways. The pull goes in favor of Hades when Demeter lets go and drops to her knees, calling upon Zeus.*)

Demeter

Oh, Zeus … this is my child. Without her, there is no

Light, no blossom, no spring … only desolation in the

Streets and in the fields.

Zeus

But she has eaten the food of the dead. Justice is

Justice.

Demeter

Five little seeds. Five.

Zeus

Five.

Demeter

Five.

Give her to me for five days, five weeks, five months, five years

But give her back to me.

Zeus

Five months.

Demeter
Five months!

Zeus
Five months of the year will she be with Hades and seven with you.

Chorus
And so it came to be that for seven months of every year
Persephone lives with her mother.
And so the earth began to bloom
And a skin of grass crept over the
Bare soil.
Plants grew, budded, burst into
Flowers
Crops sprang up in the fields
And the world was beautiful
And flourishing again.

(Transform to a mother telling her small child the story)

Demeter/Mother
And so Persephone returns to her mother and the earth
Comes to life in spring and summer. And every fall
When Demeter is left alone, she weeps and it is winter.
And when Persephone is with her
She laughs all summer long.

(The End)

The "Persephone" example comes from my story theatre work with teenagers in the Young People's Company. However, the process of finding the encounter through game exploration and the Doings is equally effective in work with traditional play texts. Here are three examples culled from my adult acting classes and professional productions: Shakespeare's *Richard III*, Chekhov's *Three Sisters*, and Ruhl's *Dead Man's Cell Phone*.

Scenes: *Richard III, Three Sisters, Dead Man's Cell Phone*

Shakespeare's Richard III [3]

In *Richard III* (Act IV, Scene 4), the scene between Queen Elizabeth and King Richard best illustrates the confluence of metaphor, game, and the Doings. First, what are the literal circumstances? What happens in this scene? Richard is suggesting that the Queen speak for him in proposing marriage for her daughter.

Second, what is the core emotional experience we can relate to from the Queen's perspective? Great fear and desperation – a royal mother/lioness protecting her cub from the danger presented by her King. Not unlike Demeter's dilemma, Elizabeth is fighting Richard for the life of her daughter. The Queen will do anything it takes to save her. She replies to Richard,

> And must she die for this? O, let her live,
> And I'll corrupt her manners, stain her beauty,
> Slander myself as false to Edward's bed,
> Throw over her the veil of infamy.
> So she may live unscarred of bleeding slaughter,
> I will confess she was not Edward's daughter. (4.4.206–211)

Elizabeth will do all this rather than give her daughter to Richard in marriage. The stakes are that high. And she does this because Richard has killed her daughter's uncle Clarence, her uncle Rivers and her brothers. And in this scene Richard is asking Elizabeth to woo her daughter for him. To paraphrase Elizabeth's response: "You want me, the mother, to communicate to my daughter that the 'murderer' wants her to marry him. The murderer of her brothers!" Could anything be more grotesque? More outrageous?

The encounter metaphor operating here is "bargaining for a life." Richard entreats Elizabeth: "Say that I did all this for love of her" (4.4.288). But Elizabeth counters: "Nay, then indeed she cannot choose but hate thee,/Having brought love such a bloody spoil" (4.4.289–290). Elizabeth will not collaborate with evil. She will not sell her daughter to Richard for any price. So the core is bargaining for

---

[3] Siemon, James R., editor, William Shakespeare's *King Richard III*. London: Arden Shakespeare, 2009.

the daughter's life (the one price the Queen cannot pay). The obstacle for Richard and why the Queen is scoring points is THE FACTS, THE OUTRAGEOUS FACTS.

Richard raises the stakes by offering to make Elizabeth's daughter queen of England: "Bound with triumphant garlands will I come/And lead thy daughter to a conqueror's bed;/To whom I will retail my conquest won,/And she will be sole victoress, Caesar's Caesar" (4.4.333–336).

Elizabeth retorts:

> What were I best to say? Her father's brother
> Would be her lord? Or shall I say her uncle?
> Or he that slew her brothers and her uncles?
> Under what title shall I woo for thee,
> That God, the law, my honour and her love
> Can make seem pleasing to her tender years? (4.4.337–342)

Elizabeth volleys well with Richard. She does this by giving back the outrageous facts of Richard's bloody actions. Elizabeth's most powerful arguments involve the "admit," the "lament," and the "admit to the lament" of the Doings. (For a fuller explanation of "The Doings," see chapter on specificity.) In the following exchange, each time Elizabeth responds, she does so with an "admit" or an "admit to the irony of the facts," as in her last line.

Elizabeth
Shall I be tempted of the devil thus?
Richard
Ay, if the devil tempt you to do good.
Elizabeth
Shall I forget myself to be myself?
Richard
Ay, if your self's remembrance wrong yourself.
Elizabeth
Yet thou didst kill my children. (4.4.418–422)

Elizabeth is gaining strength and in this final exchange shows her mettle.

Richard

> But in your daughter's womb I bury them,
> Where, in that nest of spicery, they will breed
> Selves of themselves, to your recomforture.

Elizabeth

> Shall I go win my daughter to thy will?

Richard

> And be a happy mother by the deed.

Elizabeth

> I go, write to me very shortly,
> And you shall understand me from her mind. (4.4.423–429)

And though Richard says as she goes: "Relenting fool, and shallow changing woman!" (4.4.431), we know that she will find a way to save her daughter (as indeed she does).

In all of these quoted examples, the Doings of the lines confirm over and over that Elizabeth is simply reading Richard's deed back to him and thereby stating the logic of the facts: "But thou didst kill my children." "Shall I forget myself to be myself?" The Doings convey the specificity of the communication.

Armed with this evidence, we can formulate a preliminary metaphor – bargaining for the life of her child. To begin to explore the metaphor, we need to identify high-stakes games that will allow us to capture that feeling of intensity required by the scene. The game makes the scene present and alive and raises the stakes because we, the audience, do not know who is going to win.

The Daring Proposal game is a particularly effective choice for this kind of high-stakes exploration. In this game, one player makes a daring proposal or proposition to another player, one who is sorely tempted but afraid to accept. The proposal in this game can take many forms; for example, to fire someone, to hire someone, to try to relocate someone who clearly must be relocated but is unwilling unless totally reassured. Any one of these proposals can be played at a nine or ten level of intensity to match the intensity and high stakes that Elizabeth and Richard are playing. The game Make a Deal, if played for high stakes, would also work. Any game that has to do with high-stakes bargaining would be a good choice for this exploration.

While the actors played The Daring Proposal game, I was reminded of a quote from W. B. Yeats' poem "The Second Coming": "Mere anarchy is loosed upon the world/The blood dimmed tide is loosed/And everywhere the ceremony of innocence is drowned." That for me became another metaphor applicable to this scene: the drowning of the "ceremony of innocence." Richard represents "mere anarchy loosed upon the world" and, if Elizabeth stands passionate and secure, we the audience know she will maintain the order that needs to be restored.

As the director or actor coach, finding that balance between giving and taking with the actors in rehearsal is critical to the work. I am always asking, "How much can I help the players make a transformation?" The goal is to play and to integrate the play with the meaning of the encounter. That's the trick! The whole process of what we do relies on impulse. Living theatre – going for the live, spontaneous creative moment.

Chekhov's Three Sisters [4]

Here is an example of scene work from an advanced acting class using calls to bring the players into play and closer to the underlying encounter. The actresses are working on the opening scene of act III in Olga and Irina's bedroom. Quotes are from Sarah Ruhl's English version of Chekhov's Three Sisters. The act begins at 2 a.m.; a fire is raging in the neighborhood. The sirens are ringing; no one has gone to bed. In this scene, Olga, the eldest of the three Prozorov sisters, is collecting clothing for all the people who have found refuge in the house. The servant Anfisa, a nanny who has been with the family for a long time, has fallen asleep in a chair. The portion I'll be discussing is between Olga and her sister-in-law Natasha.

The challenge in directing Three Sisters is how to unearth the passion behind a certain acceptance that appears on the surface. The central encounter of the play exists in the "do or die" struggle against a dying regime. So much is at stake and so much is lost at every turn and the characters are not fully aware of this. How do you find the encounter in a slowly eroding, insidious time span? For our purposes and, of course, for Chekhov as the master of subtext, it is important to go beneath the surface to find the visceral encounter. And yet, it is more tangible and visible than it first appears.

The "fire scene" between Olga and Natasha in the attic-bedroom is Chekhov's

---

[4] Ruhl, Sarah, Chekhov's Three Sisters. Unpublished manuscript, 2009. Reprinted here with permission from Sarah Ruhl.

metaphor for the destruction of the old life. How this gets played out is for us to find. The scene begins with Olga and Anfisa, the old nanny, sorting clothes to give to fire victims. Natasha enters and the struggle (hardly articulated or expressed directly) between Natasha and Olga takes place. It smolders like the fire, ready to burst into flame and devour everything in its path. And yet, in true Chekhovian fashion, we often do not even smell the smoke. And yet it is all there, ready to be realized.

Shortly after Natasha enters, she kicks the nanny out of the room for "sitting around" disrespectfully in her presence. Upset by Natasha's treatment of Anfisa, Olga says, "Excuse me, I do not understand *you* –" Natasha cuts her off, saying: "She has no purpose at all here … Useless people have no place in the home" (55).

Olga is hurt and offended to the core but powerless in the name of gentility and sensitivity to take a firm stand in the matter. Although Olga is strong and used to being in control in her work as a headmistress, she has respect for her brother's wife. Olga needs to take a stand and claim the attic for herself, but she doesn't have the words to confront. She has been raised in an aristocracy that will not, cannot, traffic with petty fighting or petty and crude expressions of emotion. Direct confrontation is not an option. Instead, denial and philosophical acceptance is the mode. For the Chekhovian hero, good taste, appearances (think of the wrong color worn by Natasha earlier in the play) count for everything. The thing that interferes with finding the visceral is what I call the "cover-up," the ways in which the characters mask their passions.

Natasha escalates the fight by manipulating the conversation to Olga's future as headmistress, a future Olga rejects at this point. Olga tries to explain in terms of her sensibility: "Even the smallest blunder, a word said without gentleness, makes my stomach churn" (55). They go back to the fight about the nurse. Natasha is unafraid to be blunt, unafraid to manipulate, to take charge, to – in effect – reorder the house in which the sisters are systematically taken out of the picture. Under the surface, a fierce battle is raging between these two women parallel to the actual fire burning outside.

To explore the scene and attempt to move toward the encounter, the actors and I decided, on the basis of the above and Natasha's reason for being in the bedroom, to make the scene about territory. Natasha, we know, has already moved people in and out of their bedrooms to make room for Bobik, her baby. Clearly she has an eye on the attic-bedroom for a nursery. If Olga is booted out, she will be relocated to the school where she will be headmistress. Natasha's whole stance is of the one being in charge, "the Overseer." But Olga is neither timid nor a fool. She simply has not the right tools to deal with a street fighter like Natasha. In my view, there is no scene unless we get to the visceral. I see the basic conflict of the scene as a clash between Natasha's wish to reorder the house, specifically the attic-bedroom, and Olga's desire to maintain her beach-head.

We began to devise a game to play during the scene to get at these assumptions while keeping to the text as written at all times. Our exploration began with the following premise:

> **The game:** To fight to make the attic the way each one wants it. They can do anything they want with the furniture, props, etc.
> **The encounter:** The war between them for control of the house.

At the beginning of the scene, we agreed that the room is a shambles because of the fire and the sorting of clothes. To simulate this disorder, we overturned chairs and threw clothes all over the stage. Natasha entered, "figuratively measuring the drapes," with the intention of making the attic into a nursery for the baby. The game then became "the war of the chairs." In every way possible, subtle or not, charming or not, Natasha began to bring order to the room by restoring the chairs to their upright positions. Olga, in her way, took them apart and returned them to the way they were at the opening of the scene. These actions become their individual tasks. The scene started out quietly enough, but, when we improvised, it ended with Olga taking the coat rack and planting it like the flag on the moon as victory of possession, reducing Natasha to hysteria:

> Let her sit? She's a *servant.* (*through tears*) I don't understand you, Olya. I have a nurse and a wet-nurse; we have a maid, a cook – why do we need that old lady? Why? ... Let's come to an understanding, Olya. You live at school, I live at home. You have your teaching, I have a house to run. And when I say something about the servants, well then I know what I'm saying, *I know what I am saying!* ... And by tomorrow morning, I don't want to see that old bag, that old thief ... (*stamping her feet*) ... that witch! Don't you dare make me mad! Don't you dare! (*catching*

herself) Truly, if you don't move yourself downstairs, we'll be at each other, always. It's terrible. (56)

Olga has won the battle but lost the war, but not without seeing her flame.

The basic game, The War of the Chairs, as well as other games we used, Give and Take working with chairs (finding which moments in the text could count when performing these actions), and Interrupted Destination (while in the act of moving a chair or a piece of clothing, a point could be made that would suspend the action or interrupt it; the action could then be completed after the verbal point was made), also helped create stakes. The games gave Olga a point of concentration. I am not suggesting that the scene be played this way in performance, but the actors now had enough to work with to find their relationship. All of the games played were a way of making everything count in the scene in terms of the encounter.

Always remember, the goal of this work in encounter is to get to the deepest level in the play – to ask: "What is going on here? Really going on?" The games I used here are only some of the tools available to make this kind of investigation. The use of the encounter metaphor should not close off other possibilities, other kinds of questions or other kinds of game sequences. To explore other options, let's look at the rehearsal of a scene from Sarah Ruhl's *Dead Man's Cell Phone*.

Sarah Ruhl's *Dead Man's Cell Phone*[5]

Dead Man's Cell Phone is about an ever-expanding universe in which, ironically, as the technology of our century widens, so does our ability to be intimate. Jean, the heroine of the play, takes possession of the cell phone of a man named Gordon who has died suddenly in a cafe. She becomes the surrogate for this man as she answers his phone. Consequently, she implicates herself in the lives of those who survive him. She inherits all of his unfinished business, including his inability to express love and empathy.

While finding an encounter metaphor would be productive in the Gordon–Jean scenes where the moral center of the play resides, a different approach served to illuminate the following scene between Jean and Gordon's wife, Hermia. In this

---

[5] Ruhl, Sarah, *Dead Man's Cell Phone*. New York: Theatre Communications Group, 2008. Reprinted here with permission from Sarah Ruhl.

scene, Jean makes up a letter that Gordon "might have written" to Hermia. Jean must convince Hermia through the letter that Gordon loved her. Hermia is cynical. She suspects Jean was another of Gordon's lovers. Jean, in order to cope with the situation, supplies herself with this fantasy letter to make up for Gordon's absence.

In this scene, a transaction has to occur for Hermia to authenticate Jean's letter from Gordon. Hermia has to receive it and be changed by it. As I said to the actors performing this scene in class, the lines alone do not entitle you to any kind of change. A transformation has to occur that is so profound that Hermia is changed by it. The love between Hermia and her husband has to be restored. The challenge here is to find the transformation that will reach Hermia. Jean must convince Hermia that Hermia had a real intimacy with Gordon. Jean's task is further complicated by the fact that Jean never actually knew Gordon and that the truth about Gordon is he was a charismatic womanizer and low-life whose business was selling people's organs.

How to accomplish Jean's task by the words of the letter alone is quite a feat. When Jean tells Hermia that Gordon left a letter for her. Hermia asks what it says.

Jean
> I forget exactly. But I can paraphrase. It said, "Dear Hermia. I know we haven't always connected every second of the day. Husbands and wives seldom do. The joy between husband and wife is elusive, but it is strong. It endures countless moments of silent betrayal, navigates complicated labyrinths of emotional retreats. I know that sometimes you were somewhere else when we made love. I was too. But in those moments of climax, when the darkness descended and our fantasies dissolved into the air under the quickening heat of our desire – then, then, we were in that room together and that is all that matters. Love, Gordon.

Hermia
> Gordon knew that?

Jean
> I guess he did.

Hermia
> Well, how about that. (*Years of her marriage come back to her with a new light shining on them.*) You've given me a great gift, Jean. (72)

To direct a player to say these words sincerely, passionately, doesn't seem to fit the bill. So we turned to games to further our exploration.

To take this step into game exploration is to accept the chaos of the unknown, just as we have stressed in the experience of improvisation and play. The actor/player must trust that, in such a submission, something will come of it. It is only when we pull back from the edge that we prevent our intuition from arising spontaneously in the moment.

In rehearsing this scene, it seemed to us that Jean had to be spectacularly convincing. We began to explore with the games to see if we could uncover a transformation that would make such a transaction possible. The actors opted to try any and all games we could think of for their rehearsal process and then presented the scene for the class. They used slow motion, double time, give and take, full-body whisper, train overhead, and contact. All were alive and interesting, but not until they came to the game of Contact and played fully did they begin to hit it.

By fully committing to Contact, Jean became Gordon, the lover (all the time reading the letter). At one point, Jean made a new contact with Hermia by taking her to the floor and stretching out on top of her, physicalizing the encounter. The contact was bold, shocking, and intimate. In the script, Jean does it by listening to the needs Hermia expresses when she conveys Gordon's lack of presence in their lovemaking and, most of all, how she, Hermia, secretly compensates by imagining him with his mistress. The actress playing Jean found a way to reach Hermia by physically replicating the lovemaking posture while speaking the words of the letter. Now, could such a transformation be playable in performance? Most likely not, but it pointed to the specificity needed for this transaction to be made and for Hermia to be moved and believe that the letter was from Gordon.

The scene demands that Jean summon up a Gordon she never knew and deliver the words a man would write to his wife just before his death. The specificity of the transformations and the games (whisper, give and take, slow motion, and, most importantly, contact) led us into dangerous territory. Only then could we begin to experience what it would take for Jean to give Gordon's love to Hermia.

Remember that the search for the encounter is an ongoing process throughout rehearsal, not a fixed intellectual decision. The goal is always to open up possibilities for the actors – to explore all the different ways there are to get what the character wants or needs. Early ideas lead to game choices; games lead the actors closer and closer to the encounter, the most visceral emotional experience at the heart of a set of given circumstances.

3 Story Theatre: The Bridge Between Games and Play Texts

"In a sense, the Workshop was my first true experience of community, of feeling like I belonged somewhere. I often think of the Auden poem (*Musée des Beaux Arts*) that you incorporated into your staging of 'Icarus,' and the sensation of embodying the verse while we spoke it together, a group of sailors coming upon a shimmering sea, ruled by the sun; how the power of collectively imagining the waters deepened them, reinforcing the true meaning of myth as well as who we were as performers, a bunch of 'ordinary' high school guys in black jeans and white shirts, talking about a boy who fell out of the sky one afternoon when no one was looking. Bearing witness."[6]

What is story theatre?

Story theatre, as practiced at the Workshop, refers to the adaptation and performance of a story told through a combination of narration and dialogue, movement, mime, and music. Instead of an outside narrator, the entire group shares the narration in a give-and-take fashion. The narrator at any given time is determined by whose point of view the story is being told from at that moment. This shifting point of view is related to the transformational nature of the story theatre form. Sets and props are minimal. The group establishes place, character, activity, and ambience through transformations in movement and sound.

Theatre, like all the arts (and this is what we forget), is an integral and organic

---

[6] Mozes, Jon, e-mail to Susan Applebaum, 15 February, 2000. Used with permission from Jon Mozes.

part of our lives. We are sung to, told stories from infancy. And when the first story is told, the child enters the world of theatre in a profound way – loses himself in the story, is alternately delighted, frightened, amazed in a journey that engulfs him and allows him to experience an aspect of life – a dangerous aspect – and come back, restored, satisfied, and wiser. So it is not a coincidence that we explore fables, myths, fairy tales, as well as literary tales through story theatre. We create our stories through games, evolving scripts from the group, using the games to illuminate moments in the story and to create pockets of improvisation and spontaneity in their re-creation.

In story theatre, it is the actor's job to transform the space using the words of the story, similar to telling a story to a child. As I have said before in this book, the actor employs all her artistry to accomplish this task, drawing the audience into the world of the story, making the magical transformation to an imaginative world with everything at her command – body, voice, the space itself – in sync with the other actor and, ideally, the audience to make a transformation.

We teach story theatre form and technique to bridge the gap between improvisation and script, to retain improvisational spontaneity, point of concentration, and the sense of play in scripted work. Since each story has its own organic nature, our process for realizing the story takes into account, always, a respect for the nature and inherent demands that make each story unique. Whether we are working with folklore or literary pieces, our efforts are focused on finding what serves and illuminates that particular story, on how to activate the narration and communicate the text, while keeping the frame open to the kind of play that will make it a viable theatre piece. Once this form is found, the stories are scripted, but we leave space for pockets of improvisation to retain that sense of play and vitality.

The key principle of story theatre is the open admission by the actor that "I am a player; this is a story. Come with me and I'll make a transformation." The player is always present. Reminiscent of Tom's opening monologue to the audience in Tennessee Williams' *The Glass Menagerie*, the actor in our work becomes a guide to the journey into the heart of the story or play.

As I have noted in Chapter 1, all aspects of the work – character, object, activity, location, sound – are springboards to making that transformation into the story. Key to the principle of transformation and to story theatre, this assertion bears repeating: **To make a transformation, a player must be in the space, connected**

to the other players, connected to the audience, and open to creative possibilities. You cannot force a transformation; it cannot be mechanical. It is something that occurs right before your eyes, an event that is spontaneous and unexpected both to the player making the transformation and to the audience. Finding those moments of transformation is the essential task of the story theatre process.

Brecht and his presentational form of theatre influenced Paul Sills. Paul was drawn to Brecht's theories on the demonstration of character. Story theatre follows this principle – "Let me tell you about … let me show you" – leading into a transformation. Even once the player is in the moment, he must still be showing the character. The player must avoid obligation in which he is locked into communicating that obligation with every line and movement. The player must, instead, find the moment when he and the audience can experience the moment together, when something happens that is larger than both of them. That moment is beyond technique; it's the opening up of the frame and the entering of a shared space. These aspects are the heart of theatre, and we, in teaching this work, are concentrating on them in a self-conscious way.

Story games

Theatre games exercise the impulse life and reinforce play. Story games build on those two components and add an additional focus on the discipline of detail, specificity, and third-person narration, skills necessary for the performance and improvisational development of a story theatre piece. Introductory story games include Round-Robin Storytelling, Two-Deep Tag, Story Tag, Word Machine, Papa La Chaise, Give-and-Take Storytelling, Give-and-Take Detailing of Environment or Verbalizing the Where, Gibberish games, Poetry Workshop, Invested Object, Fairy-Tale Moments, Hook-Up and Twist Narration, Queen's Trunk, Who, What, Where Scenes with Narration and Dialogue.

Round-Robin Storytelling lays the groundwork for transformation. Players must first learn when, as the player/storyteller, to go into the story and when to step out, how to make a transformation and still keep in third-person narration, and how to exercise the discipline of detail. The game Round-Robin Storytelling gives players practice in these concepts, particularly in the transformational task of alternating between narration and dialogue. Round-Robin Storytelling in some form or other plays a role in almost all story theatre classes. The essential point of concentration in this game is to tell a story in give-and-take. Other skills to focus on include:

getting the word out, remembering and filling in detail from a known story or an imaginary one, handling objects while narrating, transforming into character, and dialogue. The three basic rules are: tell the story in third person; pick up the story in mid-sentence; no backtracking allowed.

Players are seated on the floor in a circle. The leader begins a story and then points to another player who picks up the story at the exact instant, mid-sentence, without repetition or "backtracking." Eventually the leader stops pointing to players and the players continue telling the story in a give-and-take fashion. The story is told in third person. It can be an invented story or a retelling of an existing story, fairy tale, folklore, or literary story.

During the playing, the leader might make any of the following calls: full-body whisper, slow motion, double time, shout it, sing it. To help players stay focused on the point of concentration, the leader calls: "Keep it in third person. Stay in narration. You must earn the right to become that character. Try to get the story out into the space – so no thinking ahead or playwriting." When players master the basic game, the leader may increase the difficulty by asking them to handle and transform objects as they pass the story along. The ultimate goal is for the player, mid-story, to assume the character or Who in the story and give and take the action in a scene. The scene can take place in the middle of the circle and, when the beat is over, the tellers can return to the circle and other players can pick up the story and continue.

In this final step, the players learn to transform into character and into the given circumstances of a dialogue-based scene, making that leap into the requirements of acting in a traditional play. The players have "crossed the bridge" between improvisation and the play text.

Story theatre from page to stage

To give you a better sense of the entire story theatre process and how it connects to our concept of encounter, here is an example of the analysis, rehearsal and performance of one story, "The White Dove," a fairy tale by the Brothers Grimm. The point of concentration for this particular rehearsal process was on finding and realizing the "encounter" at the heart of the story. The following transcripts were taken from a series of conversations we held over a one-year period. I directed this tale with the Young People's Company for the 2007 Spring Story Theatre

Festival. Notes from the rehearsals and performance of this story demonstrate the movement from research through exploration to performance.

In order to understand the references I make to the story in our conversations, I have included a summary of the story and a beat analysis of "The White Dove" prepared before rehearsals began. To make a working script, I divide the story into narration and dialogue assigned to various speakers. The working script is a director's tool – a starting place for exploration.

The White Dove *by the Brothers Grimm*

Once there was a poor servant girl who was traveling with a family through a large forest. In the deepest part of the forest they were attacked by robbers. The robbers murdered everyone except the girl, who had escaped the carriage at the first sound of trouble and found a place to hide. When she was sure that the robbers had gone, the girl came out of hiding and looked upon the terrible massacre.

Not knowing what else to do, the girl began to look for a way out of the forest. She started to weep, thinking, "I'm lost and alone. The robbers might still find me! No one lives here. What shall I do? I will probably starve!" Out of panic and desperation, she began to run, searching everywhere for help. Darkness fell and she had not found another soul or a way out of the forest. Overwhelmed, she surrendered to her exhaustion and put herself in the hands of God. She sat down under a large tree and waited for whatever might come.

Time passed. Suddenly she saw a white dove flying toward her. He had a little gold key in his beak which he dropped into her hand. He told her to take the key over to the tree on the opposite side of the clearing where she would find a little lock hidden in its trunk. The dove said, "Open the lock and you will find food and drink. You need not be hungry anymore." The girl did as she was told and when she opened the lock she found milk in a big white saucer and freshly baked bread with a thick crust and soft center. Hungrily, she tore a piece off of the bread, dipped it in the milk and ate greedily until she was full.

It was completely dark now and she felt very tired. She wanted to sleep. The white dove showed her another gold key. He told her to find the lock in a tree further off. When she opened the second lock, she found a lovely bed made of twigs and covered with a large, inviting white comforter. She climbed into the bed and said her prayers, asking for protection while she slept. She dozed off as soon as her head touched the plump pillow.

On the morning of the third day, the dove returned with yet another key and directed her to a third tree. There she found clothes fit for a princess. The dresses were woven with gold thread and covered with expensive and colorful jewels. From then on, the dove came every day and attended to all her needs. And she lived in comfort for many days. It was a good life.

One day the dove came to her and asked her to do something for him in return for all his help. She replied without hesitation, "Anything you ask." So the dove described to her what she must do. He told her that he would show her to a small cottage. When she went inside, she would see an old woman sitting in front of a fire. The old woman would wish her a good day, but he warned the girl not to answer. The girl was to pass by the old woman on her right side and find a door deeper inside the cottage. The girl was to enter the room where she would find rings of many shapes and sizes. Some would be expensive and set with jewels, but she was to ignore those. She was to look for a plain ring and bring it back to the dove as fast as she could.

The girl did as the dove instructed her to do. When the old woman tried to grab her gown and prevent her from going into the room with the rings, the girl said nothing, yanked her dress out of the old woman's hand and walked into the room. There she found a table filled with more rings than she had ever seen – shiny, beautiful, bejeweled rings. She ignored the glittery ones and looked frantically for the one plain ring, but she could not find it. Out of the corner of her eye, the girl spied the old woman trying to sneak away with a large birdcage in her hand. And in the cage, the girl saw the plain ring in the bird's beak. She ran after the old woman and grabbed the cage. The girl struggled with the old woman over the cage, finally succeeding in taking it away with her. The girl took the ring from the bird's beak and ran home as fast as her legs would carry her. There she waited for the white dove to come for the ring. But the dove did not come.

The girl was determined to wait for the dove, so she leaned against the tree and looked up at the sky. Suddenly she felt the tree become soft and she felt movement. Two of the branches became two arms that embraced her. And when she turned to look, she saw a handsome young man who took her in his arms and, to her surprise, kissed her. Holding her tenderly, the young man explained that she had rescued him from a curse. The old woman was a witch who had turned him into a tree. For a few hours every day, the witch let him be a white dove. But as long as the witch held the ring, he was her captive and could not become human.

Suddenly all the trees turned into the young man's servants and their horses. For, of course, the young man was a prince. He led the girl to his kingdom. The young man and the girl were married and lived happily ever after.

Analysis

The Beats

The "caption" for each beat defines the literal circumstances and sometimes early ideas as to the encounter. It gives you a point of concentration for the game exploration needed to express the encounter.

1st beat: Traveling through the forest
2nd beat: Overcome by robbers and murderers
3rd beat: Girl is the only survivor
4th beat: She flees
5th beat: Lost
6th beat: Gives up and surrenders herself to God under tree
7th beat: Awakened by Dove
8th beat: Instructed: 1st tree ritual
9th beat: Ritual 2nd tree
10th beat: Ritual 3rd tree
11th beat: Instructed about the Witch/Pass on right side/Say nothing/Get the ring/

Bring it back to the Dove
12th beat: She does all this and (dream ritual)
13th beat: Dove turns into Prince and he makes her Queen

Conversation #1: 24 May, 2006

Susan and I met at a tea parlor one afternoon to begin talking about the Principle of Encounter in relation to the Grimm brothers' story "The White Dove." I had recently done a workshop with the Piven Theatre Workshop teachers focusing on this very subject. Susan was a participant. At one point in the workshop, the teachers were trying to identify the "encounter" occurring when the girl attempts to get past the Old Woman carrying the cage with the bird. The group offered many answers but that moment continued to elude them. Susan asked me to explain what we were missing.

SA: When you were working with Grimm's "The White Dove" in the Teacher Workshop and the Girl was doing what the Dove had told her – she was trying to get past the Old Woman without being stopped in order to find –
JP: Find the ring and bring it back.
SA: You asked the group what the encounter was. We were agreeing that it was a life-and-death matter. It was very high stakes. It was all those kinds of things, but you kept pushing us that that was not really at the core. Can you speak to that? Where was the core? And how did you intuit it?
JP: What many people don't do when working on a story is to say – what was the story about and how does it pertain to us? One way to know what it's about is to take it step by step and to take a look at the journey.

And the first thing that happens in "The White Dove" is tragedy – tragedy, murder, violence (a daily occurrence in parts of the world), loss, fear – being lost and trying to find her way out of the woods. Everybody's had that. Terrifying feeling to be lost in the woods. Everybody can relate to that and that's an example of trying to personalize and find out – what are you looking for when you're in the forest and you're lost? Specifically – how do you survive? Do you look on the ground? Do you look up at the sky? Do you look at the trees? Do you look around for animals? You're in a clearing. Do you run to the end of the clearing? You know, all of that, all of the above.

So then, the Girl came out and we can only imagine how exhausting that must be and she's stopped crying and she surrenders herself to God, to Fate, to Destiny. If it's Grimm, to God, and there is a whole human area of exploration.

What about the person who wants to be something – an artist – and who tries and tries and tries? How often when he gives up, when he stops trying – the trying gets in his way. Anxiety gets in the way. Fear gets in the way. Fear is part of that and the way I'm talking now is in the story. So when she surrenders herself to Fate and stops trying and, in stopping trying, she encounters the Bird. What is that all about?
SA: You mean the Bird?
JP: Yes. He gives her clothes and food, all that stuff. What that's about is, he nurtures her. He nurtures her just the way God would see to it and the way a good family and a good mother would. She was a servant girl without a family of her own. She's nurtured and the

Dove bestows all these gifts and then he wants something in return. And she, in her journey, she wants to grow up and be responsible and conquer her fear and find her way home. In quotation marks, "find her way home." She trusts in what she has been told, in what she's been taught. She's been taught by a nurturer. So she follows directions and doesn't give in to her terror or her fear. And this is what is involved in such an encounter. It's pretty frightening to go by a witch and not know what to expect. But he gave her tools. Don't engage; go straight to the treasure and bring it back home. Which she does. And in that, accepting her fate and in accepting her responsibility and conquering her fear, she grows up. It all has to fit.

If one knows that this is a test − two events: a test to get by the Woman (conquer fear) and a surrendering herself to her mother, in a positive sense. From that, everything else can be intuited and, when it can't, you say, does this moment advance the story? Can we cut it out? Could we leave out that she was afraid and tried and could hardly breathe and she'd been terrified? Could we leave that out?

If you don't deal with the story on this level, then it could be left out. Not everybody thinks on this level. The actor deals with the truth of the situation and finding the truth is that exploration. The truth resides in the fear, the specific fear that you're portraying. In order to make it real, you need to deal with the story on the level of metaphor.

SA: How is this different from working on a scene or a play in traditional ways and getting at the emotional journey the character is taking?

JP: In a scene it's already structured and we're following the text and a playwright, but we still have to find the encounter. In story, we use the games to open up a way of communicating and sharing the story with an audience. It's another tool to explore what we can find on impulse or spontaneity and we also want to have pockets of improvisation when we tell the story. Explore and heighten the Encounter − happy one, tragic one. So it's a flexible tool.

SA: So the ultimate goal of Encounter is to?

JP: To get to the heart and nature of that encounter − to communicate what the story is about from a personal and emotional place and then to find a way to communicate that essence in specific ways.

SA: How does this relate to form?

JP: Form is the next step. The encounter dictates the form. Once you've explored the encounter through the games, through talking about it, through personal research, through given circumstances, that exploration will lead you to the form of the performance. Very rough, but that's where the "organic" nature of the work comes in.

SA: I think what made the story work a little differently at the workshop was that it wasn't a director coming in and imposing some sort of concept − that the process was organic, not only to the director's connections to the material, but also to what the group brought to the table, the ensemble.

JP: The ensemble participates in exploring the encounter. They participate in expressing the encounter. The teacher is their guide.

Conversation #2 (edited transcription): 6 June, 2006

After our first conversation, I went back to the text of "The White Dove" and began to take the story apart beat by beat. The italicized sections denote the text of the story. The bracketed sections are to clarify references or make comments on the narrative.

JP: Let's go back to the beginning. (Speaking of the first beat of the story) I had to redefine what the beat was. The description in the story is: *A poor servant girl traveling with a family through a large forest. In the deepest part of the forest they are attacked by robbers who murder everyone except the girl.* This is the description. If possible your description should encapsulate the Encounter – like a newspaper headline: "FAMILY BESET BY ROBBERS – ALL MURDERED!" How about "ALL MURDERED IN FOREST EXCEPT GIRL." This is the Encounter. The swiftness of the murder then becomes the event and our job is to encounter that event – how swiftly we can lose our way, how swiftly life can be destroyed.

(Before I begin my discussion of this first beat, I want to clarify the relationship between the games I would use to explore this moment and the principle of story theatre narration. In past explorations, I would use the game Four on a Moving Object to find the essence of the carriage ride. In this game, four players improvise being in the same moving vehicle. The teacher changes the type of vehicle and the players respond as a group. This is just an attempt to give it form. The carriage does not have to be represented literally. It can be suggested just by actors using body in a rhythm to convey the movement of the carriage, to suggest the unsuspecting ordinariness of what was going on prior to the brutal swiftness of violence. In the story theatre principle of narration that we follow at the Workshop, the narrator is decided on the basis of whose point of view the story is being told from at a given moment.)

JP: Returning to the story – the family in the carriage can transform into the robbers and they flee. Transformation is key to story theatre. The carriage can be in the storyteller's imagination – the Girl. And the Girl who has hidden behind the tree in the moment of the robbers' violence comes out and surveys all she sees.

The Girl who has hidden behind the tree in the moment the robbers leave *comes out and surveys the scene before her.* Here we need to look to the actor's instrument to realize the moment. That's one of the principles we mustn't forget. *She came out and looked upon a terrible massacre.* (That acting moment has to be explored.) Seeing the carnage. Hearing the silence. Worrying if the robbers are going to come back.

(This example refers back to our introductory notes about key moments that are critical to the story. One cannot gloss over such moments. They need time and space to be fully realized. They are critical for both the actor and the audience in order to experience the emotional journey.)

JP: I must have said … here it is:
Beat 3: She weeps. What shall I do? I will probably starve.
Beat 4: She looks everywhere for a way out. At nightfall, she sits down under a tree and surrenders to whatever may come.

To be explored is how to encounter the moment when we stop trying and leave ourselves open to hear ourselves and open to other possibilities. This is really key because it's related to the games (the idea of letting go and surrendering to the group or the task at hand). This is when surrender can be productive. Anxiety can interfere with letting go. This encounter should be talked out with the group and shared with the group. Can anyone personalize this?

This is the objective – to personalize the encounter. Letting individuals in the group share an experience that allows them to relate to the situation allows the solution to arrive. So the encounter here is the hysteria of finding a way out and the ultimate surrendering to God or Fate.

She sits under the tree. Soon a White Dove flew to her. He had a little gold key in his beak which he dropped into her hand. He does this three times. Three times. It's the "Encounter of Ritual" and that really has to be explored. What is the ritual? Is it a religious ritual? Is it magic? I don't know. But it has to be explored. Everybody would interpret this with their own individuality.

Okay – the Encounter of Ritual. Then the Encounter of Feeding Her Hunger, Sleep in a Bed, Being Clothed. Given food, clothing, and shelter. The encounter at each tree must be realized with the actor's need. Hunger. What is hunger like? What is it like to be afforded finally a place to sleep? After great anxiety and no sleep and no rest?

And clothes: *The clothes are fit for a princess. The dresses were woven with gold thread and covered with expensive and colorful jewels.* This becomes crucial. So far she has been rewarded for surrendering herself to God. Her entire life transformed and elevated by the rescuer.

Now we have to discover if she is worthy and can reciprocate and pass through the eye of fear. There is a choice here. The girl has to step up and be responsible for her own fate. There *is* a choice. She was content ... perhaps. *The Dove came every day and attended to all her needs. It was a good life.*

But then, one day, the Dove asks her to do something for him in return. She accepts willingly. The girl could say no. She's given a choice. He then outlines instructions: *Go to the house. Pass the old woman on the right. Stay silent. There's a door. Open it. Enter a room filled with rings of all kinds. They're beautiful and glittery, but you must ignore them and find the plain one. Bring that plain ring to me as quickly as you can.* The instructions are all to the point. They're simple. This is another test. Can she follow the directions and face her fear on her own? Open the mysterious door – that's another test – opening the door. Doors are part of our life. It's "Bergmanesque." Bergman's films are full of doors and houses. Do we play it safe or do we chance it? Yes, do we bravely open a door – do we do that? But she does. *She looked frantically for the one plain ring, but she could not find it. She could not find the plain one amidst the glitter of the others. But while she was looking, the girl spied the Old Woman trying to sneak away with a birdcage in her hand.* Ah – hah! (I slam the table as I say this and the movement is so shocking that we both laugh.)

This is crucial. If our premise is right that this is a journey and that she has a choice – but I left out that the Old Woman has caught her and tries to prevent her from going into the room. The Old Woman withholds her permission. But the Girl remains silent. She doesn't stand and argue with her. She goes into the room. Okay. So back in the room, everything is glittering. She's looking for the plain one and, when she doesn't find it, she sees the Old Woman stealing away with a birdcage in her hand!

The Girl ran after the Old Woman and grabbed the cage. The bird had the plain ring in his beak. She took the ring from the bird's beak and ran home as fast as her legs could carry her. There she waited for the white Dove. Now, I don't know if I talk about it later, but I'll give you a preview of the coming attractions (laughter). The thing is, he (the Dove) didn't say anything about if the bird is taken by the Old Woman.

SA: You're right. He didn't say anything.

JP: She's going off the instructions. OH, MY GOD! This is my point. Without really delving into the Encounter, you miss the story. It's a journey, we all agreed, that's simple. But, look, the Encounter is: How does she receive it? Does she make a choice? She's now acting on her own. She's making a true choice. She boldly takes the cage out of the Old Woman's hand and the bird has a plain ring in its bill. She takes the ring. I guess there's a fight here.

SA: I never thought about that moment. How does she get the ring? How does she deal with the bird?

JP: Right. So there's another encounter to be explored.

SA: And a bird.

JP: Yes. Right! Another bird, with a plain ring in its bill! *She took the ring and ...* it could be the Dove! *And ran home with it and waited. But the Dove did not come.* Another test. *She leans against the tree.* I had cold shivers up my arms alone here. *She is determined to wait for the Dove.* The tree transforms. The young man explains his fate – kings, servant, horses – everything is there.

SA: Another surrender. A reprise of a motif.

JP: Yes. In the beginning she sits and the tree protects her. Here she leans. She's standing. She leans against the tree and she's determined to wait because she's fulfilled it. She'll wait there forever and that's crucial.

The first time she sits and this time she stands. She has triumphed, faced fear, and given back to her nurturer so this is an *individuated woman.* She has found her own center. She has reciprocated what she has been given and is ready to be elevated to another class – to become queen. She was a poor servant girl traveling with a family through the forest. *It's a great story!* And Transformation, Narration, Game – Method Acting – all of it plays into it.

SA: This is where you stopped?

JP: Yes. I didn't really go into the last beat. When I direct, I never finish it anyway until I've gone through the whole thing and the end appears. I always leave the last beat open. It makes everybody very nervous. But that's the only way. Almost everything I do because it's done on paper but that doesn't mean anything. All the discoveries will come as you interact with the group.

Rehearsal

Moving from analysis to practice: directing "The White Dove"

Based on the excitement about the story generated by our discussions and analysis, I decided to direct Grimm's "The White Dove" for the Young People's Company Annual Spring Story Theatre Festival in March of 2007. I worked with a group of six company members, four girls and two boys, for a series of rehearsals in December 2006 before I left Evanston for the winter in Los Angeles. Since my interest in this project developed during our discussions on the principle of encounter, I made that my point of concentration for the rehearsals. Although games played an important role in the ultimate performance, I chose to subordinate the selection of any game to the necessity of realizing the encounter of the story and its beats. Susan took notes on several rehearsals and they inform the narrative here.

Rehearsal #1: 1 December, 2006

After the usual greetings and preliminaries, I began this rehearsal with a group reading of the story. I followed that reading with a discussion exploring what the story is about. My question to the group dealt with the meaning of "surrendering." I wanted the players to understand that the surrendering in the story was not a giving up but a *choice* the Girl is making. All of my questions guided the players to think of moments in their own life when they had been frustrated, couldn't find something important under excruciating circumstances, and then experienced that moment of surrender when they stopped trying and trusted that the solution would come.

Once the group had expressed their understanding on a personal level, I went back to the story and explained, "When you surrender, you are open to hearing your own voice – instinct, wisdom – those inner voices. The voices in your ear – mother, father, the devil's voice." And the group could relate to what I was saying. I went on to talk about the story not in plot terms but as the Girl's emotional and psychological journey after experiencing the most extreme trauma, likening it to what happens in war.

The players were having trouble understanding why the Girl sits under the tree, so I moved the discussion to consider the substance of fear – the driving mode after the Girl's survival, after everyone else has been killed, and her desperate search for a way out of the forest before the robbers return. When I asked if anyone had ever been truly afraid, only one of the five players present at this rehearsal could relate to that. This player then shared an experience from her childhood when she had known that kind of fear and how she overcame it. I responded by confirming that, when we are afraid, we don't submit to the fear, we fight. I talked about "shock breath" – the breathing that accompanies fear. Then I divided the players into two groups (one group of three and one of two) and sent them off to work on the "fear beat" with the admonition not to use any game unless it directly related to what they needed to communicate.

For their version of the beat, the three-person group drew on their experiences in class with Anne Bogart's Viewpoints work, focusing on running away from the robbers, from the horror. I went back to this group and had them do it again, but this time I guided them to let go of the Viewpoints grid and focus on searching for a way out. My point of concentration stayed on trying to achieve the transformation from fear and panic to surrender. As the group performed, I side-coached them to explore their breathing. I was pushing the group to a scary place. When I sensed their unconscious resistance to full commitment, I shifted gears and coached them to collapse into each other when the Girl sits under the tree. They were ready; exhausted from their running, they surrendered totally with the breath and the words! They surprised themselves at having experienced the "Encounter of Surrender."

One of the YPC directors happened to witness that moment and was amazed. She asked me how I had gotten that depth at a first rehearsal. I replied somewhat cryptically,

"Digging." What I meant by that was that I was guiding them but also taking a lot from them. Finding that balance between giving and taking in rehearsal is critical to the work. The director/teacher is always asking, "How much can I help them make a transformation?" The goal is to play and to integrate the play with the meaning of the encounter. That's the trick! The whole process of what we do relies on impulse. Living theatre – going for the live, spontaneous creative moment.

Rehearsal #2: 6 December, 2006

For this rehearsal, I stayed with my earlier focus on violence, shock, realization of disaster, panic, and acceptance. I chose to warm the group up with a familiar game – Portraits. Starting from scratch each time, the players set up five or six portraits. On the last one, I instructed them to stay in portrait mode (in contact, with their faces seen), but to make three slow-motion changes and three double-time changes on their own. Then I called out events and the players would respond in slow motion with a new portrait – The Violence, The Shock, The Realization of Disaster, Acceptance. On "acceptance," I changed the rhythm and called for four different "acceptances" in double time. Going back to a normal slow-motion portrait, I asked for an exploration of "surrender" three times. I was using the warm-ups to help the players find the physicality they had experienced at the last rehearsal. The idea behind these calls is always to keep the players off-balance and working on impulse.

To that end, I followed the Portrait game with the Viewpoints grid, exploring 1) locomotion – running, stopping, walking, skipping, hopping; 2) levels – high, medium, low, and 3) tempo – slow and fast. I side-coached: "If you meet each other, acknowledge that and let something happen." Slowly, I added elements from the story – an oasis in the forest, looking for a way out, finding obstacles in the forest, making sound and listening – until I asked them to start telling the story. As they worked, I coached bits and pieces, for example, "Keep the breath going, double-time lost, sounds of the Dove." All this preliminary work was aimed at retrieving that brilliant moment at the end of the last rehearsal.

After this warm-up, I shifted gears into a short discussion of the nature of fear/terror and then pointed out several good moments to keep from their improvisations. They went back to work. This time, I began to focus on the Dove and the giving of the key. I wanted to make it clear that they are telling a story, that they are not really a Dove and that they have to move into a non-literal way to communicate that. For the remainder of the active section of the rehearsal, we worked through the sections of the story dealing with the rituals of finding the three trees – food, shelter (bed), and clothing.

With twenty-five minutes left of their rehearsal time, I sat them down to read through the section of the story where the Girl encounters the Witch. I assigned parts for reading and then asked rhetorically, "What's this section about?" I explained that this section is all about choice. This moment was discussed in detail in Conversation #2, but just to recap – the Girl makes a conscious choice to do as the Dove asks, to repay his kindness and to be responsible for her own fate. She also makes her own choices about how to handle the Old Woman, stealing away with the cage because that action falls outside the instructions given by the Dove.

I identified the encounter with the Dove as "communicating the instructions and getting it *exactly right.*" It is a life-and-death matter. The stakes are very high for the Dove. He tells the Girl that it is critically important to be silent, not to engage with the Witch. The Girl has to trust that the Dove knows what he is about. The Dove has to trust that the Girl will succeed. Then I sent them off to work on this beat with some technical instructions: "Do not separate the instructions from the action. Do it as a montage where the present and future are melded. The future emerges as the present is going on." The players worked on this beat and then shared what they had found.

I left them with this thought: "We're trying to find the organic transformations. We're trying to find the magic and we want the magic to occur by sleight of hand." By organic transformations, I am referring to finding those moments of change (changes in rhythm, tone, ambience, locale, character, action) that arise spontaneously from the impulses of the group. These moments are not imposed from the outside. They are not planned out in advance. They come from within the group when the group is connected to each other and to the encounter.

Rehearsal #4: 17 December, 2006

For the third rehearsal, I invited a fight choreographer to work with the group. The fourth rehearsal took place on a Sunday afternoon and was the last major rehearsal before I had to leave. One more rehearsal was scheduled for the following Wednesday to run through the story for the YPC directors who would be conducting some rehearsals while I was away in order to keep the story in play.

I began this rehearsal with a warm-up of Tag, with the point of concentration on discovering "how dark and mysterious the story is." At the Workshop, we often begin Tag with the group discovering who is the It. I began with this strategy. As soon as the It was found, I instructed the group to make a sound each time someone was tagged. The group did this, adding a new sound and new way of moving with each new It. Then I coached the players to start a story – any story – that would come out of this space and to take the next transformation out of the sounds they were making. The group played this way until I coached them to shift to the game Give and Take as a way to start the story with the first line "What can a poor girl like me ... " (In Give and Take, one person at a time has stage and either gives stage to someone else or someone else takes the stage by speaking and moving. Only one person can move at a time.) The group repeated that line and continued telling the story that was emerging.

Reminding the group that all the games they had been playing were still in the space, I kept feeding them lines or asking them to "get into the space of that word" or to explore a particularly effective line improvised by one of the players like "All the trees were dead, frozen." I gave them another line: "She looked for a way out, for the road. She went to the east or the west, went in circles." I continued to feed them lines: "All she could hear was the sound of her breath and her heart." I side-coached: "Freeze. Let's keep the mystery. New beat. Going to go into the house of the Witch – very scary. Give and take. Words count. Sounds count. Everything counts." The group played and told the story of the beat. I encouraged the breath and instructed them to pick up the story as best they could. "The Old Woman ... " They played.

All through this section of playing and side-coaching, I was working to get two specific moments connected to the Encounter:

1. Girl's fear in the forest.
2. Girl's fear in her journey into the Witch's house.

I let the players get to the "Dove didn't come" and stopped them. I talked to them about losing the fear and the sense of being lost – all the specifics of fear/murder, lost – and asked them to consider what comes next. I explained, "She's alone and then a bird … Hope – the world opens up/food – nourishment – and then THE TEST." I referred to a moment when one of the players screamed and everyone jumped and told them, "That's what has to happen each time."

After working very hard with great focus, the group took a break. When they returned, I asked them to repeat "The Test" beat. Before they began, I asked rhetorically, "What's first?" and answered, "Finding the encounter – the emotion. Follow your instinct. What's the worst that can happen?" Then I sent them off to work on that beat by themselves.

While the players worked, I reflected on what had been accomplished so far. I had scripted the story in order to mark the transformations and I felt that up to the "Test Beat" they were pretty well set. The fight choreographer on Wednesday evening had been good. I wanted him to choreograph the Girl fighting with the Witch because I felt that he could translate that moment physically. But I wanted the tree transformations to be improvisational and truly creative.

The players worked for about fifteen minutes and then presented what they had found. Pleased that they now had the whole shape of the story, I asked them to do it again while I side-coached them. In telling the story up to this point, three of the girls in the group had been giving and taking the character and narration of the Girl at different points in the story and sometimes all the girls would be performing actions of the character at the same time. I wanted to try to rationalize this convention without discarding it completely, so I gave a scarf to the Old Woman and said, "Instead of everyone being the Girl, whoever is the Girl at that moment, let her be the Girl." I instructed the boy-half of the Dove (the Dove was cast as a young man and a young woman working together and sharing the narration) to tie the scarf around the Girl's eyes when he gives her the instructions. After the Dove blindfolded the Girl, I coached the players to pass the Girl literally from one to the other, guiding the blindfolded Girl around the stage. I made a point of trying to locate the Dove in the air and not literally and told the two players representing the Dove not to talk to the Girl directly.

When they came to the "Old Woman moment," I coached the group to use sounds made with their voices and bodies to create an ambience. Seeing another way to change something being done literally to a metaphorical space, I worked with the idea of using a Tug of War as a metaphor for the fight over the cage and told the players to make the cage huge so it wasn't literal.

The coaching here moves into the area of directing while playing. As I watched the group play, I noted the possibilities and guided them. My entire point of concentration in this section was to work against being literal. When I got to the final transformation of the tree into the Prince, I saw an opportunity to help them make a connection without acting out the actions in the words of the story. I coached the Prince to tell the Girl his story while rocking her in his arms. It was a lovely moment.

Having completed the story, I asked the players to run through it again, starting at the beginning with Danger Tag into the carriage. I continued to tweak a moment here and there, particularly working to move the trees away from the literal, but generally I let them have a solid run-through from memory.

I ended rehearsal by talking with them about what they had accomplished. "You all took a giant step and I'll try to articulate it – not being so literal and going for a transformation. What is it about? Transformation is frightening. We don't know what will happen. If we put it in the head, we will miss all the possibilities. QUESTION: What was different about the way we approached the story from the first rehearsal? What kept us on the path? ANSWER: The spontaneity of it – driven by the Encounter. The magic word is the Encounter. We did some games, Yes, Tag – Give and Take into Story – Soundscape. We were purposeful going into story: started with Yoga – Tag – Give and Take – Danger Tag (Danger in the air) – Key to the Encounter. Crucial piece: Tag Where All Make A Noise – Feeding into the mood. I want you to think about it. I want it to come from you. This is new territory for you. I want to put the story in your hands. Someone else will rehearse you. You're going to have to know what your anchors are so you can be aware. You can say: We need a new game because this one isn't working now. This game has become old hat. We have to be brave. You are all magnificent."

In a discussion with the YPC director who would be in charge of the story in my absence, I told her that I felt "the seeds had all been planted" and the task was to keep the story "in their bones" and in play.

Reflections on the story in performance: 9 March, 2007

The Young People's Company Spring Story Theatre Festival opened on 7 March, 2007. A few days later, I met with Susan to talk about the performance and bring closure to this process. Before the opening, I had made some changes in the staging, primarily to the beginning and the ending.

For the beginning of the story, my point of concentration became the "creation of space." To help the players stay in play, I introduced a game progression: Listening for the sound, Entrances and Exits, Space Break, Building the Carriage with Rhythm (Four on a Moving Object), and the Girl Hiding during the Slaughter. In performance, the progression looked like this: Music begins and the lights come up slowly. Girl 1 enters from behind a pole trying to locate the sound. When she gets to the middle of the stage, she says quietly, "The White Dove." The girl who will be part of the Dove "flies" across the stage. Girl 2 enters, pins herself to the wall and slowly sinks to the floor. Boy 2 (Dove/Prince) "breaks the space" with a heavy march-like rhythm. From there, the players build the carriage through its rhythm. The group, as if all in the same carriage, moves forward, leaving the servant girl behind to hide as the space transforms into the robbery and murder. All this activity was informed by the intense emotional work that had been done in the December rehearsals. For the end, I had the players return to straightforward storytelling.

Reflecting on what had been accomplished, I was pleased with the outcome of the story. It's all about communication. If you aren't communicating on the deepest possible level, why do theatre? Theatre is a place to meditate with an audience. Finding and realizing the Encounter is the central thing. All the other principles are a way of opening the material and ourselves to communicating, meditating, and exploring truths about the human condition.

PART 2:
In the Studio with Joyce Piven: Scenes from Workshops

Introduction: Concepts for teaching games: point of concentration and calls

Part 2 is made up of five chapters, each covering two sample workshops with a point of concentration on one principle. One of the workshops in each chapter explores the principle in relation to the body and the development of the ensemble. The other workshop explores the relationship between the principle and the use of language and sound. Two teaching techniques – Point of Concentration and Calls – are central to the teaching of all game work as a means for achieving play and spontaneity.

Point of Concentration is another way of expressing the foundational principle – focus on the task at hand and the other person. Each game played has a point of concentration (POC), a term popularized by Viola Spolin. We use the term "calls," instead of Spolin's term "side-coaching," to describe the teacher's guidance from the sidelines during the playing of a game

Since these two teaching techniques, "Point of Concentration" and the use of "calls," are so critical to the teaching of game work, I discuss them in more depth here.

Point of concentration (POC)

POC refers to the specific outcome or objective that the player is seeking to accomplish in the game. It is the lever that directs the player's attention outside themselves. For example, to play an ordinary children's game like Tag, the POC for one player is to tag someone else. For the other players, the POC is to avoid getting tagged. With their focus on the point of concentration, players are not worrying about how they look in space. They are free to move in the most expressive ways because they are not thinking about their movement, they are only thinking about how to avoid being tagged or how to catch a person to tag.

Any children's game will put the players into a generalized state of play. But to transform a simple children's game like Tag, or any game structure for that matter, into a theatre game, you need to add a theatrical dimension to the original game. This new POC focuses the players on exploring an element of theatre-like rhythm (e.g. slow motion, double time) or character qualities (e.g. age, occupation, outlook on life), or speech and its dynamics (e.g. dialogue, full-body whisper, train overhead), and so forth.

How does this work? I'll use the example of adding "slow motion" to the game of Tag. In this situation, players now have two points of concentration: 1) to tag or to not be tagged and 2) to become aware of the pace of the group movement so they can move at that same rate. To accomplish "slow-motion" movement, the players must get their whole body involved, reaching with everything they have rather than speeding up and being out of sync with the other players. This double focus heightens the player's sensory involvement in the game, promotes agreement, and deepens their concentration. If they are playing both points of concentration fully, they have no choice but to be released from self-concern. They become free to make organic connections, to really play and transform.

Shifting points of concentration

The teacher can also choose to shift points of concentration in a game in order to explore different theatrical elements. Take the game Give and Take. The POC of this game is to get a group of five to eight players to give and take stage. Only one person may move at a time, with sound and movement. The goal is ensemble – eyes in the back of the head – playing, taking, and giving – leaving any control or turn-taking out of it.

If I begin to explore another theatrical element using the game Give and Take, I need to shift the point of concentration to this new element. For example, say I want to have the players in the game explore the ambience of a Where, a place like a market or a park or lake setting. I have to shift the point of concentration to "being at the lake or the park." The players are still following the rules of Give and Take, only one person moving at a time, but now they are exploring the sights, sounds, and activities of this locale through the game.

And so often, when I begin to add this new layer to the game, the players get into their heads and begin to lose spontaneity. At the point where the POC has shifted to being in the Where, spontaneity often gets lost. It is important here to shift back to the POC that focuses on the playing element of giving and taking stage, on the spontaneity and fun, even if only for a moment before returning to the new POC, the Where. The group may not reach this level of spontaneity immediately but the seed has been planted.

So the POC of any game can shift depending on the teacher's objective for the exercise at any given moment. However, spontaneity is always the first objective. The teacher must work to find the balance between the point of concentration for spontaneity and the point of concentration for exploration, for exploring and heightening within a game.

Calls: collaboration between teacher and players

"Calls" are instructions given by the teacher to the players during the playing of the game. The purpose of calls is to focus the group, keeping them out of their heads, off-balance, and open to impulse and spontaneity. Using calls puts the teacher and the players into a collaborative relationship with the goal of bringing the scene to life. Watching the game or exercise, the teacher senses what the players need to stay out of their heads – to play on impulse. The calls give the players an added point of concentration.

In an open letter to all the Workshop teachers sometime during the 1990s, Byrne Piven addressed the purpose of calls and what he saw as problems with their use. He wrote:

> The goal for the teacher is to generate impulse and spontaneity in the player's body – to guide the player to use the body in its totality; to help the player get into the body and out of the head. What does "in their head" look or feel like? When the energy is stopping. When they are trying to be clever. When they are trying to think something up. When they seem to have lost impulse. When they have lost motor and energy.
>
> The purpose of calling out during an exercise or game is to stimulate, enhance, or move the group toward a point of concentration. If the call takes more than a word or two, what happens is that the flow is interrupted and the purpose defeated. It cannot stimulate because whatever energy happened to have been in the space has seeped out. It can't move toward the Point of Concentration because there is no longer any

concentration, except in figuring out what the teacher means. You are now into explanation, discussion land, and you might as well stop altogether and explain or discuss. Talking rapidly won't do the job. It just communicates your anxiety – your awareness that you shouldn't be saying all this at this moment – and yet you feel an urgent need to say it. What's the cure? Spend the time early on to establish language – code, if you will – so that if you zig, they know exactly and immediately what you mean (and zag does the opposite right away).

Byrne takes this opportunity to offer a specific example to illustrate his point. He makes reference to the game Balance the Stage. In this game, a group of players rapidly move about the stage space, in and out and around each other, until the leader calls, "Freeze." The players are to freeze in positions and locations that form a balanced stage picture. Byrne wrote:

Maybe I can give some specific examples. In the game "Balance the Stage" – "double-time" moving through the space, call "It's more urgent" or "Raise the Stakes" or "Life and Death!" Then, it's not eno ugh to call "Freeze" unless they know the rule is that everybody's seen and the stage is designed exactly as the players would like it to be. Therefore, they must know this and "Freeze" should suffice. If there is any doubt, follow "Freeze" with the call "Balance" or "Stage Picture."

The point is that the call should never throw the players into their heads, interrupting the flow of bodies and beings interacting with each other. Calls should not create questions but function as stimulants and guides. If you need to stop for an explanation, it's better to do that.

In the best of all possible worlds, the leader will take from what is going on, what the players are doing, and help them heighten their work rather than trying to impose a structure on them. The flow should never be broken. The teacher's goal is to make calls that give form, pattern, rhythm, focus, and style to what is happening improvisationally. This cannot happen if language has not been firmly established.

Establishing game language, principles, and flow

Establishing the shared "game" language that will be used to make calls is one of the most important early steps in our work. All first classes begin with this point of concentration because of its role in the teacher–student collaboration. In scene study classes, the warm-up for the day contains the games and calls that the instructor will use later in the class to free the actors working on a scene.

Every class is designed to have an organic progression both of energy and content, all leading to a pay-off at the end that is intrinsically theatrical. Because, when all is said and done, this is a theatrical mode of teaching acting. For example, when I call, "Change partners" in a game of Mirror, the point of concentration is to keep that energy and that focus and to begin mirroring with *the first eyes you meet*. We're building on energy here, not dissipating with short breaks or letting down, like stopping yourself and walking up to your partner, instead of mirroring right from the moment you meet those other eyes, even if you are across the room from your new partner. This practice of organic flow and building on momentum is crucial to the way we work.

4 Workshops on Play

The principle of play is:

To be present and creative in the moment onstage before an audience.

The point of concentration for games focused on the principle of play is:

◆ To experience and work "on impulse" with the other players.

◆ To explore and heighten – words, emotions, characters, situations, ideas.

◆ To find that creative motor that is capable of endless invention.

◆ To react spontaneously – freely and without planning (a reaction that surprises actors and players equally).

◆ To take risks.

◆ To embrace the "anxiety of not knowing," the "off-balance moment."

Foundational games that promote play and establish the language of playing with calls like "freeze," "slow motion/double time," "give and take," "break the space/ transform together," "mirror," "explore and heighten," "help/hinder," "two scenes," "full-body whisper/train overhead" include but are not limited to the following games introduced in this chapter:

◆ The Yes game

◆ Freeze Tag as a precursor to all forms of Tag games

◆ Space Break/Group Transformations

◆ Mirror/Mirror Object-Activity Transformations

◆ Machine games

◆ Give and Take

◆ Early Object Games like Ball Toss/Word Toss

◆ Three-Chair Conversation

◆ Who, What, Where Scenes.

Introductory workshop to game language

Here is an example of a three-hour introductory class I taught to a group of young adults. As you read, note both the organic design and the use of calls. The sample classes presented in this chapter mostly represent work for advanced teens and adults in groups of about twelve to eighteen players. For younger children, the classes are generally shorter in length and the games are not taken to the same level of complexity. However, the majority of the games in these classes are played with all ages.

This class has three points of concentration: to engage the group in play; to establish language through play – agreement and transformation; to create a progression of energy and flow, stopping and starting as little as possible.

Warm-up sequence
The Yes game – Your Name, Another Player's Name, Yes
Space Walk into *Space Break* into *Group Transformations*
Mirror Object-Activity Transformations in Pairs into *Machine.*

The Yes game
I invite everyone to join me in the stage space of the Studio Theatre and explain: "We are going to warm up and get to know each other by playing the Yes game. Let's all stand in a large circle. I'll begin this game by saying my name and pointing to someone else. That person will say their own name and point to another, and so forth."

The point of concentration for this game is to engage in play by sending energy out to others and, ultimately, to explore and heighten that connection through playing with the sound and movement you receive. The Yes game is an excellent game for learning names in a first class. It is also a good warm-up for any class, especially when the play moves into exploring and heightening the word "yes."

We play. When I notice that the players feel comfortable and are getting to know the other players' names, I stop them and change the rules. "This time when you point to someone else in the circle, you say that player's name instead of your own." Play proceeds along these lines until everyone has been included at least once and everyone appears to know at least a number of names. During the playing, I coach: "Begin to play with the *sounds* of the names – varying energy, intention, or rhythms." I'm taking from what I see happening in the group when I call "Slow motion" and then "Double time;" "Full-body whisper" followed by "Hard of hearing." "Take what you are given and build on that, explore and heighten what you are given." At the end of this playing, I ask the players if anyone can name everyone in the class. Someone gives it a try and succeeds. The class applauds the successful effort.

I introduce the next step: "Now the game gets a bit more complicated. Player 1 will point to another, Player 2. Player 2 must say yes to Player 1. The "yes" gives Player 1 permission to begin moving. Player 1 starts to walk toward Player 2 in order to take Player 2's space. Player 2 must now get permission to move by pointing to someone else, Player 3. When Player 3 says, "Yes," Player 2 starts to walk toward Player 3's space, leaving an opening in the circle for Player 1 to occupy. Play continues with each player pointing to another, getting permission to move (the other saying yes), and moving to the new space. A player must not move until given permission.

This last rule is the most difficult part of the game. It takes a bit of stopping and starting over to get this part going. In the beginning, the players tend to move before they hear the "yes." Encourage them to play strictly. The game can easily fall apart at this point if they do not.

Once the players get into a rhythm and work out the kinks – clearly executing the rules – I encourage them to play with the game: "Explore and heighten what's given you. When you are giving permission with the word 'yes,' you can sing it, you can give it an intention, you can say it in slow motion or double time. Take from the sound, the attitude, and the movement given to you. Don't move until you get permission. Play faster; think less."

Mastering this final section of the game takes a great deal of concentration. The players have no choice but to focus and that focus brings them into a state of play. They've now gotten to know each other's names and the fun of playing has relaxed inhibitions. It is time to move them right into the work.

Space Walk

Now that the ice has been broken, I take the class through a standard Workshop warm-up sequence with its roots in Spolin's games. The sequence starts out slowly with Space Walk and builds to the pay-off of Machine. I begin by asking the group to walk through the space, feeling the space around them and seeing the other people in the space. As they walk, I coach them: "See from a distance. Release all your holdings. Let space into the body.

Close out space, tense everything: fingers, teeth, face, legs. Release. See everybody and let space in the chest, the shoulders. See all the colors in the room. Keep sight of everybody from a distance. Explore the space *between* you." I'm looking for everyone to be walking at an easy pace with their hands and arms relaxed at their sides, aware of all the others around them, not walking in circles but shifting position to keep everyone in sight.

"Now begin to endow the space with weight. The space begins to become heavy by agreement. Cut through the heavy space with the angles of the body – elbows, knees, hips." To get the players started in this new direction, I demonstrate this cutting movement as I speak. "Now, mirror other players to discover how heavy the space is becoming. Freeze. Take a 'picture' in your mind's eye. Open your eyes and see what you missed." This "freeze-picture-check" sequence is repeated several times with the objective of keeping as many people in sight as possible. I ask players to count the number of people they see when they freeze, joking, "It will be on the test!" I encourage the players to try to see more the next time.

When the space becomes so heavy that the group is barely moving, I coach the players to begin to lighten the space: "How light can the space become by group agreement? Watch the changing patterns you are forming. Let the space become lighter and lighter." As the space becomes lighter, the players begin to skip and fly through the room, feeling released from the slow, disciplined movement of the heavy space. "Freeze. Take a picture."

In Space Walk, I direct the players to move through the space together and focus on hearing, seeing, and being aware of their immediate environment – all in order to be present in the moment and working as a group. This pattern of tension and release produced by exploring opposite movement qualities will be explored further in the next game. Space Walk flows into Space Break and Group Transformations.

Space Break

From the freeze: "Now you are going to *break* the existing space, radically, with sound and movement – one at a time. Stay with the established movement until you must surrender to the new space." One player breaks the space by initiating a clapping/stomping movement pattern. One by one the other players follow her movements. As soon as everyone is moving through the space clapping and stomping, another player stops moving and stands in frozen silence. One by one the players stop moving until all are still. Suddenly one player begins hopping and making a frog-like sound. The rest follow suit and the players continue breaking the space with contrasting sounds and movements. Once this pattern has been established and the players have been forming and breaking the space for some time, I call, "Freeze" and change the game.

Group Transformations

While the players are in a freeze, I explain: "Now begin to find the changes together to form group transformations. For this new game, instead of breaking the space, let the sound and movement change organically as you explore and heighten your activity. Begin to move right from where you left off and find a change together."

The players return to their free-form skipping movements, but shortly begin to slow down, taking a cue from their swinging arms, to find a new way of moving. They are intensely focused on each other as they move through the space in a random pattern. It is important to keep them from walking in a circle. Encourage them to change directions if that happens. Any variation in one person's movement becomes incorporated into the group movement and leads the way to more changes. Once the players have made a number of organic transformations together, I call, "Freeze." Since the group has already been mirroring each other, the game Group Transformations flows naturally into the next game, Mirror Object-Activity Transformations.

Mirror Object-Activity Transformations
Building on the group energy and connection, I take the players from the freeze immediately to dividing up into pairs: "Turn and find a partner with the first eyes you meet. Begin to have a tug of war in mirror. Agree on the weight and pull of an imaginary rope. A real tug of war can evolve only if there is complete agreement about the space between you. Now let's move from the rope to transforming object-activities while still in mirror. Try activities like pulling, sawing, folding, sorting, lifting. Find the moment of change together. It is not important that you know exactly what the object-activity is as long as it has the thrust of pulling, sawing, etc. Let each new activity arise from the previous motion by agreement."

I am guiding these new players toward transformation, starting simply with the rope and the tug of war. Since this is an introductory class, I don't stay with this exercise very long. It is just a taste. After a short exploration, I shake up the space to bring the warm-up sequence to its pay-off moment.

Transition to the Machine game
"Freeze. Drop the mirror. Begin to move in and out of each other in double time – all the way out and all the way in. Freeze." The purpose of this transitional moment is to keep and build on the momentum already generated. From this phase we go right into Machine.

Machine
"Someone start a repeatable movement that engages the whole body, and add an accompanying sound. The movement should not be random." One of the players jumps in and begins a movement/sound pattern. I call, "Find the weight in the space. Make it sharp. Go for the sound when asked to make a sound, not a word like *bang* or *pow* – a *sound*. Keep repeating your sound and motion." To the other players: "One at a time, add your own sound and movement in relation to the other person. Add on until a whole 'machine' is working together. Explore levels. The floor is a trap. Explore your rhythmic connection to the others. There is no physical contact between players in this game."

The first player goes into the space and begins to make a pulling/pushing movement and a sound that he continues to repeat. A second player goes in and makes a pounding movement and sound in relation to the first player. A third makes a stirring-type movement. Players add on until about seven people are moving in rhythm as one machine. The rest of the players stand and observe the action.

As soon as a whole machine is formed, I coach the players to wind down together to a complete stop. The players are still in their machine positions but their movement has suspended. "Listen to the breathing of the group. You are breathing together. Begin to start up the machine, no person initiating the movement. Make your movements more efficient as you get faster. Move faster and faster until you sense – as a group – when to stop, when to freeze." The group breathes together and that breath initiates movement. The machine starts up and gets faster and faster, everyone working together rhythmically. The action gets quite frenetic until out of sheer exhaustion or a sense that everyone is ready to stop, the machine stops! Ideally, everyone stops together, but, at this early stage, sometimes one or two stop and the rest follow.

The first team becomes audience to the next group. I ask this new group to scramble and get some energy going and then call, "Start a machine." The players who had been observing make a new machine, learning from the experience of the first group.

When the game is over, I make a few brief comments before giving everyone a break. "Stopping together is not an easy task. It can only be accomplished when each person is truly focused on the others. Remember that the floor is a trap because, if you are on the floor, your movement is inhibited. In this game, everyone emerges and no one is submerged. The individual is released when working in relation to others, taking energy from the other person."

Machine represents the pay-off moment for this warm-up sequence. Beginning with Space Walk, everything has led to the moment of finding the freeze together. At this point, the players have expended a great deal of energy and concentration. They have earned a break.

Core sequence

Give and Take (two groups)
Three-Chair Conversation (changing groups of three)
Three-Chair Conversation with Conflicting Objectives

Give and Take

After a good break, I ask for about eight players to go up into the space and balance the stage in total stillness. "One of you *take stage* with a sound and movement. Continue to take stage until someone else takes stage. Or continue to move until you *give the stage* to another player by standing directly in front of that person, making eye contact, and passing your energy to them. At that moment you suspend movement and the other player *must* take stage." Play begins. I coach: "Don't make up a movement, take it off what's given to you, react to what's given to you. There is no physical contact in this game."

The game proceeds with players giving and taking the stage, one at a time. Only one person can be moving. At first, the movements and sounds are generally abstract – large stomping moves, swimming movements, skipping. Many of the movements are like those explored earlier in Space Break, but here only the player moving has our full attention – has the stage. If one person goes on too long, someone else can move, take stage. If no one takes, the player can give it away.

Once the players have the general feel of the game, I call, "Now only give." This call serves to get everyone involved in the game, even those who have held back. Once the players get into the rhythm of passing the energy to others, I change the pattern: "Now only take. Work for lots of taking. Take. Take. Take! It's all right to suspend for a beat and then take the stage back by continuing your movement. No time for politeness here. Take!"

The goal is to encourage the players to get out of their heads and into taking on impulse, not holding back and censoring themselves. The call also serves to force the players to focus more intensely and work together to achieve a rapid shift from one player to another. Rapid taking reinforces the idea that you are not frozen when you don't have the stage, but merely suspended – always ready to move again.

For a last beat: "Return to giving and taking. *Every movement counts!*" As the game advances, impulse and energy are generated. The giving and taking is more shared now, with no one player dominating the stage. I see that the group is ready to explore and heighten a theme.

"When I call a theme, respond with whatever the theme means to you. Words can come up. Move from the impulse given to you. Still in give and take, explore the ambience of the theme through sound, word, and movement." I call, "A playground." The players respond. "One at a time. Don't take turns." One player begins jumping on an imaginary hopscotch layout; someone takes stage with a running scream; another starts bouncing a ball and gives that action to someone else. The sights, sounds, activities, and relationships of a group of children in a playground emerge.

"The call is a factory." When the loud, machine-like sounds and practical movements of a factory have been explored, I call a contrasting theme: "Early morning at the lake." With birdcalls, a solo runner, cricket sounds, the lapping of the water, the ambience of this tranquil scene emerges through the giving and taking of sound, word, and movement. When the players begin to lose impulse, I call a new place and guide them to finish: "Thirty seconds to make your last statement." The players make their final moves. "Freeze."

This first group finishes the game and the audience applauds their efforts. The audience has gained insight into how to play the game through watching this group. I ask for a second group to go up onstage. Another eight people volunteer. I take them through the same beginning sequence as above, but, for this group, I explore new rhythms and themes: "Slow motion. Silent film/double time. Gibberish. Sunday in the park. Stock Exchange."

After two groups have played Give and Take, I make a few brief comments: "The purest way to play is without themes, letting relationship, character, or story come up in transformation. Themes make it more manageable for new players or young players. Themes are also used to explore elements of stories."

Since my point of concentration for this introductory class is to establish game language, I shift gears to verbal work by introducing the game Three-Chair Conversation. This game will involve the entire class, three at a time, and will be preparation for the pay-off game at the end.

Three-Chair Conversation

I set up three chairs onstage in a row, facing the audience, and ask for three volunteers to come up and sit in the chairs. "The first chair is the 'occupation' chair, the second chair is the 'listening' chair, and the third chair is the 'personal' or 'anecdotal' chair. Those sitting in chairs 1 and 3 talk only to the person in chair 2 (the 'listening' chair). The player in the middle chair must respond to both conversations, trying to hear both people at the same time. When I call 'change,' everyone moves to the next chair and begins talking and listening to new conversations right away. In other words, the two scenes go on simultaneously with the middle player straddling both. The players on either end are not to acknowledge the existence of the other scene. Everyone will experience all three chairs in this game."

The first three players begin to talk. I coach: "Listen to the one who is speaking to you. Address the listener. Really listen. Change." The call of "Change" prompts the player in the third chair to return to the audience. The listener shifts to the "personal" chair and a new player takes the "occupation" chair. Each change brings a new dynamic that requires different calls. "Begin speaking as soon as you sit down. Change. Keep talking. Change. Don't let the other scene distract you. Focus on communicating. Change."

At the end of the game, I ask the players: "Which chair was the most fun?" When I ask this question, most players rarely realize that the one who is the listener is the one most in the "acting" moment, which prompts me to explore that experience more deeply by asking: "Was it easy to listen? Was the listener really listening? Were the other two people connecting with the listener while keeping up a steady stream of conversation?" I caution: "Players should watch out for 'acting listening' instead of actually hearing. One of the most important aspects of acting is in the ability to listen and receive. This game focuses on doing that. It exercises listening."

I acknowledge that there are no right or wrong answers to the favorite chair question. But most importantly, I point out that this game emphasizes the receiving, so one can engage and respond improvisationally and naturally. Some people observe that in order to stay focused you really have to have something specific to share, something concrete to tell the other person, whether it was a personal anecdote or the need to sell something or teach something in role. Without a story to tell, one player observes how easy it is to become distracted by the other scene. These insights lead right into the next game, Three-Chair Conversation with Conflicting Objectives.

Three-Chair Conversation with Conflicting Objectives

"We are going to play a similar game, but one that adds conflicting objectives and character transformations." Three people volunteer to begin. I explain, "Your situation involves two siblings trying to persuade the third sibling, the one in the middle chair, to stay home and celebrate his mother's birthday. The player in the center chair needs to come up with a strong reason for why he can't or won't stay home." The players begin to improvise a scene in pursuit of their objectives.

The main point of concentration of this game is character transformation. During the playing, I call out different ages. "You are ten years old." "You are forty." "You are college students." When I change ages, I coach: "Make the transformation right from where you are. You don't have to backtrack or start over. What has been said has been said. Transform how you are talking, transform your tactics, transform your physical movement to express the age called." For example, as ten-year-olds, the players try to threaten their sibling; as forty-year-olds, the players place a huge guilt trip on their sibling, dredging up past rivalries; as college students, the vocabulary changes to include pop culture references like "dude" and lots of "you knows." The tactics fall somewhere in the middle of the other two age groups. To keep the scene alive and spontaneous, I make calls during the playing using the language I established earlier in the class – slow motion, double time, give and take, freeze. This variation on Three-Chair Conversation leads directly into the final game.

Pay-off game: To Gets in pairs

For this game, I ask for two volunteers and then locate these players in a "Who, What, Where" situation. The Where and the "activity" remain constant throughout the playing. "You are on a train sitting next to each other. Player A is sitting next to the window. Player B wants Player A to open the window." I assign them a beginning relationship – Player B is a businessman and Player A his female administrative assistant.

The players begin to improvise a scene. I look for a moment to catch them off-balance and call to Player B: "She's your wife." The players transform immediately to accommodate the new call. As the improvisation progresses, I call out different relationships and the players must adjust without backtracking or starting the scene over. I always make my calls in terms of the person pursuing the dominant objective: "She's a perfect stranger." And finally, "She's your boss." If Player B has effectively and believably played their objective, Player A will end the scene by opening the window. If not, I will call: "Thirty seconds to find a final freeze." The audience acknowledges their good work.

Like the previous game, the main emphasis here is on transforming relationships. The player can begin a sentence talking to a grandmother and end that sentence relating to a child. To achieve the objective, the player must deepen the need. This doesn't mean giving more reasons to Player A as to why she should do something. It is not about finding the right reason. It's not about manipulating. It's about deepening the two conflicting needs within the specific relationship. For example, let's say Player B appeals to Player A on the basis that he needs her to open the window because he is about to faint. If Player A still doesn't open the window and Player B's need is real, he will indeed faint! At that point, it would be difficult for Player A to continue refusing to open the window – unless it was stuck, of course.

I ask for two more volunteers and add an imaginary object-activity to the scene. "You two are making a salad. Player B needs help with her homework. You are sisters." For the first change, I call: "She's your mother. Important people are on the way. Raise the stakes." "She's your grandmother, she's your daughter, etc." "Try all different ways to reach your objective." Player B, talking to her daughter, starts crying out of frustration because she doesn't understand how to save her file on her new computer and needs her daughter's help. The daughter can't help because her hands are wet. When that beat is played, I call, "Try a new way. Don't reason it out logically. Try a spectrum of different ways." The players take the bait and try a range of tactics: pleading, demanding, teasing. I call several more relationships: "She's your sorority sister." "She's your co-worker in a school cafeteria." "Change as the relationships change." "Stay in that relationship and explore the different ways that are needed to achieve your objective."

In response to this scene, I comment for everyone's benefit, "Let go of plot. Let go of wanting to perform well. The danger of this game is manipulation. Counter it by exploring the relationship and sticking to the need."

I invite one last pair of volunteers to come onstage. For this pair of players, I set up the following given circumstances: To Player A: "You are rehearsing for a play while your husband is doing the income taxes." To Player B: "Your objective is to get her to be quiet so you can concentrate." Calls: "She's your lover. She's your daughter. She's your employer. She's your grandmother. You are total strangers." At the end of this scene, I invite observations of how the tactics for reaching the objective changed with the changing relationships. Players noted how people get closer as the level of familiarity and intimacy grows – a lover can get closer physically than a stranger. And if a stranger violates the other's personal space, tension mounts. They also noted that emotions are more readily expressed the closer the relationship. When Player B went from dealing with his wife to dealing with his lover, the entire tone of the scene changed from directness to playful nudging. Examples of changes in power also came up. Player B could be dominant in relation to his daughter, but had to be more deferential to his boss.

After the discussion, I sum things up: "You don't want to get married to one way. I'm interested in the whole spectrum of ways to reach the objective. The game itself is a translation of Stanislavski's work with objectives and conflicts: How do I get what I want? And the principle of transformation is absolutely crucial to this game. Trust in the transformation. Don't justify it. Understand the transformation viscerally. Continue in mid-sentence, mid-action. When a new relationship is called, don't drop everything, don't rethink. Trust that the adjustment will happen."

Referring to the last scene about needing quiet, I talk about the trap of negativity. "In real life, we often have the obstacle of knowing someone is going to reject us, to say no to us. Why is the other refusing us? One way to counter the negativity is for the player not to be willful but to have some very important reason for staying with their activity, for not breaking the concentration needed for that activity. Interpret the conflict not so much as absolutes, but in terms of play and give and take. It must be related to play, otherwise you think your way out."

And finally, I address the importance of the Where. "We are never in a vacuum relating to another person – we are in a place. Stay with the activities – it is more concrete. This focus removes any sense of the obligation, of what the player 'should' be doing."

Adult players and potential teachers should note the progression and design of the class. How does the warm-up relate to the To Get games (mirror transformation of object-activities)? How does each section relate to the next? Design is integral to the teaching of this work. Everything should "breathe," be organic, and relate one to the other, culminating in the final section, what I call the "pay-off." The pay-off moment of To Gets gives the players an opportunity to perform a scene, gives them a theatrical moment to explore. Both teacher and student now have a language with which to communicate. The teacher has many games and calls to keep the players from trying "to act" or "write" the scene, to keep them from being "in the head."

Byrne Piven: on leading Three-Person Scenes and To Gets

Three-Person Scenes with Conflicting Objectives evolves nicely out of Three-Chair Conversation but you must now make it a Who, What, and Where. Get your players out of the chairs into a somewhat detailed Where with an activity. Even a train ride has activities: reading, playing solitaire, computer work maybe. I write on planes all the time. Raise the importance of these activities, for example, a book that you love, a letter to your boyfriend.

As the leader, you must find the quick and efficient way of catching the players off-balance for the change in relationship. Establish the language: a handclap means "Freeze" and you call the new relationship, which they must enter on impulse so as not to get into the head and compose a stereotype. (Clap your hands only when you know the new relationship you want to call!)

The POC in this game is finding the action. It comes from the Stanislavski system where the term *actions* refers to the way in which we go about trying to achieve an objective. Players A and C are given beat objectives like "You need to tell her this great dream you had last night" or "Get her to tell you about her date last night." These are merely opening suggestions: "Get her to vote for a certain person for class president," "Get her to forgive you." Look for objectives that will elicit a focus on the other person rather than on the indulgence of the character's need. Give and take should be the mode here.

Encourage the players to find different ways of trying to achieve their objectives. Actions are gerunds and can be preceded by the word "by" – by pleading, by demanding (an all-time favorite), by flattering (careful of over-manipulation), by reasoning (watch out for complaints that the other person doesn't understand them), by seducing (translate for kids: "by making her your friend"), by comforting, by honoring, by needling, by teasing, by making her laugh, by intimidating, by touching her emotions, by understanding her, by sympathizing with her, and on and on. Maybe some physical ways. Try these: by whispering; by making physical contact.

If manipulations and bickering are present in every relationship in the game, call your players on it. A teacher can flunk you, a boss can fire you, a parent can ground you, a friend can break off the relationship. Remind the players that there are consequences for their behavior. The player of lower status needs to make adjustments in response to the implied power of their superiors. They cannot deny that a power differential exists.

If manipulation still persists, try emphasizing "life objectives:" "You're the kind of person who always wants to be just; you're a religious person." Life objectives are juxtaposed against beat or scene objectives, thus giving the work dimension.

Introductory workshop emphasizing verbal work and play

An exploration of language through play is critical to our efforts to bridge the gap between improvisation and scripted work. Getting players in touch with their bodies and connected to one another through highly physical work is only half of the equation. In his advice to the players, Hamlet says, "Suit the action to the word, the word to the action" (Arden 3.2.17–18). That connection between the body and language plays an important role in game work, in story theatre, and in scene work. Games that explore the verbal life along with impulse, agreement, and transformation include Word Tag, Word Toss, Word Machine, all Gibberish games, Simultaneous Rap, Four-Way Telephone, Double Scene, Fingers (Amore), Poetry Workshop, Who, What, Where Scenes, and Storytelling games.

Exploring verbal life: a scene from the Workshop

My overall point of concentration in this class is to connect the player's verbal life to their body, to impulse, and to agreement. My specific point of concentration: to explore and heighten sounds and words expressing meaning and feeling. I am using this early game class to introduce students to verbal work through several foundational games as I continue to establish game language with them.

Warm-up sequence
Freeze Tag into *Word Tag* into *Ball Toss/Word Toss* into *Word Machine*

Freeze Tag

I start to warm up the class with a game of Freeze Tag: "Freeze Tag is played like regular tag – someone is 'It.' The It tries to tag someone else; everyone else tries not to get tagged. But in this version of the game, when the It tags another player, they both freeze and stay frozen until everyone else freezes too. When everyone is frozen, the new It begins to move, signaling everyone else to move and play tag again."

My first call is "Slow motion." I explain, "The point of concentration in slow motion is for the player who is the It to tag while moving in slow motion – getting to one's goal as fast as possible in slow motion. Everyone must be moving at the same speed, like a group in a slow-motion film. You can't speed up to tag another player; you must reach out while staying in slow motion." This is an important subtlety, since most players think the objective is "to demonstrate" slow motion rather than to reach your destination by tagging another player. From slow motion, I call its opposite: "Double time with shoelaces tied together." These calls are alternated to get the players into a flow.

Everyone freezes the moment someone is tagged. This widens the circle of concentration to include the others – all working together. The point of concentration here is agreement. The players are to make no sound after someone is tagged. The one tagged must sense with the group when to begin to move again.

Word Tag

Once the players are working together, I change the game from Freeze Tag to Word Tag in order to focus on the point of concentration for the class – verbal life. "Like Freeze Tag, when the It tags another, all are to freeze, but in 'Word Tag,' at the moment of tagging and freeze, the It says a word on impulse, sending it to the person tagged. The new It receives the word and then senses with the group that it is time to move again. When the new It tags another player, all freeze, and the new It says the word given to her plus one of her own. We will keep adding on words until the list becomes too long to repeat and then we will start a new list."

As they play, I help the players keep off-balance with calls of slow motion, double time/ shoelaces tied together, whisper, sing it or give it a style. I coach the players to get into the space of each word, to say the words from their own center: "Fill the space of the word and give each word its own value. Send the word to the person you tagged. Energize it. You are passing the word to your partner." After several lists of random words, we explore a theme with related words: "This game is about communication through sound and feeling; it is the first step in connecting the word to its meaning and emotional weight through the body."

The first theme is "autumn." Players make a list that includes words like "dying leaves," "cold," "colorful." Next I call, "Halloween." The first player says "Jack-o-Lantern" and the next player adds the word "spooky," but both words sound the same. I ask that player, "How does the word *spooky* sound different than the word *Jack-o-Lantern*? Try it again." The second player repeats the word *spooky* with her own intonation and play resumes. Each new player can say the previous words as they were said or they can bring their own take to the words in the expanding list. To get the players out of their heads, I call, "Sing it." "Full-body whisper." "Noise overhead." These calls help the players give each word in the list its own value. For each theme, the players generate a new list of related words.

Ball Toss/Word Toss

I move from Tag to a game of Ball Toss by gathering the group into a circle and throwing an imaginary ball to one of the players. I instruct that player to throw the ball to another and then guide the group to explore throwing imaginary balls of different weights and sizes around the circle. As soon as the group is invested in the exercise, I shift gears: "When you throw the ball, also 'throw a word' to another player. Start with colors." One player throws "Red." Another throws "Tangerine." I encourage the players to explore and heighten the quality of the words. "What does 'tangerine' sound like?" I ask.

I shift gears to new words and experiment with different rhythms by calling: "Slow motion. Double time. Short, sharp staccato throws. Leisurely playful throws." I encourage the players to reflect the physical movement in the word: "Capture the quality of the word with your movement." Then I instruct them to explore on their own, giving and taking the energy being passed around and building on it.

Many of the calls I make are repeated over and over in the games played. The repetition helps to establish the game language that will be used throughout our work. The calls embody the universal rhythms and vocal qualities important in theatrical expression as well as the gearshifts in energy necessary to keep an audience's attention. Over time players internalize the calls; they become a kind of non-judgmental short-hand. For example, instead of telling a player or actor, "You are speaking too fast" (a corrective that implies he is doing something wrong), the call of "slow motion" achieves the same purpose without making the player/actor self-conscious.

The games played to this point get the group moving and working together. It is important to encourage the players to get their whole body involved in expressing the words. These games also introduce and reinforce the point of concentration for the class − the exploration and heightening of sounds and words expressing meaning and feeling.

Word Machine

During the last playing of Word Tag, I call a freeze. "From that freeze, take that energy and, one at a time, build a 'word' machine. Your point of concentration here is to bring a word or phrase in with your movement when there is space for you to lay it in. Your word can be *slice, punch, push, pull,* etc." As the machine is getting established, I encourage and guide the players: "Let the body help the word and the word help the body. Get the action going and add the word. Give and take the word and throw it out into the space. You don't have to say the word every time you make a movement."

Once the machine is established, the players wind down and start again on the common breath, speed up the machine and find their freeze together. Break time.

Core sequence

Simultaneous Rap morphing into *Give and Take*

Simultaneous Rap

When the players return from break, I ask them to find a partner and sit down facing each other in pairs around the stage space to play Simultaneous Rap. In this whole-class exercise, all the pairs will be playing at the same time and the players in each pair will be talking simultaneously to each other. Subjects for this game are sets of opposites. I suggest several possible subjects for the group to consider: hot and cold, winter and summer, tall and short. The group chooses "hot and cold." I explain to the paired players that one will speak about "hot" and the other about "cold," but they will be speaking at the same time. "The rules of the game: you cannot use negatives, ask questions, or use the first person. This is a *third-person rap*. Be careful not to answer each other. This is not a conversation – you are rapping on the subject essay style."

The players rap on their respective subjects, speaking simultaneously.

For example:

Player A: "Hot is red and fiery, flames licking the face. Hot is like hell, an inferno of heat. Hot is Florida and Arizona in the summer."

Player B: "Cold is icy and numbing. Cold is freezing temperatures during winter with the wind howling and biting the skin."

I let the rap go on for a bit until I see that the players are connected. At that point, I call a freeze and explain, "This time, as you continue your rap, incorporate words and phrases you hear from your partner into your own rap." The players resume talking and I walk around listening to various raps and reminding the players to play strictly, to stick to the rules: "Get as much eye contact as possible. Keep the game going. No negatives. Stay in the third person. Communicate to your partner."

I notice a pair playing well – they are connected and their rap flows freely. They are staying in the third person, not using "I" or "you" or negative statements. I tell them to continue rapping while asking everyone else to suspend their play for a moment and attend to the group chosen. I highlight a couple of other pairs. In this way, players learn from each other without the need for a critique.

Simultaneous Rap in Give and Take

I tell everyone to resume playing, but this time to give and take their rap. Playing by the rules of the game Give and Take, only one person can move and speak at a time. To rap in give and take, the players must leave their simultaneous speech and begin to speak in a contrapuntal fashion. Player A will have to suspend mid-sentence while Player B takes stage, then Player A takes back the stage to complete her sentence. The rap continues in this back-and-forth manner, but in true give and take, which is not turn-taking. Turn-taking has a sense of regularity and agreement – now it's my turn, now it's your turn. In true give and take, Player A stops Player B by moving and talking without regard for the end of the sentence or pause. The taking is a surprise and Player B must react instantly by ceasing his rap. The players must have intense focus on each other to accomplish true give and take. This game is all about *impulse!*

An example of Player A and B speaking contrapuntally, in give and take:

Player A:	**Player B:**
"Hot produces/	"Cold requires bundles and bundles of/
sweat, beads of water dripping/	
	clothes – hats and scarves and down/
down the face and back. Hot is/	
	jackets so a person doesn't freeze to death. Cold is
	snow cones and Pop/
what is popular – the fad/	
	sicles and ice cubes."
of the day."	

Caryl Churchill and David Mamet, for example, use this type of overlapping or contrapuntal dialogue as a playwriting technique.

Now we enter the final phase of the game. I call freeze: "Go back to your simultaneous rap, but this time switch subjects." Once the players get actively into their new rap: "Keep the subject you have now. All rules are suspended. Fight to win." The room explodes with energy as the players are freed from constraints and pursue victory. They use "I" and "you," and negatives, speaking directly to each other, trying to drive home their point in the most powerful way possible. Some stand to gain higher ground. Some try to win on volume. At the peak of play: "Thirty seconds" and then "Freeze."

After the playing, we discuss their reactions to the game. They talk about what happened when the rules were suspended and they were free to fight to win. The players agreed that they felt a great release. Everything they had done informed the pursuit of this objective. No time to think, they responded on impulse and surprised themselves by their audacity.

Pay-off theatrical experience: Who, What, Where Scenes

I divide the class into groups of four or five players for Who, What, Where Scenes with a Simple Situation and Calls. "Decide *who* you are in relation to each other, *where* you are, and *what* you are doing in this place. The What should be some kind of shared physical activity like setting a table, raking leaves, painting a room. That is all. You will discover the nature of the scene as you play. Your point of concentration is to engage in the activity in that particular Where."

After a few moments of group interaction, I ask for a volunteer group to go up onstage and begin the scene in silence as they establish the space. Once the Where seems clear, I release them to speak. During the playing of each scene, I use some of the following, now familiar calls: Slow motion, double time, hard-of-hearing, full-body whisper, sing it, help (help everyone in the scene make contact with imaginary objects established), hinder (keep others from using the objects), give weight, shape, texture, temperature to the objects. To shake up the space, I shift gears to calling different film styles: spaghetti western, foreign film, melodrama.

My choice of calls depends on what the players in a particular scene are doing, on what I observe they need at the moment to achieve their objective or to energize the scene. Do they need help in realizing the objects? Are they playwriting instead of listening and reacting in the moment? Are they losing impulse and energy? Do they need help in exploring the richness of language in scene through rhythm and intent? Any game the group has played before can be used as a call within this exercise to keep the players in the moment and in play (e.g. contact, entrances and exits, even tag). These calls direct the focus without taking the players out of the game. They also bring humor and energy to the scene.

Sometimes when there are five or more people in a scene, the players begin to divide up and essentially play two scenes at once. I call, "Double scene" to make the players aware of what is happening and "Give and Take" to get the players to move back and forth between the two sub-scenes. That means the group of three will speak and move to play a moment from their sub-scene and the group of two will take stage to play a moment of their sub-scene while the other group suspends their movement and speech. Only one group can move and speak at a time. The two groups will give and take the stage, perform their sub-scenes, and find their way back to all performing one scene. I call, "Thirty seconds to your final freeze," and the playing ends. The other players perform their scenes. The "Double scene" call makes the players aware of others onstage and suggests ways of working together. It generates kinesthetic awareness of "other," as a concept onstage.

The final scene game in this class reinforces the connection between game work and scene work. All the physical and vocal work done in the class has been preparation for the performance of a scene that has all the basic elements of a play – a setting, characters in relationship, and an action. The improvisational nature of that performance requires the players to practice good acting technique – to see each other, to listen to each other, and to react to each other truthfully in the moment. Players learn what works and what impedes play onstage from observing others perform. They begin to understand how the calls serve to keep the players focused on the POC and in play.

Importance of organic flow

All these classes embody organic flow, a concept that guides all the class design at the Workshop. Building on the energy and focus of a group through the organic flow of a game sequence, a class, or a series of classes, is critically important to any creative process, and especially important for achieving "play" in game work.

Classes at the Workshop are developed in a way that capitalizes on this notion of flow. Instead of treating many games as single entities, sequences of games are created. Play starts simply by helping the players get connected and then builds slowly toward a pay-off experience. One of the most fundamental of these sequences is Space Walk-Space Break-Machine. This sequence is repeated many times in various configurations, sometimes adding mirror, sometimes adding words, such as Word Machine.

Many other game sequences exist. For example:

Transformation work – The Mirror sequence starts with a basic Mirror exercise. Focus is on two players getting connected by mirroring each other in large slow movements. The sequence progresses to Mirror Object-Activity Transformations. Still in Mirror, players begin to explore activities with objects in space – stirring, pounding, kneading, folding – finding transformations from one object–activity to another. This game leads to the pay-off of Mirror Scene Transformations. Here the players transform from scene to scene, returning to mirror at the end of a beat to find a new scene, if needed. The ultimate goal is to establish a motor that enables the players to be so in tune with each other that they can transform without going back into Mirror.

Mime work – The Construct sequence starts with players slowly designing the space, one at a time, when their number is called, to moving one at a time without outside guidance, to designing "constructs" (group sculptures based on nouns like *house, bird, tree*). This game can move into Adjective Constructs where each player in turn adds an adjective to the noun (*old tree/gnarly old tree/mammoth, gnarly old tree*). The coloration of the word forces the players to move in response and the shape of the original construct – the design of bodies in space – changes. Finally, after establishing the required focus and discipline for the slow constructs, the sequence ends in the pay-off – Impulse Constructs, the explosive release of simultaneous sound and movement in response to the leader's object calls, for example, washing machine, telephone switchboard, germ, a rose.

These are only a couple of examples, but, once you understand the principle of building on the group energy and momentum, you can create your own. The process is like priming a pump. In an entire class, organic flow is achieved through a design that links the warm-up games to the games in the core of a class, and finally to the pay-off experience. All the games in a given class are linked through the point of concentration for that class. So the pay-off experience is usually a scene game or performance activity that calls on all the skills explored during the class.

Spontaneity. Training the impulse. Exercising in the off-balance moment. Keeping out of your head. Not thinking about what to do. Never getting ahead of yourself in the moment. Being in the moment. Giving to and receiving from the other person. These are the elements of play. The point of concentration in the discipline of the games is the task between two people. That's all you need to be concerned about. Play allows the "thinking" brain to take its proper place in relation to the body. Left alone like this, the mind begins to do cartwheels. It can go to places it could never imagine.

5 Workshops on Agreement

The principle of agreement is:

To work together in harmony, giving and taking from one another and from the surrounding space in order to play a game, improvise a scene, find a transformation, or tell a communal story.

The point of concentration for games focused on the principle of agreement is:

◆ To be part of the whole.

◆ To experience group agreement.

◆ To discover together the sensory properties of imaginary objects or circumstances.

◆ To be connected to all the other players, united in common purpose.

◆ To follow the follower rather than initiating independently.

◆ To communicate through intent, physicalization, and melody without words.

◆ To take what's given and build on that energy.

◆ To explore and heighten through giving and taking what you see and hear.

All the games we play require agreement among players. At the introductory level, imaginary object games serve to promote agreement and prepare players for more advanced work in specificity through sense memory and emotional investment. The following games are particularly good for developing ensembles:

◆ All Tag games

◆ Fish

◆ All group transformation games, e.g. Transforming Machines

◆ Mirror in 2s, 4s, 6s, 8s

◆ Space Break

◆ Musical Transformations

◆ Give and Take

◆ Portraits and Constructs (Slow and Fast)

◆ Four in a Moving Object

◆ Many object games, e.g. Three on a Box

◆ Story games, e.g. Round-Robin Storytelling and Give-and-Take Storytelling

◆ All Gibberish games.

Workshop on kinesthetic agreement

The point of concentration for the kinesthetic agreement workshop is to experience group agreement. The warm-up sequence explores kinesthetic agreement, the core of the class focuses on agreement through work with imaginary objects, and the pay-off experience gives the players an opportunity to practice these skills in a performance situation. This workshop typically runs three hours long.

Warm-up sequence
Cat's Corner (Basic game into *Who, What, Where* into *To Gets)*
Portraits (Group 1); *Impulse Constructs* (Group 2)

Cat's Corner
I begin with the whole group of players standing in a large circle. One player stands in the middle. I explain the rules: "The person in the middle is the Cat. The Cat will approach someone in the circle and say, 'Cat wants a corner.' That player will answer, 'Go see my

next-door neighbor' and point either to the 'neighbor' on her left or the one on her right. The Cat follows that instruction and asks the neighbor for a corner. While the Cat is going from player to player asking for a corner, the rest of the players change places by making eye contact with someone across the space and non-verbally agreeing to exchange positions. The Cat tries to claim one of the vacated spaces. If successful, the player without a corner is the new Cat. If unsuccessful, the Cat continues to seek a corner."

I caution the players to play fully but to be aware of the safety of all concerned, including themselves. To play this game successfully, the players must risk losing their corner. The fun comes from those moments when numerous players are scrambling to find a corner. I make a variety of calls: "Slow motion. Double time. Full-body whisper. Hard-of-hearing. Accents: Southern, British, Italian, German, Russian." Once the players are actively playing, I encourage them to respond to the Cat in the style of the question and to "explore and heighten the energy you are getting from the Cat."

To deepen the game, I add Who, What, Where elements to the playing. My first call is "prison yard." I coach: "Respond in character to the Where and to one another. Create the ambience of that place." The players respond as if they are prisoners, with the Cat playing a guard demanding each prisoner's space. The players stay with this Where until a new Cat emerges. I call, "Tea at the palace." The players respond as courtiers with teacups in their hands or fans or canes, still playing the basic game. I call: "Playground at kindergarten recess." The players become young children seeking a swing or a turn at hopscotch. For "rock concert," the players become teens jostling for position and grooving to the imaginary music.

As their characters and situations change, the players adjust their dialogue to reflect their new circumstances. For example in the prison, the guard yells aggressively, "Hey, you, get off that bench!" and the prisoner responds, "Go pick on someone else, will ya!" The players in this scenario play a moment of challenge, staring each other down, until the guard gives in and the game moves on. For the call "Tea at the palace," instead of asking for "a corner," the Cat asks, "Tea?" and holds out an imaginary teapot. The courtier responds in a clipped British dialect, "Not for me, thank you."

At this point, I shift gears again and add a "to get" dimension to the game. The players will improvise dialogue depending on the situation established. For the first effort, I set up the following situation: "The Cat is a person who has some emergency and needs to find a phone. In character, the Cat knocks on imaginary doors in an effort to be let into the apartment or house to use the phone. The players behind the imaginary doors can improvise their own characters and reasons for not letting the Cat into their homes." The players continue to play the game *and* play the mini-scenes with a real need and strong objective. After a few scenes, I encourage them to improvise their own situations on impulse.

This variation on the basic game keeps the players in play because it asks them to focus on two things at once: the scene and the game. The player being appealed to by the Cat should engage in the given circumstances, not dismiss the Cat because that's a possibility within the rules of the game. The resistance must come out of legitimate concerns.

The original "Cat's Corner" game came to the Workshop from Paul Sills. We added the Who, What, Where and "to get" elements. This is a very physical and competitive game. Immediacy comes from not wanting to be the one left out, the one who didn't get a chair.

The game reminds you of all the times you lost or you weren't good enough. Players abandon themselves to this game. It has surprise, laughter, play, and the "off-balance" moment. It takes you out of your head and into impulse and visceral space where anything can happen, what you hadn't anticipated and you couldn't choreograph. The actor is present and spontaneous there. It takes courage to enter that area.

Portraits

For this game, I have a group of six to eight players stay onstage. Everyone else becomes the audience. I introduce the rules of this game: "One at a time, you are going to build a portrait." I point to a spot on the floor and explain, "The first player will run to this mark and strike a pose." I point to a place on the wall over the heads of the audience and tell the players to pretend there is a camera out there: "When you hit your pose and freeze, make sure your face is seen and your eyes are focused on the camera." The next player will run up and strike another pose that makes some kind of physical contact with the first player. "You can have your foot touching their foot, your elbow touching their waist – any sort of contact as long as you support your own weight. Each player must be in contact with one other player in the portrait."

The players build a portrait, running up to join the frozen group, one at a time, on impulse. Calls: "Be in contact. Get your face seen. The floor is a trap. Support your own weight. Keep your focus out here. Use levels. Go back and someone else start a portrait."

These calls are made to help the players play strictly – to keep them focused on the task at hand and away from grandstanding. For example, if someone takes a pose on the floor, that pose may draw the audience's attention but it will be more difficult for that player to move with the group into a new portrait.

The players must build the portrait on impulse and not hang each other up by pausing to think too much. Players are not given numbers or any prescribed order for joining the portrait. It is important that they negotiate with one another non-verbally in a give-and-take fashion, moving *on impulse* rather than pre-planning. Right from the start of the game they are learning how to be in agreement.

"Now, in slow motion, when I say 'change,' make a change in the portrait beginning and ending at the same time and in contact." I suggest that the players make the adjustment in really thick space, in slow motion, while keeping the space buoyant. In other words, moving through the heavy space without physical tension. It's almost like taking one slow-motion breath as a group and coming to rest on the exhalation.

"Change." All the players change position simultaneously. "If you are right, go left. Left, go right. Up, go down. Down, go up. Use levels. Change." On each of these changes, the players move as one body, not looking where they are going so much as sensing where they need to go, and coming to their new portrait at the same time, in agreement.

"Now, on your own, make three fast changes, beginning and ending in agreement. Staccato!" Sharply, one player turns a head, another changes an expression and focus, another kneels, another makes a sharp gesture – all at the same time. "Bup ... Bup ... Bup!" I call out, marking the rhythm of their changes.

I encourage them to explore levels and different body positions, and to stay mindful that they are in contact and getting their faces seen. When I feel they are working together well, I change the rhythm and give them agency: "Now make three slow-motion changes *on your own* and then three double-time changes." The only way the players can accomplish this task is by group agreement, sensing the movement impulse in others and responding to it.

For the finale, we play Captions. I direct them to take that same energy and build a portrait based on a caption. The first call is "Why me?" The players respond individually and as a group. New call: "I've won!" And the last caption: "It's my turn now!"

I'd like to reinforce the idea that players are not assigned an order to joining the portrait. In this game, it is important that you *take a chance* and that you move in a give-and-take fashion, one at a time. This open form puts the players in touch with one another in a non-verbal way. Assigning numbers and an order undermines the point of concentration of the game – impulse and agreement.

Impulse Constructs

I call up another group of six to eight players. They will respond, on impulse, all at once, through sound and movement to the **sound, feel, or shape of a word** that I will call out. In this game, you don't need to be in actual physical contact, but you should end up in a big clump of bodies working in tandem, not spread out all over the stage space.

I tell the players, "Your sounds can take the form of actual sounds or they can be repeated words, even short phrases. For example, if 'telephone switchboard' is called, you could respond verbally by repeating a buzzing sound, repeating the word *hello*, or the phrase *one moment, please*. You'll all be making sounds and performing movements at the same time and your movement should be connected to your sound or word. For example, if you are repeating *one moment, please*, you might be pressing and holding a button as a phone operator would." The class laughs. "I think I'm dating myself here! Do you even know what a phone operator is?" They don't!

In this case, the call of telephone switchboard wouldn't be a good choice for this group. It would put the players into their heads and stop the energy. Because the leader is making calls in the moment, working improvisationally with the group, sometimes a call that seems perfectly understandable to the leader will not resonate with the group. If the call doesn't move the players into immediate action, you know they are confused. The remedy? Make a new call right away! This situation is a good example of the kind of non-verbal dialogue that takes place between players and leader in this method.

To get the group started, I have them run around the stage quickly, in and out of one another randomly. "Go all the way in and all the way out. How close can you come to someone else passing through the middle?" When I see that the players are focused on playing, I call, "Freeze. A blender!" The group responds with the sound, shape, and feel of the word *blender*. "Give and take the words and sounds." One player is making karate movements and chopping sounds. Someone else is whirring. Another is repeating *purée* in a high-pitched voice and making a squishing movement. "Freeze." "Scramble – a balloon!" Players respond with some holding balloons, some blowing up balloons, some being balloons.

The game Impulse Constructs is similar to Machine in the sense that each member of the group is part of a whole, working rhythmically in tandem with everyone else. However, impulse constructs are more loosely structured than machines; the players make an individual contribution to create a cumulative effect expressing the sound, feel, and sense of the word.

"Freeze – old sneakers!" In this one, one player is putting on and taking off an imaginary sneaker. Another is smelling a stinky sneaker and repeating "Phew!" A third is simulating running in place. Still another is repeating "Adidas" and holding up the "product" as if in a television commercial. I call, "Get the word out. Throw the word into the space from the sounds that you have."

"Freeze – scramble – prison searchlights." As the players explode in a cacophony of sirens and the chaos of a prison breakout, I coach: "Be a part of the whole." I call a freeze to bring the game to an end and the audience applauds appreciatively for the commitment and creativity they have witnessed. Break time.

The point of concentration of this game is to respond on impulse with the first thing that comes to your mind rather than thinking about what you are going to do. The fun of the game for the audience is to see all the varied responses together. The humor lies in the juxtaposition of all kinds of different responses. It isn't about who is the clever one. It's about the group response.

Core sequence

Make a Deal into *Moving a Large Object* into *Problem with a Large Object*

Make a Deal

I ask everyone to come up into the playing space and make a large circle. "Shake up the space with your entire body – not just hands, but hips, stomach, back," I say, demonstrating. "Begin to shape the space with your whole body until an object emerges. No balls, no toothbrushes. Now use the object that you've found in the space in an extraordinary way, a way that it would not normally be used. For example, balance it on your head, stroke your cheek with it, and so on." The players do this exploration with their own objects. One player walks on his broom as if it were a tightrope. Another smells a necklace and then uses it as a slingshot. "Now use the object in its accustomed fashion – sweep with a broom, roll dough with the rolling pin, and so on."

Once the players have firmly established their objects, I instruct them to pair up. "Demonstrate your object to your partner and have your partner demonstrate her object to you. If your partner is confused or has no idea what you are doing, you might have to demonstrate your object over again. You can trade objects when your partner indicates that she knows what your object is and you think you know what her object is. Once your first trade is made, go around the room and find new partners. Make as many trades as you can."

It is important to note that a player cannot make a trade unless his partner indicates that he has an idea of what the object is. He may think that the object being demonstrated is a broom when the demonstrating player meant it to be a shovel, but that doesn't matter at this stage of the game. The players are agreeing to trade on the idea that each thinks they know what the other's object is.

As I watch the trades being made, I often notice that a player is struggling to demonstrate their object without the help of speech. In this case, I might call: "If you feel you must speak while demonstrating, you can speak in gibberish (nonsense language). And your partner must ask questions in gibberish."

After everyone has made about five or six trades, I ask the players to take the object they have ended up with and sit in a circle. Going around the circle, the players demonstrate those objects one at a time. After everyone has had a turn, we discuss what the initial objects were, how the objects changed as they were passed along (much like the game of Telephone), what they thought they had and how others interpreted what they were given. We all laugh as we discover that the rolling pin became a baby carriage and the bell rope turned into a plunger.

Moving a Large Object

With this game, I build on the mime and agreement work done previously. I divide the class into groups of four and ask each group to decide on a large object. When the groups have come up with their objects, I tell the first group to volunteer: "You are to move your object across the space from that corner to this one. Your point of concentration is on the group agreement as to the size and shape of the object." I vary the calls for each group, depending on their needs and to keep things interesting. For Group 1, I call, "Help each other," to get the players connected and then I introduce a conflict with "Now hinder each other." I raise the stakes for Group 2: "The building is closing down and you have limited time before you're locked in." For Group 3: "You hear your parents coming home and, if they catch you, there will be hell to pay." For Group 4, I reprise the help and hinder calls and remind them to explore the shape and weight of their object. "Thirty seconds."

In this game, watch for agreement in knees and hands and movement. The paradox of this game is that, in order to successfully hinder each other, the group must be in total kinesthetic agreement about the object, otherwise they only argue.

Problem with a Large Object

For this game, we form new groups of four. "In this game, you must decide on a large object and its problem. Your point of concentration is to agree on the weight, shape, and size of the object as it is handled and to solve the problem agreed upon. For example, you have a locked trunk and have lost the key or you have a Christmas tree that is too large for the room. You will then *improvise* three possible solutions with no success and solve the problem on the fourth try." I send the groups off to decide on the object and the problem but advise them not to plan out anything else.

Each group performs their scene. Calls: "Slow motion. Double time. Full-body whisper. Give and take. Deal with the object physically. Help. Hinder. Agree on the weight, the size, the shape. Solve the problem. No playwriting. Focus on the object." Each call is made based on what each group is doing. The call keeps the players focused on the task at hand and out of their heads.

As a player, you must keep focused on the task of solving the problem – the doing of it rather than the talking about how to solve the problem. Remember that, as players, you really don't have anything to play off of except the other players, which is all you'll need. The life of any game or scene is in the agreement of the players. By using large, full objects, you are compelled to agree, lest chaos reign. And it's wonderful to watch players in full and total agreement using and moving things like imaginary cars or couches. By agreeing to the object's size and mass and weight or bulk and every other possible detail about that object, it becomes real for you and for the audience. The alternative is like the five blind men and the elephant. Each individual knows what they have got, but nobody knows what anyone else is about. For example: "Grab this wheel here." "You mean the pillow there?" Aaargh! If you have faith in what's going on in the space, the audience has faith. Avoid making up a plot; just deal with the problem.

Pay-off game
Where relay
The whole class plays this game, but the players are onstage two at a time. I decide the place – backstage at a theatre. I locate the entrances and exits and put a couple of chairs and cubes in the stage space for the players' use. I explain the rules: "The first player will enter the space, establish an imaginary object in it, and stay onstage engaging in an activity as someone who belongs backstage at a theatre. The next player will enter the space, relate in some way to the first player's object, and establish an object of his own. The first player must make contact with the second player's object before she can leave the stage. A third player will enter the space and establish another object. The second player must make contact with that new object before he can leave the stage. And that is how the play continues until everyone has had a turn. We are creating a Where through a series of two-person scenes. We are also, in effect, improvisationally creating a one-act play. The point of concentration in this game is to make contact with the object established by the new player and then to exit the space. You are also to establish the physical qualities of an imaginary object and use it as you would if it were real."

One player goes up onstage and begins to apply make-up to his face. The second player enters the space and grabs an imaginary broom and begins to sweep. The first player drops an imaginary box of face powder on the floor and borrows the broom to sweep it up. The first player exits the stage. The third player enters the space carrying a costume, but, as she takes the costume off the hanger, Player 2 has his back turned. I call, "Make sure the other player can see what you are doing." Player 3 asks Player 2 to hold his jacket so he can put it on. "Don't name the objects; just use them." Player 2 exits. Player 4 enters and engages Player 3 in conversation, forgetting to establish his own object. I call, "Accomplish your task. Give the object weight. If you don't know what the object is, use it in the same way you saw the other player using it." Play continues until everyone has had a turn.

In this game, a focus on the other player is *crucial*. In order for a player to leave, they must see the new object so they can make contact with it. It is important to keep focused on your task in order to maintain a forward movement for the scene. Your task is to make contact and leave the scene. You should not get bogged down in "playwriting."

Agreement workshop focusing on language and melody – Gibberish

"Gibberish" is an exercise where the player substitutes nonsense language for normal English speech accompanied by an action. It is not a word-for-word translation of an English phrase or sentence. In gibberish, intention and melody are important. The intended meaning is carried not by the actual words, but by the tone, rhythm, and feeling state; for example, anger, sorrow, fury, joy, grief. Since the players don't have real words, they convey the meaning through the melody of the gibberish language used and the energy in their bodies. In Gibberish, it is important to have something real to say.

The point of concentration is to communicate through intent, physicalization, and melody. This workshop could stand on its own or become the core of a class with a more extended warm-up sequence. It works well for teens and adults.

Warm-up sequence
Gibberish Practice into *Gibberish Anecdotes in Pairs*

Gibberish Practice
This warm-up is a whole-class exercise. "Find a partner and sit down facing each other in the stage space. Try out some gibberish sounds in simultaneous rap." As the players begin experimenting with sound, I encourage them to use both consonants and vowels and to get their mouths and lips moving.

The space explodes with gibberish. It is interesting to note that everyone has a distinct sound palette that is uniquely their own. Some people gravitate toward a gibberish that sounds vaguely Eastern European, some sound Scandinavian, some French or Spanish, some Asian. They may speak none of these languages, but gravitate toward the sound pattern anyway. Others get stuck on a single sound that they keep repeating. I call, "Use as many different sounds as possible. Use consonants and vowels. Exaggerate your mouth movements." When the players have warmed up their vocal apparatus, we are ready to move forward.

"Now each of you will tell an anecdote or highlight of your day to your partner in gibberish. When you finish your anecdote, your partner will convey what he or she has heard in English." I coach the players to vary their tone, but keep to usual speech rhythms – to let the gibberish flow as they try to communicate to the other player. "In this practice, don't expect your partner to interpret what you are telling them. You can support your gibberish with gesture, but this is not charades. At any point, correcting the listener should be done in gibberish."

I walk around to listen and select some of the most successful to repeat the exercise for the whole group. The class discuss their responses, difficulties, and the types of gibberish that emerged, noting the various language patterns they found themselves speaking. I stress that it helps to mix consonants and vowels so that the gibberish takes on the character of real speech.

Gibberish is about melody of language and has as much to do with "The Doings" (see Chapter 6, "Workshops on Specificity") as with exploring how we can expand the different ways we can communicate. The actor has to act with his back, with his eyebrows, with melodies of communication.

Core sequence
Gibberish Translation in Threes into *Gibberish Storytelling with Translator*

Gibberish Translation in Threes
Three volunteers go up onto the stage and find cubes. They arrange them in a straight line, facing the audience, and sit down. I explain the rules: "The player sitting in the middle will translate into English a conversation between the other two players who are speaking in gibberish. If the player translating is confused, she can ask the other player *in gibberish* what was said. Don't invent translations out of the air. Try to translate to the best of your ability what you think they are saying. When you converse in gibberish, really concentrate to convey your meaning. Insist that the translator says what you mean." To help the translator, it is a good idea for the gibberish speakers to be very specific and have strong needs to communicate what they want.

Before moving on to the next game, I make a few observations: "In this game, if you know what you are talking about, the audience will too. Generally try to get more vowels into your gibberish and avoid repeating the same phrase over and over. It is critically important to connect the gibberish to the body, to imaginary objects, and to the English translation."

Gibberish Storytelling with Translator
After a couple of groups have played the last game, I move on to a game played in pairs: "In this game, two players are going to tell an original story together. One player will start to tell the story in gibberish and the other player will translate into English. Begin with 'Once upon a time ...' in gibberish, of course. If you are the gibberish player, try to collaborate with the translator to tell the story. The translation doesn't need to be letter-perfect. The general idea is good enough. Translator, don't make up a story independent of your partner. Try to work together."

Once the story has been established, I begin to have the players switch roles back and forth between gibberish and English. I coach the players as to when to change, trying to keep them off-balance: "Switch. Switch again. Pick up the story right away." I keep switching the roles faster and faster until they no longer have defined roles as separate storyteller and translator – they are both telling the story and both translating it. I signal them to finish the story: "Thirty seconds." Several pairs try this game.

Players learn from watching others and incorporate that knowledge into their own playing. I leave the game with a final thought: "Don't be afraid of putting the body into it, but don't charade."

Pay-off game
Who, What, Where Scenes in a Foreign Country

The idea for this game came from Byrne. It was inspired by a trip he made to Japan on a USO tour. He needed cleaning fluid for his toupee and tried to purchase it in a Japanese department store!

I divide the class into groups of four or five. The Where will be a shop. In each locale, one player is a seller or clerk who speaks English, the other players are foreign tourists who have come to buy things. The shoppers must try to convey their needs to the clerk in gibberish. I start each group in a different place – a clothing store, a hardware store, a butcher shop, a jewelry store. As a group is playing the scene, I call different locales and the players must make the adjustment to the new situation without starting a new scene. For example, Group 1 started in a clothing store. I made the following calls: an outdoor marketplace, a flea market, a church bake sale, an upscale department store, a swap meet, a black-market bazaar in a war-torn country. I also switch the gibberish speakers to English and vice versa as I did in the previous game.

Players use the energy in their bodies to help them speak. Melodies and tunes lead to clarity in gibberish. Gibberish cuts out the extraneous and gets the body involved. The effort is to communicate; you can't lie back. Gibberish also frees you. You don't have to be a playwright. Gibberish helps players get in touch with the moment and with each other – what is really happening.

Both physical agreement games and verbal ones like Gibberish require the players to work together, building off of each other, exploring and heightening what they see and hear. They must be present in the moment, focused on the task at hand and on the other person. In any one of the examples in this chapter, if the players are playing to the audience and not working with their fellow players, if one or more players are grandstanding or calling attention to how clever they are, the game or scene will fall apart. The ability to be in agreement is a fundamental skill to master for all improvisation, for scene work, and for any ensemble-based activity.

6 Workshops on Specificity and the Doings

The principle of specificity is:

> **To bring to life on the stage the defining characteristics of fundamental dramatic elements – objects, environments, people, relationships, and emotional experiences – through sense memory and emotional investment.**

The point of concentration is:

◆ To develop sense memory – seeing, hearing, smelling, tasting, and touching.

◆ To make specific choices when exploring imaginary objects and environments regarding the qualities of weight, shape, texture, function, and emotional investment.

◆ To find the character's specificity that relates to your own specificity.

◆ To find the specific nature of your relationship to another character in any given moment in a scene or play.

◆ To exercise the discipline of detail when telling a story.

All object games and sense memory games can be played with a point of concentration on specificity and/or agreement depending on the focus for a given class. These exercises include:

◆ Make a Deal

◆ What Am I Seeing? Hearing? Eating?

◆ Heavier when Full

◆ Four Moving a Heavy Object (bringing in elephants and coffins)

◆ Three on a Box

◆ Circle-Object Transformations

◆ Mirror Object-Activity Transformations

◆ Invested Object.

The following two games, Circle-Object Transformations and Invested Object, demonstrate how we have built on Viola Spolin and Uta Hagen in our own work.

1. Circle-Object Transformations

Spolin calls this game Transformation of Objects. You can find it played in many beginning acting classes. At the Workshop, we play it as a stepping-stone to more advanced transformation exercises like Invested Object or Round-Robin Storytelling with Objects.

In our version of this game, all the players are seated in a circle. The leader usually starts the game by creating an imaginary object. As the leader in this example, I might begin shaping the space substance into something that takes on the character of a necklace. As I explore the emerging necklace to discover its particular properties, maybe it becomes a rope necklace. I handle the necklace in its appropriate ways and then pass my imaginary necklace to the player sitting next to me. That player takes the object and handles it as I handled it, with the same weight and size, even if he doesn't know what it is. He knows it's a rope-like thing – it isn't heavy, you can swing it. He must explore it, heighten its properties and let it transform. The goal is to let the necklace transform into some other object.

I encourage the player to take his first transformation, handle it with authority, and pass it on. Committing to the first transformation keeps the player connected to his impulses and prevents him from starting to plan and think too much about the new object. The player might start with the imaginary rope necklace and begin pulling it in different ways until it *becomes* a bow and arrow. The object found should be a surprise to both the player and the audience, not something made through pre-planning. The point is to explore and heighten the properties of the object, *not* to mold it like it was clay. Play continues around the circle in silence with everyone's focus on the transforming objects. After the game, we talk briefly about what objects emerged.

2. Invested Object

In our attempt to relate the theatre game to acting, Byrne took the basic Spolin game of Object Transformation and, referencing Uta's work, developed it into Invested Object. In this way, the game doesn't become an abstract experience for its own sake. It is important in our training to make those connections between the games and acting onstage.

I begin by asking the players to think of an object that has special meaning to them, special value not in worldly terms but in emotional associations with a person or experience – something they treasure, something of value to them personally. One player volunteers to go first. As they explore and move the space substance, I side-coach: "Describe the object as you handle it in imaginary space – remembering its texture, temperature, delicacy if fragile or very old, very heavy and sturdy if that's it. Whatever. As you handle it, you are talking about the object and recreating it hands-on." The focus here is to describe and realize the size, shape, weight, and other sensory aspects of the object. Once the object has been fully realized, you can move on to the next level.

To help the player realize as much of the object as possible on a sensory level, I prompt them to remember: "What are its physical properties? Who gave you this?" If that object is attached to a special occasion or a special relationship, that emotional memory will be revealed and should come up because we've delved into the past and conducted an exploration. "Now share the object with another player. Continue to talk while the other listens and maybe handles the object. Maybe it's an object that can be taken apart and fixed or polished or restored in some way."

In the third phase of the game, the shared moment continues but I put the play into the context of a scene by giving the players a To Get improv as they are handling the object. For example, I tell the player with the object to get their partner to lend them some money. A scene takes place and a kind of magical thing happens – a subtext emerges. The simple task of handling a special object when engaged with the other and doing an independent scene has more depth than an ordinary improv. The important thing is that we see the dramatic possibilities of a subtext.

Workshop for exploring sense memory and emotional endowment

Point of concentration: sense memory and emotional endowment. I've taught this workshop to advanced teens and adults.

Warm-up sequence
What Am I Seeing? Hearing? Eating?
Mirror Object-Activity Transformations

What Am I Seeing? Hearing? Eating?
The focus in this warm-up is to prepare the class for the more complex emotional involvement of Invested Object and scene work. It will help the players remember to stay grounded in the physical environment while they explore relationship and emotional terrain in the more advanced games. This warm-up game gets the players connected through its requirement of group agreement and it allows them to start out simply by focusing on a single sensory experience. Their only task will be to find the specificity of that one experience as individuals and as part of a group. If they keep focused on the point of concentration and find the specificity, they will stay in the moment, out of their heads, in connection with each other. For example, how is the experience of watching a football game different from watching a chess match? How does listening to rock music differ from listening to a lecture? How does the body react to eating something sweet? Savory? Sour?

To form groups, I ask the players to count off by threes. Each group of five players will explore a different sense. Group One will watch a spectator sport like football, baseball, basketball, tennis, and so on. Group Two will choose an event that focuses on listening, for example, a concert of classical music, rock 'n' roll, children singing holiday songs, or a spoken-word event like a political debate or poetry reading. Group Three will decide on a food to share: caramels, fancy chocolates, or fried grasshoppers. I let the groups deliberate for a short time, enough to agree on an activity but not enough to start planning what they are going to do. They choose basketball, Lollapalooza, and chocolate-covered grasshoppers.

Group One goes onstage. I coach: "You are facing front with your focus above and over our heads. Start watching your event without speaking. Your point of concentration is to find the event together and to explore and heighten what others in the group are seeing. Begin when you are ready." The players begin to watch what appears to be a basketball game. One player begins to start shouting out the plays, prompting me to side-coach, "Just watch. Don't tell us." I give them time to play as they absorb that call before encouraging them to be aware of those around them: "Take from others. Don't lead the group to watching." The group quiets as they try to integrate the call. They've become more focused but I can see they want to talk, so I release them to start slowly: "If you need to make sounds, go ahead, but don't tell us what you are watching. Focus on just watching the game together." As the play continues, I keep encouraging them to tell less by letting the scene grow together: "Don't tell each other so much. Focus on each other watching that event. Explore and heighten it together." As they play, I see they need a way to find each other in the space, so I call, "Know what others are doing through your peripheral vision."

Sensing that the group has fully explored the moment, I coach them into finding an end to the scene: "Something important is going to happen. Someone made a basket. Respond to it. The game is ending. Find the end. Thirty seconds." As you can see, I am always taking from what is happening in the group to make a specific call. And it is important to remember that, each time I make a call, I must give the group time to integrate it. My role is not to interrupt the flow of the playing with a constant stream of directions, but to guide the players toward staying focused on the point of concentration.

Before the other two groups share their exercises, I reinforce the task at hand: "Your point of concentration is on showing agreement with your bodies and your focus, but you are also exercising your sense memory. Try to be as specific as possible. For example, it's not just any game – it's a basketball game. What is specific to that particular game? Is it a championship? Do you know the players personally, or are you a lifelong fan? Respond to what you are seeing."

The other two groups share their exercises. In these exercises, the players are not performing scenes. There is no dialogue per se. The sole focus is on accomplishing the task together: seeing the same event, hearing the same sounds, eating the same food.

After each group has played, we briefly discuss what they were seeing, what they were listening to, and what they were eating, highlighting a moment or two where they were showing rather than telling.

Showing is a real human being watching something, hearing something, tasting something that has temperature, texture, aroma, etc. Telling can be as obvious as a player literally telling us what he is seeing and imposing that vision on everyone else by shouting, "Look at that guy jump for the basket!" He has told us that the group is watching a basketball game without earning the right to do so, placing the cart before the horse, so to speak. Or, telling might take the form of describing through action what someone looks like when hearing something. For example, a player might start snapping her fingers in an effort to tell the audience that she is listening to something with a particular beat, or someone might nod their head vigorously in assent to tell us that she is in agreement with a person speaking. The players here don't trust the audience to know what they are listening to. Those players are not in the moment, they are focused on giving the audience information, not on listening.

The player who is really listening in her mind to her imaginary music might let the rhythm of what she is listening to move her in some way, causing her to begin swaying slightly. If the group is working together, another player might notice and take up that movement by swaying in concert with the first. A third might start snapping his fingers quietly in response to the first two. All of these players are focused on listening to the imaginary music and each other, letting what is happening in real time affect them. They trust that the audience will hear the music with them.

When a player is telling, he is not in the moment. He is in his head, thinking and planning how to tell the audience something. When the player is showing, he is responding through sense memory to the imaginary stimulus and to what is coming from the group around him – his awareness is heightened to what is happening in the present.

Mirror Object-Activity Transformations

To complete the warm-up section of this workshop, I move the players into a more physically active exercise in object work by bringing the whole group up into the space and asking them to find a partner for Mirror Object-Activity Transformations. This isn't the first time they have played this game, so I move them quickly into mirror, telling the players to find an activity with an object between them – pulling, stirring, sawing, kneading. Once they have explored that object-activity in mirror, I instruct them to let it change, to let it transform into another object-activity and to keep transforming, seeing how many object-activities they can find.

During the playing, I make calls to keep the players on task: "Find an activity in the space. Stay away from just movement. What is between you? What object? What activity? Get it in your body. What's in the space *between* you?" To make a transformation, the players must work with the space substance that exists between them. All the good stuff happens in the "space between" because that is where the players are in connection, focused on the task at hand and on each other. They need to grab that space, give it weight, manipulate it in a specific way, with a specific rhythm that can change. Speeding up an action like pulling taffy can lead to pulling string; slowing down and giving more weight to that same action can lead to shoveling. Moving your hands in the air randomly, even in mirror, will lead to little. General dance-like movements and those that involve the self, touching your own hand or face, impede the player from connecting with the imaginary space substance and the other player. For some, general movement leads to self-consciousness, causing the players to feel silly and taking them out of the experience altogether.

In my coaching, I continue to drive home the same point: "Try to stay away from yourself. Get into the space between you. *Extend it!* It needs to go somewhere. Commit yourself to the object – deal with the object. *Grab it.* Extend it. Make a full-body commitment. Explore quietly each change."

Once the players have made numerous changes in their object-activities and are working with good energy, I call a freeze, and say, "Take that energy and find a new partner. *The first eyes you see* will be your new partner." I will repeat this instruction several times with the goal of building on the energy created and spreading it throughout the group. When I sense that everyone has played with several people, I will bring the exercise to an end: "Thirty seconds. Find your final transformation." If they have been playing well, they will have expended a tremendous amount of energy and need a break.

Core sequence

Circle-Object Transformations into *Invested Object* into *Conversation with Independent Activity*

For the core sequence of this class, we play the games described earlier in this chapter. Circle-Object Transformations, played in a circle sitting on the floor, leads directly into Invested Object. The first volunteer begins to describe an old soup pot that belonged to her great-grandmother. The player grabs the space substance as if it were the pot and starts to detail it. "This pot is quite large and heavy. It holds about eight quarts of soup. It is made of some kind of dull gray metal and the sides of the bottom are rounded. The bottom is permanently burnt in places because the pot would always sit on the stove for many, many hours, simmering soups or stews. On its side, here, you can see several small dents where my grandmother, as a child, dropped it while she was drying it for her mother." As the player speaks, she is handling the pot, pointing out its imperfections, its texture, its construction.

When the pot has been fully realized, I begin to shift the narrative to more personal considerations: "Tell the person sitting next to you the story of who the pot belongs to and what it means to you. While you answer, begin to polish or clean the pot in some way, involving your partner in the activity." The player talks about how the pot came to be a family heirloom:

"My great-grandmother brought the pot with her from Bohemia when she came to the United States. Her father had sent her to live with his sister in Hungary after her mother died, but her aunt used her as a cook in her boarding house. When her father found out, he brought her home and then sent her to America where she was married off to a countryman. Every weekend, she would cook a big traditional meal for her extended new family – roast duck or pork, sauerkraut and bread dumplings, cherry strudel. And she would make liver dumpling soup or stuffed cabbage in the great pot. Before she died, she gave the pot to my grandmother who gave it to my mother. I remember helping my mother cook Sunday dinners at our house using this old pot. When I complained that she should buy a new pot, my mother would tell me that it had magic powers, that it made the food taste better. We would laugh together and that became a running joke between us."

During this narrative, the two players have developed an intimacy. The listener has been helping the teller polish the pot and asking questions that stimulated the narrative above.

To move into the third phase of the exercise, I assign the players a relationship – mother and daughter – and explain that the mother is to get her daughter to cut her hair. The players play a few beats of this improv. The intimacy established in the earlier narrative sets the tone for the beginning of the improv. The mother gently brings up the idea of the haircut by suggesting that she saw pictures of the new styles in a teen magazine – short and curly is in. The daughter initially laughs off her suggestion, reminding her mother that she hates curly hair. As the improv continues, the mother becomes more insistent and the daughter more belligerent. They end in a stalemate. The earlier shared activity and narrative gave texture and subtext to the scene.

We play a couple more scenes. A second volunteer describes a dirty old Chicago Bears jersey that belongs to his father. A third volunteer chooses to share the story of an antique Christmas nutcracker. The sequence played remains the same. The exercise always begins with a detailed description of the object in terms of its weight, shape, texture, temperature, color, and unusual properties. Once the object has been realized in the space, the exercise moves to a shared telling of its personal significance. Sometimes I stop here; other times we move into an improvised scene with an independent topic or a "to get." These scenes all take place sitting on the floor. They are intimate conversations, not fully per-formed events. Their purpose is to make connections between the physical world and the emotional one.

Pay-off game: The Daring Proposal game: Two-person scenes dealing with a difficult and emotionally charged task (firing, hiring, breaking up, or making a daring proposal)

Here I instruct the players: "Find a partner and decide between you where you are, who you are to each other, and what you will be doing. You are going to choose something difficult to do. You can be hiring, firing, breaking up, or making a daring proposal of some kind to the other person. For example, you could be breaking up with your best friend, you could be firing your brother (roommate, grandparent, an upstart) from a job, telling your best friend you can't help her do something impor-tant to her, asking your girlfriend to marry you. You decide between you." I give the group some time to discuss and decide before asking for volunteers.

The first pair begins the scene of two lovers meeting. The woman has some wonderful news. She tells her fiancé that she is pregnant, expecting him to be thrilled. The male player blanches at the news. He cannot handle the prospect of being a father and makes the daring proposal that she get an abortion. The woman is shocked and informs him that she could never do that. During the course of the scene they explore the emotional landscape of this painful dilemma. How can she love a man who wants to murder their baby? How can he say he loves her if he is repelled by her pregnancy? How can he make her understand how much fatherhood frightens him? He isn't ready to be a father – the financial and emotional responsibility of it all!

During the playing, I make calls that help the players raise the stakes of the scene and keep them in the moment. By now, many of these calls will be familiar to you because they form the basic language of our game work and keep the players off-balance so that surprising things can happen: "Slow motion." "Double time." "Full-body whisper." "Hard of hearing." "Contact." "Unacknowledged actions." "One word." "Explore the love between you." "Thirty seconds." Remember that any game played can become a call within an improvised scene. For example, the game Unacknowledged Actions asks one player to do outrageous things that would make no sense in the reality of the scene while the other player continues the scene as if nothing is happening. In the above scene, the man started walking around as if he had a book on his head, singing his dialogue, while the woman sobbed that he didn't love her. When the call was made for her, the woman began rolling around on the floor, crawled under the table, sniffed his leg like a dog, and barked. This call shakes up the space and opens up possibilities. It gets the players out of a rut, out of playwriting, and forces them to focus on the task at hand.

Other pairs perform. One group of three set up an intervention where two children proposed that their father seek help for his alcoholism. Another pair played a scene about skydiving for the first time. All of the work done in this class on specificity, sense memory, and emotional truth, our point of concentration, comes together in this final pay-off performance experience where players improvisationally explore those elements through scene work based on emotionally charged situations.

The Doings: relationship and emotion through language

"The Doings" come from the methodology taught by Mira Rostova to Byrne Piven. Byrne evolved it and I carry it on today. The Doings are the melodies of relationship that speak to the heart of communication and to our common understanding. They refer to an active process of communication. The actor is never giving information. Information is for calculus class, or the newscaster's neutrality. Instead, the actor is always evolving, always communicating the emotional encounter. By inhabiting the word (getting in touch with what it is doing, what it is communicating), we can share it with spontaneity, coloration, variation, and variety. The Doings are not line readings. The melodies of the line cannot be written down on paper. An actor can spend a lifetime training the ear to hear the Doings, and training the instrument in order to connect with the encounter of the line.

As Mira said, "The recipe is the other person." The doing of a line is derived from who you are talking to and what, on the deepest level possible, you are communicating to them. Even a comedic "throwaway" line speaks to this depth: the more serious you are in the doing, the funnier the line becomes to the audience. The doing changes with changes in the relationships. Think of the way you communicate with a lover, a stranger, a parent, king, president, cousin, sibling, best friend, or acquaintance. The doing is influenced by the status of the person you are speaking to – their class, occupation, achievement, authority or no authority. The Doings come out of who you are communicating with and what you are communicating.

The process of the Doings involves letting the text be your teacher. Within every Doing is the specificity of these questions: What is the line doing? What emotion is the doing communicating? Astonishment? Discovery? Admission? Lamenting? Celebrating? What irony (or loss) is one sharing? Looking at the emotional encounter: What are you lamenting to? What are you defying? What are you celebrating? What are you admitting to? The actor needs to find the encounter in the moment and translate that encounter into his or her instrument.

When we retell a story, we are always the hero of our own story. We are always dramatizing. When we tell a story about a bus driver, and we imitate him, saying, "Hey, lady!" we are imitating his tone, his melody. We are not imitating the sound of his voice nor are we necessarily repeating verbatim what he said. We are certainly not relaying information. We are not giving line readings. We are capturing and communicating the encounter of the story. In the same way, when we work on a play text, the Doings convey the encounter of the story, the emotional content, the tone, rather than giving information.

There are four basic kinds of Doings that identify what the line is doing: the "admit," the "lament," the "defy," and "the demonstration of amazement." Shakespeare is the ultimate model of the Doings. All Shakespeare quotes in this chapter are from Arden Shakespeare editions.

The admit

The admit is a dead-level melody. It is admitting to the inevitability of an act; assenting to the truth of the matter. Lines like "If you ever do that again, I'm going to kill you"; "I hate you"; "You're worth it." The lines in comedy known as throwaways are good examples of a comic admit. An example of an admit from Shakespeare is the messenger line to Macbeth about Lady Macbeth: "The queen, my lord, is dead." The queen has been mad and sick and quite out of Macbeth's priority. Stricken as he is, this is not unexpected news. More to the point, the fact of her death is the weight of things and need only be communicated as fact. The news is deep and sorrowful enough without the messenger adding one iota of himself into this mix.

The event of her death is enough to convey. Getting out of the way of the line is sufficient. Admitting to the truth of the line is enough. There is no need to "dramatize" the line; the communication is enough. Seyton, the messenger, is communicating with King Macbeth. The king is neither an intimate nor a relative. Seyton can only respectfully "admit" to the event, which, in itself, is of grave import.

In life, the communication "You're grounded" is an "admit" when a parent wants to convey there is no room for negotiation, when the parent means it. The specificity is in the history of the child's behavior and the circumstances. "You're fired" is an "admit" if the boss is serious and the specificity resides in the history between the boss and the employee. In any case, specificity is where the art comes in.

The lament

"Ah, the lament," I say "lamentingly", because you and I share the struggle to understand and identify the melody. I am here also lamenting with humor the irony of the "wink, wink" I, as teacher, am sharing with you, my audience. The "lament" also speaks to the shared condition of life we all have. "That's life." "The good die young." The lament is the melody of commiseration. We are commiserating our common condition. Be careful that you do not confuse the lament with the melody of complaint. We always avoid the complaint onstage. Variations on the lament include the lament with irony, the lament with humor, admitting to a lament, lamenting to an admit.

"We lost everything in the hurricane." After Katrina, we heard people simply get out of the way of communicating the tragedy. "We lost everything," sometimes even admitting to the lament and sometimes lamenting, "It's gone. Everything. The house, the land, the trees are all gone." We are speaking to the common understanding – the vulnerability of life.

One example from Shakespeare: The chorus (usually one person) says in the opening of *Henry V*:

Chorus

O for a Muse of fire, that would ascend
The brightest heaven of invention,
A kingdom for a stage, princes to act,
And monarchs to behold the swelling scene!

(Prologue. 1–4)

This speech is the ultimate wish of a great playwright/actor/director. It is a celebratory lament to the irony of the size of this passion that can never be fully realized, confined as it is by the limits of reality. It is a lament to the celebratory wish (almost a prayer) to the powers that be to transform this coming event (the telling of the story of Henry V) beyond the mere confines of a bare stage, imperfect actors, and an audience that doesn't always know enough to receive it.

It is a prayer, a profound wish that could only be lamented. It is a lament to the irony of the intensity of such a hope that could never be fulfilled. It is the wish of every person in love with theatre. The line is energized by the most extravagant and yet specific of words – fire/brightest, invention, kingdom/stage, princes/act/monarchs/to behold/swelling. There is a world in that "O" – the largest, deepest, most fervent wish and prayer a theatre artist could make.

Another example of lament is from Shakespeare's *The Winter's Tale*, after Leontes has accused his wife, Hermione, of adultery.

Hermione

> How will this grieve you,
> When you shall come to clearer knowledge, that
> You thus have publish'd me! Gentle, my lord,
> You scarce can right me throughly then to say
> You did mistake. (2.1.96–99)

This is the ultimate lament – an expression of love where Hermione puts her husband, Leontes, above her own pain. At that moment, she thinks not of her predicament nor of defending herself, but – knowing she is innocent – laments the pain that he will feel when he realizes he has accused her unjustly. For me, the lament unlocked the meaning of what can seem a very strange play. In the language, in the doing of the line, in the communication of the beat, she is expressing her deepest love – a lament to the deepest pain that will be caused (by the discovery of her innocence) to the one she loves. She laments to that irony. It is one of the ultimate expressions of real love.

And from *Hamlet*, another ultimate lament:

> What a piece of work is a man – how noble in reason; how infinite in
> faculties; in form and moving; how express and admirable in action;
> how like an angel in apprehension; how like a god; the beauty of the
> world; the paragon of animals. And yet to me what is this quintessence
> of dust? Man delights not me, nor women neither, though by your smil-
> ing you seem to say so. (2.2.269–276)

This lament is the ultimate expression of depression: "And yet to me what is this quintessence of dust?" All this life, *all this beauty in man* ... and yet ... and yet ... it is a lament that also includes amazement.

An example from *Antony and Cleopatra*, Cleopatra's final scene:

> I dreamt there was an Emperor Antony.
> O, such another sleep, that I might see
> But such another man! (5.2.75–77)

What else could the line be doing other than voicing this visceral wish? Look at the sound that is repeated: "UH," "such," "uhnuther sleep," "that I might see buut suuch uhnuhhther man." It's like giving birth, only it's before she dies by her own choice. Brilliantly Shakespeare has Cleopatra's servant standing throughout trying to get a word in. Cleopatra has someone to be audience to her most fervent, visceral utterance. Read the rest of her speech:

> His face was as the heavens, and therein stuck [uuh]
> A sun [uhh] and moon, which kept their course, and lighted
> The little O, the Earth [uhh]. (5.2.78-79)

Remember the O? But instead of being pulled downward in the pain, Cleopatra moves in to the "defy."

The defy

The defy is celebratory because it is energized by the thought of defying the fates. To defy is to look fear in the eye with courage. "I will win this game no matter what the odds." "No matter what the odds, I will triumph!" "I will pass this test!" I will *win!*"

To continue Cleopatra's speech, she becomes airborne in celebrating this man, Antony, who defied the fates as a colossus:

> His legs bestrid the ocean; his rear'd arm
> Crested the world. (5.2.81-82)

In and with the line, she is defying the fates by celebrating instead of being pulled earthward and defeated by her loss. The search for the nuances of the Doing doesn't end until the actor finds all the personalizations (who is Antony to you?), all the colorations of words she uses to describe this man, this god. The actor's arsenal, so to speak, must be formidable to bring the variations of Doings throughout.

Another example of "defy" is in *Henry V*. Henry himself is rallying his soldiers to jump into the fray:

> Once more unto the breach, dear friends, once more
> Or close the wall up with our English dead. (3.1.1-2)

He is celebrating the glory of fighting and possibly dying for their country. The defy is a celebration!

The demonstration of amazement

The demonstration of amazement is the sensation of discovery. You are discovering the word and the phenomenon at the same time. It is the melody of a child discovering light for the first time: "Light!" The demonstration of amazement is a particularly improvisational state to be in. When we describe something while doing a demonstration of amazement, we are in the act of discovery rather than giving information or being illustrative. Put an "Oh my God" before each line: "(Oh my God) He's so tall and strong!"

Cleopatra's scene quoted above contains a myriad of defy/amazements:

Cleopatra

> For his bounty,
> There was no winter in't; an autumn it was
> That grew the more by reaping. His delights
> Were dolphin-like; they show'd his back above
> The element they lived in. (5.2.85–89)

In this Doing, one is entering into the wonder that discovery contains. A simple example from life: "I opened the door and there it was!" The wonder of the thought hits one, so to speak.

From *A Midsummer Night's Dream* a "demonstration of amazement":

Helena

> Lo, she is one of this confederacy!
> Now I perceive she has conjoin'd all three
> To fashion this false sport in spite of me. (3.2.192–194)

She is literally (and this is what the line is doing) putting two and two together to get three! "Demetrius and Lysander and now Hermia are conspiring to trick me!"

Remember, in general, the Doing – what the line is giving expression to – is found in relation to its deepest specificity. Any Doing can be loud, soft, very soft – even a defy or a demonstration of amazement can be whispered. The recipe is the other person. It is always respectful no matter what the circumstances – and by that I mean you speak to the common understanding.

The lament is the hardest to hear for us. It seems to come more naturally to

Europeans, possibly because their culture is much older and shaped by great trag-edy and war on their own soil. We Americans suffer from what I call "entitlement." We are either chiding or complaining about things when those things are not going right for us. It's our common melody. If you "complain" instead of "lament," the moment becomes about you and not about your deepest wish, your deepest prayer, your deepest rage, your deepest compassion. The lament is more philo-sophical, more accepting of the fact that sorrow is part of life. More than this, it is a shared melody, for example, we all share that this is part of the human condition.

Who we are speaking to shapes the specificity. We speak different melodies to different people: babies, intimates, family, children, parents, strangers, neighbors, old people, people we care about. If I comfort someone, it is to lament a condition of life we all experience. Lamenting to a child contains my empathy of shared experience: "I know how disappointed you must feel; I identify with your pain." Another example: "It's snowing again." If I complain and whine, it's about me. If I share my distress in a philosophical way, it's about our shared existence: "We must suffer yet again with snow storms."

I want to make it clear that this process includes all the work that is needed to perform – personalization, emotion, tears, and laughter – all of it. I firmly believe that all methods are good if they help you to add to your very demanding craft.

Workshops on Transformation

The principle of transformation is:

◆ **To let a change happen – in the physical, vocal, emotional, or spatial dynamic or in the imaginary circumstances of a moment in a game or scene.**

◆ **To let a change occur suddenly or slowly – from slow to fast, heavy to light, soft to loud, high to low, crying to laughter, and so on, or from the real world to an imaginative one, from storyteller to character, from locale to locale, or from character to character.**

The point of concentration is:

◆ To be in the space, connected to the other players, connected to the audience, and open to creative possibilities.

◆ To submit to the "chaos of not knowing," to the unknown.

◆ To take a chance and let go of the need to control.

◆ To let the transformation happen rather than making it happen.

◆ To be aware of all the possibilities for change – a sound, a movement, an object, an activity, a location, or a character – anything that is in the space between players.

The primary games to foster transformation and ensemble include:

- Circle-Object Transformations

- Mirror Object-Activity Transformations

- Group Transformations

- Criss-Cross Sound and Movement Transformations

- Scene Transformations

- Musical Transformations

- Polymorphs

- Character Layers

- Fingers (Amore)

- Four on a Moving Vehicle

- Hook-Up and Twist/Activate.

Workshop exploring transformations

Warm-up sequence: *Mirror Object-Activity Transformations* into *Scene Transformations*

Mirror Object-Activity Transformations

See the chapter on "Specificity" for a more detailed description of this game. Mirror Object-Activity Transformations appears often in our class sequences because of its importance to the training of transformation, agreement, ensemble building, and specificity. Here it is the first step toward an advanced game: Mirror Scene Transformations.

The point of concentration in the Mirror Object-Activity Transformations game is on *change*: "How many changes can you make? How many activities can you find together? How many partners can you work with?" The players are encouraged to focus on the space *between* them and to make a full-body commitment to the object-activity. The only way to make a transformation is to commit fully. Players change partners many times.

My calls keep the focus on changing activities, changing partners, while keeping the energy up. I don't let the players settle into any one activity or start over every time they change partners. All of these calls keep the pressure on the point of concentration: "Take that focus and that energy and find a new partner. *The first eyes you see* will be your new partner." "Keep the energy at the level it was. Don't take a break. New partner. You should be going into the activity even if you are a mile away from your new partner. Pulling, push-ing, tugging, sawing … Freeze." I am working to get a motor going between the players as preparation for the next game.

Mirror Scene Transformations

While the players are in the above freeze, I tell them to go back into mirror, but this time to think about what they might be saying or doing with their partner. And to open up the space, I coach them to try to balance the stage while they are in mirror.

I see that everyone has established a connection with their partners – one pair is per-forming a sawing activity, another is pulling something with the consistency of taffy, a third pair look like they are sorting small things, and so on. At this point, I call a freeze, saying, "Scene. Go into scene with your partner. Everyone at the same time." The pair that was sawing play a scene as lumberjacks sawing a huge tree. The players pulling the taffy-like substance play a scene as artists stretching a large canvas together. The players sorting small things are kids counting money from a broken bank. Another group plays a scene about movers packing crates. The players are no longer in mirror, but are people engaged in scenes dealing with objects found in the mirror activity.

I let the players get involved with their scenes and then tell one pair to continue work-ing while the others watch. I guide that pair into finding one transformation before moving on to highlight each of the seven pairs of players in the game. The lumberjacks are the first pair highlighted. During the course of the scene, as they are looking up to watch the tree start to fall, I call, "New scene!" Right from there, the players transform into soldiers, diving to avoid a low-flying plane that is shooting at them. The players are on the ground, crawling, and I call, "New scene!" They transform into retriever dogs sniffing out a bird for their mas-ters. Before moving on to another group, I tell this pair to find their own transformation. They end their moment in the spotlight with a scene about two workmen finding a gas leak, the transformation prompted by the sniffing activity.

We applaud their efforts and I turn my attention to the other groups, telling everyone to go back into mirror. "When I highlight you to take stage, play one beat of a scene and then see if you can transform into another scene." After everyone has had a turn, I tell the players to find a new partner and continue to play simultaneously for one minute, exploring scenes and transformations, trying to make as many transformations as possible. Learning takes place while being audience to others. Highlighting and simultaneous playing gives every-one a chance to take what they have learned and apply it to their own practice.

The point of concentration in this exercise is on transforming from scene to scene, not on playing the scene for its own sake. Anything can spark a transformation – a look, a sound, a repetition of a sound, a physical stance, or a gesture. Once the players are con-nected, there is no need to go back to mirror. One scene can transform into another scene on a dime. The purpose of the mirror exercise is to establish the connection between play-ers and to find the motor. Mirror always remains an option if the players lose their connection.

Core sequence: *Character Layers*

Byrne and I initially developed this game as a way to teach character transformation in story theatre, but, after playing it many times, I came to appreciate what a good tool it was for acting in general. It taps into the actor's observational powers and into the discipline of detail and specificity as well as transformation.

Point of Concentration: To describe physical traits in detail and find their expression in the body, the voice, and the emotional instrument, adding on until the full character emerges.

Character Layers

I begin: "Think of someone you know, someone you can describe verbally in detail – a person with strong enough characteristics in terms of movement, physical details – the most unforgettable person you've ever met."

One player volunteers to demonstrate a person to the rest of the group. "Begin in neutral, as yourself. As you describe this person, take on each characteristic and add on until you create this whole person." It is very important that every characteristic be held as the player moves to describe another characteristic. It is a process of layering to get to the transformation. The following abbreviated dialogue between the player and me will give you an idea of how this game goes:

Player: "This person has long blond hair and is very, very thin."
JP: "How thin is she? How does that influence her movement or how she carries herself?"
Player: "She has long, thin limbs and she kind of glides because she is so light."
JP: "Take that on. Glide like she would as you talk about how tall she is. What does it feel like to be tall?"
Player: "This person is quite tall; maybe five-foot-nine or ten and her long arms and legs reach like a ballerina when she moves. She kind of leads with her hips."

The player is doing this movement as she is speaking. Exploring it, trying it on, trying to find just the right way to move. The more she describes, the more detail she remembers.

JP: "What does her face look like? Her nose? Her eyes? Her mouth? Take that on. Be as specific as possible. Keep everything you've described so far."
Player: "She has a long face as well. A long, thin nose. Her lips are thin too, and kind of pursed. But her eyes are really large and almond-shaped. She looks like a figure drawn by a painter. And she tends to keep her head up and tilted to one side as if she's surveying the world. Kind of aloof."

The player has stopped walking, but has drawn her own short body up to its tallest stance, and she is trying to lengthen her face, purse her lips and reshape her eyes as she talks. When she tilts her head back and surveys the audience, she is beginning to look like this person she describes.

JP: "Go back to her hair. How does that influence her head and arm movement?"
Player: "Her hair is long and thin and straight. It reaches down her back and sways with her body as she moves. She sometimes flicks it like Cher or puts it behind her ear with a languid arm movement."

JP: "What does her voice sound like? How do does she talk? Begin to take on that voice along with the thinness of face, the openness of the eyes, the pursing of the lips."

Player: "She talks very softly and has a kind of hoarse, sexy sound. And she says 'Hmmmm' a lot, especially as she moves her head – to punctuate a thought or reflect on something."

JP: "You have the voice. Begin to walk again. Get all that height and thinness in your body. Whatever you describe, take it on. As you walk, tell us how she would relate to objects or people. Direct your attention specifically to things in the character's world – coat, shirt, shoes, personal objects. What would she say while using that object? Tell it to someone in the audience."

Player: "This is my favorite coat. It's made of fur and it's very warm and soft. Hmmmm. My guy gave it to me for Valentine's Day. Doesn't it look rich and luxurious? He likes to give me expensive things. And he admires how they look on me. I like that. Hmmmm."

By this point, the player has made a complete transformation into the character she has been describing. Her final interaction with someone in the circle completes the exercise by bringing this new character into dialogue with another.

After several players have attempted the exercise, I talk about this challenging game. "Be aware that the player is demonstrating. It is more demanding because the actor must be very specific. The actor's job is not to impersonate but to present with everything at their command – voice, body, emotional instrument, craft, artistry."

It goes back to principle again. Everything is kept because we're working for a transformation. We want to see a new person emerge. The important part of this exercise is that, as the player details the physical traits, they must keep whatever they have described. For example, if a person talks like I'm talking now, they would keep that and then they might say, "She's very short." DETAIL: "How do you look at the world if you are short? Have the body connect with that." IT'S ABOUT TRANSFORMATION. It's about breaking down the process of transformation.

Pay-off game: Who, What, Where Scenes in Transformation

I divide the players up into groups of threes and fours and explain: "The What or activity for the scenes will be 'trying things on.' Decide in your groups where you will be doing that." The possibilities I give them include: ski shop, tailor shop, dress shop, bridal salon, costume shop, postal workers, nurses, construction, etc. The players quickly determine where they are, who they are to each other, and some basics about the location – entrance/exit, where some key pieces of furniture are, etc. I tell them not to plan out the scene beyond that. I give them some time to make those decisions.

The first group goes onstage, sets up some cubes and begins playing the scene. This group starts out in a bridal salon where a saleswoman is helping the bride try on wedding dresses for her mother and the maid of honor. The saleswoman tells the bride how lovely she looks, but the maid of honor disagrees. All the players start talking at once, so I call, "Give and take." Back on track, I call, "Slow motion" and then "Double time," to keep them off-balance and to get them away from playwriting.

Once the scene is in progress, I call a change of location – ski shop. The players are to transform immediately. They must make the adjustments to the new locale without starting over from the beginning. To create some conflict, I call, "Hinder." The mother begins to get in the saleswoman's way, creating one scene, while the two girls start trying on their own skis. When the group splits up their focus, I call, "Double scene," and have them play those two scenes in give and take until they find a reason to come back together as one group. To aid them further, I call, "Help," and everyone finds a way to move back into playing one scene.

Right from there, I call, "Costume Shop." The players adjust to this new situation right from where they are, immediately transforming into two middle-school girls with their mother buying costumes for Halloween. I note that the costume shop is not being realized with enough specificity, so I call, "Six-Sided Where," which tells the group to describe the space on all six sides in a give-and-take manner. The players, one at a time, begin to describe a space crammed to the ceiling with all manner of costumes that are hanging from clothes lines drawn across the room. There are costume pieces littering the floor and spooky masks in glass cases along the walls. There is a display of different kinds of make-up and wigs on one side of the room and a bank of small dressing rooms on the other. Now that the space has more definition, I call, "Normal," and the players begin to play the scene in response to what is around them. To bring this scene to a close, I call, "Thirty seconds, find an ending Portrait." The scene ends with the mother paying the saleswoman while the two girls pose as if wearing ghoulish masks.

For the other scenes, I add, "Gibberish" as a call and have the groups explore some foreign locales. For the last group, I move into calling different styles (e.g. melodrama, spaghetti western, Swedish art film, opera). In addition to calling changing locations, I continue to make calls to keep the players off-balance and in the moment: "Slow motion," "Double time," "Give and take," "Help," "Hinder," "One Word at a Time," or "Gibberish," whatever the playing requires. However, no matter what the calls, the point of concentration on immediate transformation, without backtracking or starting over, remains primary.

Joyce's signature poetry workshop

Out of my love for Shakespeare and poetry, I devised this sequence of games before we began working with the Doings. It was my way to link the principle of transformation to the exploration of language. The point of concentration for the workshop is playing with sounds and words – *exploring and heightening sounds and words to express meaning/feeling.* This workshop also became an important tool for our work in story theatre.

Warm-up sequence: *Circle Pass* into *Ball Toss* into *Word Toss*

Players stand in a circle. They pass a look, a clap, a sound, a word, a phrase around the circle. Next, we begin throwing an imaginary ball around the circle. To start, I change the weight and size of the ball each time it comes to me; after a few rounds, the players each change the ball every time they throw it.

Then we segue into Word Toss. This time, as we throw the ball, we also "throw a word." As played before, we start with colors. I demonstrate by throwing the word "Blue!" to the player across from me in the circle. We explore and heighten the quality of each color word, using different rhythms and vocal qualities.

Say the word as you throw it. It is key here that the movement and the word express the same quality simultaneously – slow, fast, staccato, light. The point is lost if a player throws and then says the word or vice versa. For example, in this particular workshop, one player throws "mauve" with "full-body whisper" and a light toss. Another throws "black" in slow motion with the "a" extended. She says, "blaaaaack," and moves her body in slow motion. A third player throws "pink" in a high-pitched and staccato voice with a similar mode of movement. Another group might physicalize and vocalize the colors differently. The point is that there is no right or wrong way to say the word as long as the player makes a full and clear commitment. We end the game with a short burst of "Hot Potato" where the players simulate tossing a very hot potato around the circle, responding both physically and vocally to the catching and quickly getting rid of the potato.

These activities get the group moving and working together. It is important for players to be encouraged to get their whole body involved in expressing the words. These warm-up games introduce the point of concentration for the class – the exploration and heightening of sounds and words to express meaning and feeling.

Core sequence, poetry exploration: *Criss-Cross Sound and Movement Transformations* into *Poetry Transformations in Mirror* into *Poetry Machine* into *Musical Transformations*

Criss-Cross Sound and Movement Transformations

The point of concentration is: To establish a repeatable sound and movement through physical exploration on your own; to "teach" this movement to a partner non-verbally through mirror; to let the sound and movement transform through full-body commitment; exploring and heightening of the original.

After the warm-up sequence and a short break, the players gather to begin the more advanced section of the Poetry Workshop. The players stand in two lines, facing each other, with a generous amount of playing space between the lines. Think of profile staging with the audience on two sides of the playing area. I point to the first player in Line 1 and say, "Begin to make a sound with a corresponding movement. Bring that sound/movement phrase into the center. Move around the space, walking in a circle, and explore and heighten that sound and movement to find a transformation. Let your sound and movement transform. Accept the first change and commit fully to it."

Player 1 begins to make a slow pulling movement with her arms as if she is ringing a bell. She continues to explore that movement as she walks into the playing space. As she incorporates the original movement into her whole body, doing it faster and faster, the movement and the sound change. She is now drawing something across her chest with each arm moving in turn, first one, then the other – like putting a seat belt first on her right side and then on her left. The sound has gone from something low and guttural to something high and siren-like. She has made one transformation.

When I see that the transformation is complete, I tell Player 1: "Move toward a player in the opposite line. Go into mirror and teach your sound and movement to your partner, Player 2. Mirror the arms, mirror the hips, mirror the feet." This new player then emerges with the sound/movement given to her and enters the "circle of change." To the new player: "Let the sound and movement transform. Make it your own." Player 2 begins to consciously push her movement into something that looks like she is dancing very beautifully. She is not finding that movement organically, she is in her head. I coach: "Get off your center. Risk it. Find something ungraceful. This is not a dance class." She makes her transformation and gives it to a new player in the opposite line and so on. The name "Criss-Cross" comes from the transfer of sound and movement between players criss-crossing from one line to the other after they have made their transformation in the "circle of change."

Poetry Transformations in Mirror[7]

When the last player has had a turn at Criss-Cross Sound and Movement Transformations, I ask the players to form a circle and introduce them to a poem for exploration:

---

[7] After a good faith effort, we have been unable to confirm the original source of this poetry or the copyright holder. These games were originally conceived over forty years ago.

The man said,
After inventing poetry,
"Wow!"
And did a full somersault.

I tell the last player from the previous game to go into mirror with someone else in the circle and for both players, while in mirror, to move to the center of the playing area. To the players in mirror: "Say the poem simultaneously, in mirror. Find transformations throughout the poem. For example, after saying, 'The man said,' you can work physically for a transformation of rhythm before saying the next phrase."

Responding to my calls, the players work in mirror until they find a different rhythm and action. The slow-motion, heavy space of "The man said" yields to a lighter activity. The players are now moving as if they are quickly tossing handkerchiefs or scarves in the air. The line "After inventing poetry" is said quickly in a light, staccato fashion, one word for each toss of the hand. From there the players find an enormous imaginary ball between them and toss it high into the sky, following it up with their eyes, as they say "Wow!" in amazement. After the ball is tossed, the players find a double-time, antic rhythm as they repeat, giggling, "And did a full somersault" three times. Having explored the entire poem once through, this pair of players goes back to the basic mirror exercise.

As they work, I coach two more players to join them in the playing space. We now have a four-way mirror arrangement, something like two sets of bridge partners at a table for four. The purpose of this overlap is to give the new players a chance to build on the energy of the first pair. Once the new players are connected, I coach the original pair to slowly exit the playing space by fading back into the circle, staying connected in mirror until the last possible moment. This action allows the original players to wind down rather than abruptly drop their activity and provides an organic flow to the whole exercise.

The new players find different rhythms for the poem. "The man said," in this iteration, is whispered, as if a secret is being shared, as the mirroring partners sort tiny imaginary beads. The sorting gets bigger and bigger, yielding to large slow-motion movement. "After inventing poetry" is almost sung in a deep, operatic voice, building to a soprano exclamation of "Wow!" The pair come back into their mirror and find their sorting activity again, ending the poem as it began, in a whispered intimacy.

After three pairs have worked on the first poem, I introduce a new one:

Neatness, madame,
Has nothing to do with the truth.
The truth is quite messy,
Like a windblown room.

This time, I coach the players to find three changes within this poem around the words neatness, messy, windblown. The point of concentration is to find the expression of these very different states through the sounds of the words and the physicality attached to them.

For example, the first pair finds a movement in mirror akin to wallowing around in the mud as they say, "The truth is quite messy," infusing the word *messy* with their disgust at their filthy hands and bodies. The second pair begins to throw what seems like stacks of papers in the air, giving their expression of the "messy" line a feeling of joyous abandon. The third pair engages in a very precise style of movement as they say the line in a clipped, disapproving tone of two prissy British schoolteachers. The mirroring provides the conditions for this kind of exploration, for finding the expression of meaning through sound and movement rather than imposing it.

Poetry Machine

Time to shake up the space. Starting with four volunteers, I give each player a phrase from the following poem:

#1 – The earth; #2 – voomed out; #3 – like a baseball. #4 – Creation!

After an initial scramble to build energy and unpredictability, I tell the players, "Create a machine without worrying about the order of the phrases."

Player 1 (The earth) jumps into the space making a repeatable scooping motion, as if scooping up great clumps of dirt from a mound and dropping handfuls into an imaginary bucket. Her whole body is involved in this motion and she gives weight to the "dirt" in her hands. Player 2 (voomed out) adds on to the machine with a breaststroke-like movement, arms close together at first and then opening out as she says her line. Player 3 (like a baseball) contributes a pitching motion to the machine. And Player 4 (Creation!) dips down and thrusts his hands and arms to the sky in a triumphant gesture as he says, "Creation!" The machine is complete and the players are repeating their words with each movement, talking over each other. I call, "Give and take the words," so we can get a clearer sense of the poem. I encourage the players to layer in the words: "Slow the machine down, finding that space to say your word. You don't have to say your phrase every time you make your movement."

The machine has stopped. I call, "Start the machine on the breath and accelerate to freeze." The players are so connected to each other that they find a communal freeze together. We applaud their beautiful effort.

Discoveries about the dynamics of the poem – how the phrases relate to each other, how emphasis on one rather than another changes the impact of the poem – come from this kind of exploration. To play machine, to be a part of the whole, you must be listening intently with your ears and also with your body. The poem, its various meanings and interpretations, emerges without forethought, often with surprising results.

Musical Transformations

I ask five to seven players to come onstage: "Begin to sing 'Mary Had a Little Lamb.' Other simple tunes like 'Row, Row, Row Your Boat' would be fine too.

"I'm going to call out different song styles. Transform to these styles from wherever you are in the song. Transform both vocally and physically.

"Barbershop quartet." The players move physically into quartet position and sing in harmony.

"Jazz." The players begin to move around the space randomly in slouchy body positions like cool cats! Some begin to snap their fingers in response to the jazz rhythms.

"Gregorian chant." Bodies become more formal as if a line of nuns or monks were intoning and marching to pray.

"Opera." Someone bursts forth as a leading soprano and another as lead tenor, with the others taking on supernumerary roles as they all grandly sing the ditty.

Other calls include: children, witches, or different cultures like Russian, Italian, British.

"Now find your own transformations as a group." The players explore "gospel," and "call and response," oration, rock, pirates, the blues. "Thirty seconds. Find your final style." The group ends with a lullaby sung over an imaginary crib.

All the games played in the warm-up and in the body of the class are designed to prepare the players for the following final exercise. As you can see, all of the games in this section have explored the connection between the body and the word, they have explored and heightened the meanings and feeling tones of the words, and they have focused the players on taking from each other and from the space between (out of their heads).

Pay-off game

Group work on Ariel's speech from Shakespeare's *The Tempest.*

Full fathom five thy father lies;
Of his bones are coral made;
Those were pearls that were his eyes;
Nothing of him that doth fade
But doth suffer a sea-change
Into something rich and strange.

For this final exercise, I divide the players into four groups and tell them to find games to explore Ariel's speech from Shakespeare's *The Tempest.*

"Learn the poem, as a group, in round-robin style to see what phrases pop out, for example, 'rich and strange,' 'pearls,' 'sea-change,' 'coral made.' Then think of games that will help you get into the space of the words." I release the groups to work on the verse, letting them prepare for fifteen to thirty minutes, depending on what I see in terms of involvement and energy. I try to stay out of their way so they feel free to be silly on the way to being serious. Bonding as a group is an important component of this process.

Words, no matter how descriptive, can never truly capture the dynamism of players improvising and transforming in the moment as they explore and heighten beautiful language, especially the poetry of Shakespeare. The unique and fluid connection between word and sound and rhythm and movement, unfolding in real time, cannot be translated to the page, or even to film. The danger and the electricity are always lost. That said, I will try to give you some idea of how two groups approached this exercise at the end of this particular workshop.

Group 1 began the line "Full fathom five thy father lies" with jazz-like rhythms, repeating some of the words in the line, scat-singing with the sounds of the words. Next they began to play the game Space Break by exploring new rhythms or other game structures. "Of his bones are coral made" became a poem machine and morphed into Word Toss with the players tossing "bones," "coral," "pearls," and "eyes" to each other in different rhythms and with different attitudes. Using the same two lines, they broke into an echo game and then started to explore and heighten "dem bones" in the spirit of the Musical Transformations game. They ended their performance by reciting the entire poem through a group mirror with slow-motion emphasis on the final line of transformation, "Into something rich and strange," winding down like they would a machine. This group had developed a strong motor and could have gone on endlessly transforming, so organic were the shifts from one game to the other.

Group 2 took a more structured approach. They played the game Whip-Statues for the first line, "Full fathom five thy father lies." One player spun another and then let them go. That player spun out and froze in a pose as they said the first word, "Full." The leader spun another player for the word "fathom," and so on. Whip-Statues is a common children's game.

The whole group was now arranged in frozen statues all over the playing space. For the second line, "Of his bones are coral made," the group drew on the game 1–2 Decroux or Slow Constructs. They explored the words "bones," "coral," and "eyes" for sound and shape by making portraits, moving one at a time, to design the space in an abstraction of each word.

For the third line, this group used the game Ali Baba to repeat the line numerous times with different movements and rhythms, and ended with an Impulse Construct based on the words "pearls" and "eyes." Embracing the meaning of the poem as one of transformation, the players started a game of Object Transformation. As they found objects in the space, one at a time, and passed them along after transforming them, they repeated the line "Nothing of him that doth fade/But doth suffer a sea-change." After several individual object transformations, the group came together in mirror to explore the words "sea-change/Into something rich and strange." Mirror morphed into Ball Toss as they tossed key words of the poem to each other. To complete their performance, they repeated the entire poem through a game of Phrase Tag, adding a new line with each new tag until they came to the last line, "Into something rich and strange," which they performed by building a final portrait (each player taking one word and finding a pose). Each game grew organically out of the one before, so that the exploration was seamless and beautiful to behold. The poetry and the movement served to complement each other and to illuminate the poem in surprising ways.

After all the groups presented, I ended this workshop with a few brief comments: "Exploring and heightening the sound and meaning of the word reveals the whole spectrum of the word and leads to finding another phrase of the poem. Game connection helps us leave out anything we would impose on a great poet. We must trust the poet. We can only enter the poem and explore, but cannot bring our own interpretation until it has been explored, or maybe we never need to interpret. Submit to the word and connect with the word, and you get everything: character, emotion, meaning, depth."

8 Workshops on Story Theatre

Story theatre is:

The adaptation and performance of a story told through a combination of narration and dialogue, movement, mime, and music.

The point of concentration is:

◆ To bridge the gap between improvisation and script.

◆ To retain improvisational spontaneity, point of concentration, and the sense of play in scripted work.

◆ To discover what serves and illuminates a particular story.

◆ To transform into the imaginative world of a story with everything at the player's command – body, voice, the space itself – in sync with the other players and the audience.

◆ To establish place, character, activity, and ambience through transformation in movement and sound.

◆ To physicalize and activate third-person narration.

◆ To find the right moments to move from narration into dialogue and back to narration.

◆ To earn the right to transform into character and dialogue.

Key games for work in story theatre include:

◆ Two-Deep Tag

◆ Round-Robin Storytelling

◆ Circle-Object Transformations

◆ Guided Mime Transformations

◆ Invested Object with Independent Conversation

◆ Round-Robin Story with an Object Hook-Up

◆ Character Layers

◆ Fish

◆ Papa La Chaise

◆ Three on a Box

◆ Fairy-Tale Moments

◆ Slow (1–2 Decroux) and Fast Constructs

◆ Adjective Constructs

◆ Portraits

◆ Group Problem Solving of Individual Beats from a story.

The following introductory story theatre workshop demonstrates how the game Round-Robin Storytelling functions in a class progression. This workshop is designed to explore the Greek myth "Arachne."

Introductory workshop focused on Round-Robin Storytelling and the Greek myth "Arachne"

Warm-up sequence

Fish

I begin the class with Fish, a Vietnamese children's game, asking five people to come up and stand in a line. I instruct them to hold onto the waist of the person in front of them and explain that the point of concentration for this game is to keep the fish in one piece: "You are all part of a whole – the fish must stay together; it is one fish. The object of the game is for the head of the fish to tag the tail (the back of the person at the end of the line) without breaking the fish apart. When this is accomplished, the head moves to the tail and the second person in line will become the head, and so on, until everyone in the fish has had a turn as the head."

Awkwardly, the players begin to move as a group, the head testing out how she's going to tag her tail. Her first instinct is to go directly for the tail, but, in doing so, she forgets about the attached players and the fish falls apart. The lead player now becomes the tail and the next player in line tries her hand at leading the group. This time I caution the players before they begin moving: "Get the feel of the body. See what it can do." The lead player begins to explore her "body." I continue to encourage her to see how the fish moves as a whole: "Get a sense of what's behind your head as you move. The head must move as a part of the whole." I slow them down with the call "Slow motion," and guide them to do more exploring before trying for the tag "Try different ways of walking and moving. Double time … normal … change directions." As the players get the feel of moving as one body and begin to move one way and then the other, the tail magically and organically presents itself to the head player who then effortlessly tags her tail.

The head player moves to the tail and the next in line becomes the new head. For this leader, I suggest that she explore massive, larger-than-life movement, adding, "What is the personality of the fish? Maybe offer a sound." During this exploration, the fish becomes a blown-up fish moving with large slow-motion steps and swaying from side to side. This movement gives way to a tiny fish drawn into itself and tiptoeing through the space in a zigzag fashion. When the tail presents itself at her side, the head tags the tail-player's back easily.

For the next leader, I make calls for different kinds of fish, starting off with "A Russian, man-eating fish!" The players begin to stomp and become threatening as this fish, yelling "Nyet" repeatedly. I call, "French fish," and the players respond by making gibberish sounds with a French accent and moving in a dainty, precise fashion. To end the game, I call, "Chinese dragon fish." The movement and sound the players find is reminiscent of a dragon in a Chinese New Year's parade.

There are two pitfalls in playing this game. Either the players are so into being "parts of the whole" that they never tag, or they are so intent on tagging that the whole fish falls apart. The goal is for the head to discover how the fish moves and use that to tag the tail. The secret of the game is as indicated earlier (if the head gets into a weaving rhythm, the tail will virtually present itself to be tagged with very little effort), but the players must discover this secret through playing the game. This game is a good warm-up for story work.

Guided Mime Transformations

From Fish, I shift gears into a mime-transformation game with the point of concentration on endowing imaginary objects with weight, shape, size, texture, and movement. I begin by teaching the group how to do an "earth walk."

To do an earth walk, you walk in place – toe-heel/right-left. Use the foot to release into the ground, like you are crunching snow, before bringing the heel down and releasing the other foot. The "earth walk" is best played in slow motion. As the players simultaneously experiment with this walk, I coach them: "Feel the ground beneath your feet. Focus up and out. Permit help of arms, swinging from side to side."

Once the players have gained some mastery, I lead them in the following sequence of transformations as I work with the imaginary objects along with them: "Find a very heavy sack in the space. Start to pick it up and put it down." I repeat this action several times as I say the words "Pick it up ... put it down." Through this repeated action, the sack changes to a fishing pole with a fish on the line. I start by casting forward and drawing the pole back. The act of catching a fish leads me to a transformation. The fishing pole changes into the string holding a big balloon; the balloon bobs up and down vertically. As the players follow/mirror my physical transformations, I call, "The pull of your feet keeps you grounded. Explore the feel of the balloon and then let the balloon change to a kite. Pull it in and freeze/wind change/blowing against your back – free-flowing kite – play with the kite. Now the kite changes to a large umbrella – wind in front ... wind in back." We explore this action several times before the next transformation. "Now the umbrella changes to a dog leash. The dog is in control. The imaginary dog suddenly pulls us forward." I call: "Now *you* are in control." The players rein in their dogs. We repeat this alternating action several times before I call, "The dog runs away," and the game ends.

Between each of the above calls, we all explore the individual object. For example, as I described earlier when I had the fishing pole, I cast a line, let it bob up and down to see how it feels to catch a fish. At the height of a casting movement, I found the transformation to the balloon. My point of concentration is to find the transformation through the movement rather than pre-planning the whole sequence. Even though I know that I want to end with the dog on a leash, the way to get there may change from exercise to exercise. For example, the balloon could transform into a bell rope instead of a kite.

Mime work with imaginary objects gives a concrete connection with the space. It prescribes a way to deal with space. One is constantly connecting with the space in story theatre and scene because: 1) props are never the real thing onstage, but we must deal with them as if they are; 2) in teaching children, mime allows one to deal with their non-verbal life. When a child is comfortable in space, he or she can speak up; 3) mime helps to create the particular Where of the moment, opens up the space of the creativity, enhances one's whole stage life. I developed this mime sequence after studying with students of Etienne Decroux.

1–2 Decroux or Slow Constructs

I now shift to another game inspired by my work with Etienne Decroux. I took Decroux's basic mime game, adapted it to explore images from stories, and called it 1–2 Decroux in honor of my teacher. The point of concentration for this game is to create designs in space – to sense the movement of others using your peripheral vision and kinesthetic feeling.

For many years, I used this game before I was aware of Spolin's Give and Take game. Sheldon Patinkin introduced me to Give and Take, which is sometimes called "the actor's game" and is more on impulse than slow constructs. Give and Take has largely replaced this game at the Workshop today, but 1–2 Decroux is still an excellent game for story theatre exploration. Here I lay specific groundwork for the pay-off experience of this class – performance of beats from the Greek myth "Arachne."

I ask for five to seven players to come up onstage. I give each player a number and tell them: "Balance the stage and stand in neutral. Neutral means standing, no holding, weight on the balls of your feet, ready to move. When I call your number, you are to move in slow motion to make contact with another player. When I call another number, you will freeze and the new player will move. The freeze is ideally a suspension of movement that will continue as if uninterrupted when your number is called again. You will move one at a time, in slow motion, to fulfill your objective, which is to make contact with someone else. Once that contact is made, you may break that contact and seek a new contact with another player. You must keep moving until another number is called. Since the point of concentration for you all is to create designs in space using your bodies, you don't need to be facing front, proscenium style, all the time."

I begin calling out numbers, not in order, with the goal of getting everyone moving and seeking contact. I am also trying not to leave any one person frozen in an awkward position for too long. Once everyone's number has been called several times, I tell the players, "Now move on your own, one at a time, in a give-and-take fashion, to explore new designs."

The players begin to move in slow motion to design the space but the discipline of "one at a time" begins to erode. I remind them as they continue to play: "Suspend your movement when another person begins to move. Only one person can move at a time. Move one at a time. Don't wait your turn; just move and the others have to suspend for you." The players have now re-established their "one at a time" movement but have lost the sense of connection. They are moving in space without touching one another and they are only exploring standing positions. I remind them to stay in contact and encourage them to find different levels and designs in space. On this prompt, the players begin to bend and kneel and use the floor as well as reach to the sky. The space becomes more dynamic immediately.

As the players move, I continue to guide them: "Take stage, if you wish. The minute you see someone move, you must suspend." One player is hiding behind the others, so I call, "Get yourself seen." To break up the slow movement and get the players off-balance, I shift gears: "Freeze. Small staccato moves – strong, tight, small, precise. See how little you can move and still be effective – how small and still take stage. Let anything come up." I make a sound for them every time someone makes a small movement like the turn of a head, the flick of a hand, the shrug of a shoulder: "Bup … Bup … Bup."

Now we move into the "construct" phase of the game. I explain to the group, all frozen in their last design, that I will be calling out nouns and that they are to respond to the word by creating an abstract design of it with their bodies, one at a time. "The object is not to be literal; try to go for the feel of the noun, the sculptural qualities – shape, line, space, mass, levels."

I call: "Build a tree. Not a literal tree. Tree-ness ...whatever that means to you. Try to get the feeling of the object." The players move on their own, one at a time, to build on each other's movements to create the design of a tree. One player stands tall as a trunk. Another player lies down on the floor holding the "trunk's" legs to give the impression of the tree's roots. Someone else stands next to the "trunk" and leans out with her arms to create a drooping branch. Another player mirrors that movement on the other side. The last player, a very tall guy, stands behind the "trunk" with his arms reaching out above his head. The "tree" is complete.

I call, "A bird." The players move to create a bird. One player creates a beak with his arms and hands. Another stands behind him, making contact with her bent head to form a body. A third creates a large tail by standing upright with arms stretched to the sky. The last two players create the sense of wings. A large, beautiful bird emerges from the movement and the tableau.

And finally, I call, "A fish." The "beak" player stretches out flat on the floor with knees bent and feet in the air. Several more players huddle around the first to create a massive body. The final player creates a huge open mouth at the head of the mass with his bent body and his arms reaching forward. A whale or shark-like fish has formed.

When the fish is complete, I tell the group to relax and shake out. They have worked hard. The audience to this group can see that it is just as interesting, if not more so, to watch the image form through purposeful movement in heavy space as it is to see the beautiful finished design.

Adjective Constructs

I ask for another group to come onstage and move this group quickly through the basic game (they know what to expect from watching the first group). When I call, "Tree," the players form a generic tree, but this time I tell them to add an adjective, one at a time, to create a specific kind of tree. When the initial player moves and calls out the adjective, all the players in the construct are to move at the same time to adjust the design, to reflect the feel of the adjective, forming a whole new design. One player says, "*Oak* tree" and the players respond by making all their shapes and positions larger and more commanding. The next player says, "*Old* oak tree" and the shapes move to communicate the weight of age. The next: "*Gnarled* old oak tree" and the shapes of each branch become gnarled through the use of many fists.

New object: I call, "Gate." The players, one at a time, form a gate. One player stands center and swings his arms and one leg for the opening and freezes mid-movement. Other players arrange themselves on either side, variously taking on the character of fence posts, some linked by outstretched arms. When one player says, "*Strong* gate," the rest stand and the central two players lock their arms to form a closed gate. The third player calls out, "*Rusty*, strong gate," and the players respond with small staccato moves to indicate cracks and age. The final player surprises everyone by changing the nature of the gate altogether with the call "Picket fence." The players don't miss a beat. They alter their positions to get the feel of "white picket fence" out of a Norman Rockwell illustration.

From here, I return to the earlier game and we explore some images from "Arachne" – water plants, nymphs, forest. To reward and release the players from the discipline of the slow constructs, I finish the playing with Impulse Constructs, where everyone moves simultaneously in response to the sound, shape, and feel of the word called. Still referencing "Arachne," I call: "Bubbling brook; tree spirits; weaving machine." The players respond to this final call with something akin to the familiar Machine game but with one player doing the weaving as the others form groups to indicate the shifting parts of a loom, one group moving horizontally and the other vertically.

1–2 Decroux is a mime game that focuses on creating designs in space with the body. Through mime the players can feel the connection viscerally and move toward true ensemble playing. The game begins controlled, but then progresses to the give and take. Even without calling numbers, the play retains enormous definition. The rules give the players a frame of reference to connect with others.

The players have played with enormous focus and discipline. Break time.

Body of the class

I shift gears into playing an introductory story game, Two-Deep Tag, to prepare for Round-Robin Storytelling. I ask the players to form two circles (one inside the other), instructing each player in the outer circle to stand behind a player in the inner circle. I solicit two more players to be runners. I explain: "These two players will run around the outside of both circles. Player 1 will pursue Player 2. Player 2 can escape at any time by standing in front of someone in the inner circle, releasing the outer player (the new Player 2) to run in their place. If Player 2 is tagged while running around the circle, the play reverses with Player 2 now pursuing Player 1." We play the basic game to learn the rules.

Once the class is comfortable with the game, I ask the person being pursued to sing a simple song, in this case "Row, Row, Row Your Boat." If the singer is tagged, the play reverses and the new singer must continue the song with no backtracking – no repetition of words previously said. For example, if the player being pursued is singing "Row, row, row" and gets tagged on "your," the new singer must pick up the song with "boat." That player cannot repeat the "your." The same rules apply if the runner stands in front of someone in the inner circle. The new runner must pick up the song exactly at the point of release, no backtracking. That way the game constantly keeps the players off-balance and gives them two points of concentration – the Tag game and the song. It forces the players into playing in the moment.

My goal all along is to get to the storytelling. For the last phase of this game, I ask the players to tell a story instead of singing a song. The same rules apply to picking up the story without backtracking. To help the players through the singing and the storytelling portions of the game, I use the calls "slow motion, double time, full-body whisper." To bring the playing to an end, I call, "Find an end to the story."

Now that the players have practiced some of the principles of Round-Robin Storytelling in the form of a warm-up game, I ask them all to be seated in a circle to play Round-Robin Storytelling in earnest.

Round-Robin Storytelling

"I will begin a story in **third-person narration** and then point to another person who must pick up the story in **mid-sentence with no backtracking** (no repeated words said by the previous storyteller)." I begin, "Once upon a time there was a strong young woman who ..." and I point to someone in the circle to pick up the story right from there. That player continues the sentence "was lifting huge blocks of" and I point to someone else. The new player picks up the sentence with "wood that she has just cut with an enormous ..." New player: "ax." In this manner, the sentence "Once upon a time, there was a strong young woman who was lifting huge blocks of wood that she has just cut with an enormous ax" was created by four people.

I continue to point to different people in order to change the narrator, catching the storytellers in mid-sentence as much as possible. After everyone has had a turn narrating, I encourage the players to continue the story on their own in a give-and-take manner. I caution the tellers to speak with a sense of putting the story out to be taken, yet able to be continued if no one takes. In other words, if they are telling very fast and not leaving any room, no one can pick up the story. You need to slow down to allow space for the taking. I remind them to give and take mid-sentence and to pick up the story with no backtracking. To keep the players "off-balance" during the storytelling, I call, "Slow motion, double time, full-body whisper, sing it" (folk song, lullaby, opera, jazz).

As the story progresses, I ask the tellers to go into greater detail and begin to relate to each other. For example, I coach one player to detail the physical attributes of the young woman in the story. One player starts by saying, "The young woman was unusually tall, with long ..." Another player takes: "legs and arms. She has big features too – a large ..." New player: "nose and enormous eyes, and big red lips." You might have been thinking that the first player was going to say "long, blond hair." The story could go that way, but didn't because it is a group effort. The players who take the story surprise us all with their contributions. No one person controls the narrative for very long.

My next goal is to get the players to a place where they can narrate themselves into a scene in order to communicate the encounter at the heart of the beat. I coach the tellers to physicalize what they are saying – to open the door physically as they say it, seeing what's inside; to go into the space for real and create it. Ideally, the players can stand up and move into the center of the circle through narration, go into a beat of dialogue and scene, and return to the circle through narration. A story emerges about this big, lonely woman who lives in a forest cottage and encounters a woodsman who has lost his way. When one transformation into scene has occurred, I guide the players to find an end to the story.

"How can you get someone to pick up the story? You have to leave space, a moment for them to pick it up. Rule 1: the story must be told in third person. Keeping the story in third person maintains the literary form and makes it easier to transform (distance and objectivity). Once into dialogue, the obligation is a heavy psychological and subjective one. Rule 2: You must pick up in mid-sentence with no backtracking."

Round-Robin Storytelling exercises three key skills for story theatre performance – earning the right to transform from narration to story, finding that moment of transformation, and detailing the Who and the Where. This is an important step toward working with stories.

Pay-off: theatrical moment

I have the players read the Greek myth "Arachne" in give-and-take, round-robin style. The myth tells the story of Arachne, a woman from Lydia renowned for her skill at weaving. Arachne challenges the goddess Athena to a weaving contest. She is transformed into a spider as punishment for her arrogance.

After reading the story, I divide the players into groups of four or five and instruct each group to go off and explore one beat from the myth, explaining: "Any game may be used to deepen the segment and realize the encounter of the moment." The groups go off and rehearse for about twenty to thirty minutes, at which point they return and perform for each other.

One group sets up a frame for transforming into story. They take on the characters of high school students complaining about their English class, which is studying mythology, and find a way to transform into telling the story by creating a weaving machine for Arachne. Another group creates a series of constructs as they describe the images Athena weaves into her tapestry – an Apollo construct, a Pegasus construct, and so on. A third group explores the character of different gods and figures mentioned in the story through a transforming Fish game – an Athena fish, a Calypso fish, a Zeus fish, and so on. A fourth group explores the scene where Arachne challenges Athena to a weaving duel while speaking to an old woman. The old woman transforms into Athena. After improvising the first part of the scene in dialogue, the group went back into narration to accomplish the Old Woman-to-Athena transformation by detailing the emerging Athena as a character layer.

In story theatre, action precedes narration: see it, receive it, and then give it to the audience. Be careful not to jump into character too soon; let it evolve. Add on slowly. If you jump into character too quickly, you cut off the process of transformation and the audience doesn't get to see the transformation. Each character is free in this form to narrate herself into scene. Players can occasionally involve the audience, narrating but still sharing it with the audience. When there is no sharing, you are closer to what makes a play. The moment of transformation is the moment between two characters.

Some early explorations found their way into the final performance version of the Arachne story. See the following Young People's Company working script for "Arachne" to get a sense of how these discoveries got shaped and developed for performance.

The following story theatre script for the Greek myth "Arachne" was adapted and directed by Byrne and Joyce Piven and the 1986–7 Young People's Company. It was performed as part of the YPC show *Medicine for Melancholy* in the Piven Theatre Workshop's annual Spring Story Theatre Festival for that year. Raphael Beck provided the original music and keyboard accompaniment to popular songs. The story featured Jacki Greenberg and Rachel Ablin, alternating, in the role of Arachne with Laura Weisenberg playing Athena. The Young People's Company members whose improvisations contributed to the development of this script included Rachel Ablin, Raphael Beck, Jeff Broitman, Leslie Brown, Colinne Byrne, Eric Fine, Jacki Greenberg, James Meredith, Jon Mozes, Julie Pearl, Lisa Ritts, Anne Ryan, Eric Saiet, Jeremy Wechsler, Laura Weisenberg, Caroline Wilkinson, and Marc Wilson.

ARACHNE

(*Students coming into a school lounge*)

James

God, that teacher's such a bore.

——. I'm so tired!!

——. Thank God! Free period.

——. Look at him. The "dedicated student."

Jon

I hate Greek mythology

James

Awwww. Poor baby.

Leslie (*Leslie improvises from a popular song, singing under the dialogue that follows, and is joined by other members of the ensemble.*)

Ensemble (*Others join Leslie in song*)

——. What's so tough about mythology?

Jon

Just look at all these names. Cerebus ... Menelaus ... Achilles ... I'll never keep them straight.

——. You can handle mythology.

——. Let me help. We studied myths in Latin.

Jon

You're taking Latin?

——. Took.

Jon

Will you guys keep it down? I can't study

(*Song begins to top dialogue.*)

(*Jon continues to talk about mythology under the song and then the dialogue gains prominence.*)

——. Let's break it down. Start with just one name.

Jon

Okay, Okay. Uh ... Arachne. The Spider Woman.

——. Spider Woman?

Rachel/Arachne

Remember what the teacher said? Relate it to something else ... somebody you know.

(*Song ends. Other students become involved in mythology discussion.*)

——. What's Arachne like?

Jon

Someone that's really arrogant and rotten, who really thinks a lot of herself.

Leslie

(*singing*) Johanna. I love you!

——. She's great.

——. Yeah. But she knows she's great.

——. She's so-o-o talented.

Leslie

Hi! My name is Johanna and I'm going to the Olympics!

——. Excuse me. I'm going to throw up.

———. How many times did she tell you she was going to play basketball at the Olympics?

———. She doesn't have to flaunt it.

James

She gave it to me four times. "Guess what, James? I made it to the Olympics."

Rachel/Arachne

Hey, can you just picture her in the Olympics?

(*Ensemble becomes basketball players and crowds at a game.*)

———. And she puts it in!!!

(*Ensemble cheers.*)

———. The problem is she's running around for hours in her own glory and people have already gone home.

———. They've been gone for hours.

———. The janitors are sweeping up.

———. And she's still taking her victory lap!!

Arachne

Don't be so down on her. Johanna is so talented. You're just jealous. She's just sure of herself.

———. She's too sure of herself.

———. She has a right to be. She's good.

———. She was born with talent.

———. So relate her to Arachne.

Arachne

Arachne's an awesome artist. She's like Picasso or Da Vinci or something.

Jon

Yeah. But I don't know exactly …

Arachne

Okay. She was renowned throughout the country of Lydia for her skill as a weaver.

———. She was as nimble with her fingers as … as …

———. Calypso, that nymph who kept Odysseus for seven years in her enchanted island.

———. She was as untiring as Penelope.

(*Tug of war*)

Jon

Penelope?

——. The hero's wife who wove day after day while she watched for his return.

Arachne

And day in and day out Arachne wove, too.

(*Player transforms into Arachne as she weaves.*)

And all the children of the village of Lydia would gather around her loom to watch her.

James

Dig them threads, man!

——. Check out those fingers. They're so nimble.

——. As nimble as Calypso.

——. What threads did she use on her loom?

Arachne

Silver like spun glass.

Ensemble

(*echoes in whisper*) Glass.

Arachne

Gold like the liquid sun.

Ensemble

(*echoes in whisper*) Sun.

——. The design is brilliant.

(*Jealousy beat in counterpoint.*)

——. Look how the designs seem to breathe … and move.

——. I wish I could weave like this and be the center of attention.

Leslie

A goddess must have given you your talent.

——. She was born with her talent. She didn't have to work for it.

——. Pallas Athena herself must have graced your fingers.

Arachne

Athena!!!

Jon

Athena?

(*End counterpoint.*)

——. Yes, Athena inspired all the household arts.

Ensemble

(*each member takes one art*) Cooking, pottery, basket weaving, embroidery, sewing, kneading, baking, weaving.

Arachne

All those things are crafts. Weaving is an art. You can't compare them to weaving. I was inspired to weave.

——. Aha! Inspired!! The spirit comes into you from the gods and gives you your talent.

James

What kind of jive is that? That's what my momma says. Check it out. When I get home from a good night at basketball, she says I owe her stuff. "I gave you your uniform. I gave you your sock. I gave you your sweat pants." But check it out. I don't owe her nothin'.

Jon

Or this one. "Young man, look at me when I'm talking to you. Eric, I gave you life." What does that mean to you?

Eric

That's pompous. Over-blown, corny and stereotypical.

Jon

"As long as you live in my house, you live by my rules. One of those rules, Eric, is respect."

Leslie

My mom does that to me all the time.

——. (*as mom*) "I gave you your talent. You wouldn't have it if it weren't for me. I'm the one who got you involved in singing."

Leslie

Yes, but it's my craft now.

——. "I got you to take lessons and encouraged you …"

Leslie

"I perfected it, though. It's my talent."

——. "You were given it."

Rachel/Arachne

What difference does it make? It's her talent now. That's the point. No one can take it from her.

Athena

Somebody gave you this talent. Athena.

Arachne

Athena!! I'm not afraid of Athena. You hear that, Athena? I'm not afraid of you. You didn't give me this talent. She didn't give me this talent.

Ensemble

Ssssshhhhh!

Rachel/Arachne

Don't shush me. I don't care if she hears me. In fact, I'll shout it. Look at this, Athena!!! Can you weave like this? If Athena can weave any better, let her come and try.

(*Freeze – silence*)

——. The children, frightened, shrank away.

Athena

And only an old, old woman remained. She looked at Arachne's work and said, "You don't know what you're saying. Perhaps if you beg forgiveness, the goddess might forgive you."

Arachne

I've worked hard for my art.

Athena

You must be grateful.

Arachne

I know everything there is to know about weaving.

Athena

Arrogance will bring you down.

Arachne

Arachne broke her thread and the shuttle stopped humming. "Keep your advice to yourself, old woman. If Athena can weave better than I, then let her come and try it. I challenge the Gods!" And as she glared, Arachne was amazed to see the old woman …

Ensemble

Change …

——. Suddenly …

——. Into a tall, majestic …

——. Maiden.

Athena

It was Athena herself.

Arachne and Athena

In silence, the two began to weave …

———. And the children stole back.

———. Coaxed by the sound of the shuttle …

———. That seemed to be humming with delight over the two looms,

———. Back and forth like bees.

Lisa

They gazed upon the loom where Athena was weaving and slowly
shapes and images began to form.

———. And magnificent designs emerged, showing the greatness of the
gods.

———. Their power!

———. Their great accomplishments!

Jon

The King of the gods, reigning supreme in the heavens with all the
gods and goddesses around him.

(*Elvis Presley construct*)

Zeus

Zeus!!!

Jon

Driving his shining chariot through the heavens, bringing light to the earth.

(*Apollo construct*)

Apollo

Apollo!! (*sings, accompanied by Ensemble*)

Jon

Riding to slay the Flaming Dragon chimera.

(*Pegasus construct*)

Ensemble

Pegasus!! (*singing*)

Jon

Who's this? Lifted up to heaven and throned among the stars.

(*Andromeda construct*)

Ensemble

Princess Andromeda!!! (*singing*)

Athena

And, last of all, as a warning to Arachne, Athena pictured a vain woman
of Troy who was turned into a crane for her arrogance.

(*Troy construct*)

Ensemble (*singing*)
Athena

All these and more Athena designed with immortal skill and beauty.

——. And everything was bordered with pale olive blooms and fruit.

——. And the whole tapestry shown like a rainbow.

Arachne

Meanwhile, Arachne embroidered her web with stories against the gods.
(*As the Ensemble creates the next series of constructs, Arachne and they sing.*)

Jon

Bound in misery, while vultures tore at him.

Ensemble

Prometheus!

(*Prometheus construct*)

Jon

Wearily bearing up the weight of all the heavens.

Ensemble

Atlas!!

(*Atlas construct*)

Jon

The princess carried off by Zeus in the form of a bull.

Ensemble

Europa!

(*Europa construct*)

(*During the following speech, the Ensemble does quick constructs for "birds," "peacocks," "donkeys," and "Niobe."*)

Jon

Arachne, making light of all the gods, she portrayed them as birds, peacocks, dogs ... donkeys ... and Niobe – all tears, weeping over her slain children.

Arachne

And all of this she bordered with flowers.

James

Flowers of the kind dropped by the young Persephone when Hades stole her from the bright upper world and carried her down to the dark realm of spirits.

——. But, yet, she wove with marvelous skill.

——. And the creatures seemed to breathe and speak.

——. And it was all as fine as the gossamer that you find on the grass before the rain.

(Ensemble continues singing throughout the above segment until they end the verse. Then they freeze. Pause.)

Athena

Athena herself was amazed … so much so that she forgot her anger at Arachne for an instant as she stood entranced. Then slowly, imperceptibly at first, she … began to undo all the threads and then … Suddenly … Slashed the web across …

And she took her spindle and touched Arachne's forehead three times.

Since it is your glory to weave, you and yours shall weave forever.

So saying, she sprinkled upon the maiden a certain magical potion.

(Ensemble becomes a weaving machine.)

Arachne

Slowly, Arachne's beauty began to fade and then her very human form shrank to that of a spider. And as a spider, she spent all of her days weaving and weaving.

Athena

You may see something of her handiwork among the rafters.

(Ensemble continues to weave, then suddenly break to become students in the lounge.)

James

I hate it when this stuff gets in your eyes.

Marc

All these spider webs. What a sticky situation we got here.

James

Awwww, Marc.

Marc

Did you know webs are made of spider spit?

——. Spider spit?

——. It's bad luck to kill a spider.

Eric

Look at that one! It's beautiful.

Leslie

> I'll get it.

Eric

> No, it's perfect.

Jon

> You guys, I got it!! Arachne, the spider woman.
>
> (*End*)

Workshop exploring narration to scene using Fairy-Tale Moments

The ability to move from narration into dialogue in story theatre form is a key skill that students must master. I developed a game called Fairy-Tale Moments to address this skill specifically. My game Invested Object provides a perfect vehicle for this type of transformation. The following sample class uses impulse, mime, and agreement games to build toward the Fairy-Tale Moments pay-off experience.

Warm-up sequence

Papa La Chaise

The players stand in a circle. I ask for someone to volunteer to be It and tell her to walk around the circle and tap another player on the shoulder. The volunteer does so. I tell these two players to walk in opposite directions around the circle until they meet at a place equidistant from where they started. "You two will have the following dialogue: The player who is It will say, 'Good evening, Papa La Chaise. And how are you?' (If your partner is a woman, you address her as Mama La Chaise.) Your partner will answer, 'Fine.' You will then say, 'And what shall I say when I get home? Shall I say, "How are you?"' Once these words are repeated, you both race around your half of the circle to home base (the space vacated earlier). Whoever gets to home base first is safe. The player who reaches there last is the It and finds another player in the circle to tag."

We play the game until everyone has the idea of how it goes. The first time through, the It makes it back to the empty space first. The new It taps another. The players begin to play around with the rhythm of how they say the cue line to move, the second "How are you?" They get the idea that the goal is to catch the listener off guard.

Now I shift gears. Instead of the formal dialogue, I give the It a made-up line to say. That line becomes the first line in a little beat or improvised scene between the two players. This time, when the It repeats the first line, the two players run for home base. I give the following line to the It: "You plug the first hoochamagigger here." The It grabs an imaginary object and mimes plugging it into a huge imaginary machine as he says the line. His partner says, "Why there?" The It explains, "Because this cable connects to the computer." The two players have a short scene about hooking up a new computer, when suddenly the It says in exasperation: "You plug the first hoochamagigger here!" and starts to run. He has caught the other player by surprise and arrives safely at home base. I give the new It this line: "You wrap the noodles around the fork this way." For another scene, "Screw the light bulb in tightly." We play until almost everyone has had a chance at a scene.

Papa La Chaise is a Haitian children's game that I turned into a theatre game. It is an excellent warm-up for reinforcing the connection between object work and dialogue.

Body of the class

We shift to a group object/agreement game, Three on a Box. I divide the class into groups of three and explain the rules: "Decide on the nature of some kind of box and discuss the types of things it might contain. You should also decide where you are and who you are to each other." I make some suggestions to give the players an idea of the types of boxes they can consider, "The box could be a Christmas box full of toys, a costume trunk, a thrift shop storage box, a box of summer clothes, an old attic trunk, a treasure chest, a laundry bag, and so forth. Your point of concentration is to detail the physical qualities of an imaginary object together." I give them some time to confer but not enough time to plan out the improvisation.

The first group goes onstage. One player reaches into the box and pulls something out. It seems like something long and thin. I tell the group to discover what the object is together by exploring its qualities: "You can't name any object until you have realized it. Naming the object won't make it happen. You have to earn the right to name it. Use texture, color, smell. Don't worry about the audience." Absorbing my call, speaking one at a time and handling the object, the players marvel at how soft the object is, explore its length, play with a lovely fringe it has until a hand-knit winter scarf emerges. Once they know what it is, they can lay it aside and find another object.

The second player grabs something and pinches his nose at the smell. "It's so musty." Another feels the fur around the collar of what starts to emerge as an old winter coat. A clump of fur comes off in her hands! The players hold the object up, discovering its shape and length. One player tries it on. It itches, so she takes it off and they move on.

I call, "Detail what's inside the box. Explore and heighten that object. No preconceptions. No questions. Get into the object. Keep exploring. Trust. Help. Give and take." The audience slowly recognizes that this group is in the attic of their parents' house and that the box contains very old vintage winter clothes.

Once everyone has found one object, I guide the players to end the scene by telling them to reach in and find one object together. "The realization of the final object should be a surprise, if you leave yourselves open to all possibilities." They find an old fur muff from the nineteen-thirties or forties and let their scene come to an end.

The other two groups choose a costume trunk in an abandoned theatre and a pirate's treasure chest. This game calls on the players to explore the contents of the box through give and take and to discover by agreement what is in the box, one piece at a time. The players must discover together the qualities of each object before it is named. Once an object is given a name, it is put aside and others are explored. For example, each player exploring the trunk full of old costumes found a different imaginary costume, used it to give it some initial shape and substance (to make it real), then shared it with the group. Agreement by the other players heightened and developed the object's reality.

When the last group finishes presenting, we move on to the other two preparatory games:

Invested Object into Conversation with Independent Activity
Round-Robin Story with an Object Hook-Up
(See earlier descriptions of these games.)

Pay-off: theatrical moment

Everything we have done so far has been preparation for the game Fairy-Tale Moments. I divide the class into groups of two to five people and give each group copies of various fairy-tale moments that involve important objects. I ask them to explore how to use the objects to transform into scene, sending them off to work on these moments using games and narration for their presentations. I caution: "The moments and descriptions I gave you are just suggestions. None of them is sacrosanct. The samples here are only ONE WAY to transform into scene or dialogue. It is whatever connects you into scene (like walking into a picture) – the time of day, the ticking of the clock, the sound of music, a strand of hair – virtually ANYTHING with specificity."

The sample moments handed out are:

1. Spindle (*Sleeping Beauty*)
Player begins describing the spinning wheel and the action of the spindle the moment before the princess enters the tower room. The princess narrates herself into the room and the two characters move into dialogue: the princess is curious about the needle and the spinning process; the old woman draws her in until the moment is accomplished in the pricking of the finger.

Opening line: "The spindle was long and sharp as she slowly began to wind the soft brown thread around …"

Ending line: "And the princess slowly began to fall asleep" or "Just then the clock stopped and everyone fell suddenly asleep."

2. The poisoned apple (*Snow White*)
Player begins as an old woman describing the apple to the young princess while standing in the doorway of the cottage. The stranger (the Queen in disguise) needs to convince the princess to accept the apple.

Opening line: "The old woman held the bright red, shining apple up to the light and under the nose of young Snow White as she said …"

Ending line: "The young princess thanked the woman, and closed the door as she bit into the delectable apple."

3. The oven (*Hansel and Gretel*)
Gretel details the oven and the actions of the witch. The scene: Gretel tricks the witch into showing her how to get into the oven. This scene involves conflicting objectives: each wants to get the other into the oven.

Opening line: "The oven was old and black and the witch motioned for Gretel to light the oven and climb in."

Ending line: "And as the witch climbed in … Bang! … Gretel shut the oven door."

4. Mirror/Queen (*Snow White*)
One or both players narrate the mirror: "The mirror hung on the vast wall. It was heavy, made of pewter or brass" (whatever) … and then the players who divide

into the mirror and the Queen detail the ritual of the Queen in give and take. The Queen goes into Character Layer as well. They work slowly into the moment when the mirror tells the Queen she is no longer the fairest in the land. "Mirror, Mirror on the wall; tell me who is the fairest of them all."

Ending: Beat ends with the smashing of the mirror.

5. Magic wand (*Cinderella*)
Begin with the godmother describing the wand (surely it's not an ordinary stick) and transforming into dialogue with Cinderella. Or, start with the transformation moment.

Opening line for second option: "The godmother lifted her wand and transformed her rags into a beautiful ..." Detail the clothes until you can transform into scene.

Ending with the slippers: "But best of all on her feet ..."

6. Beans/magic seeds (*Jack and the Beanstalk*)
One player narrates into the scene by detailing the beans and transforming into Jack presenting the beans to his mother. Scene: Dialogue/argument with the mother.

Opening line: "The beans were small and black in his hand, gleamed in the light, he could hardly wait to show his mother the wonderful thing he had bought with the cow in the market."

Ending line: "And so, furious, the mother threw the beans out of the window."

I give the groups plenty of time to work on these moments. We come together and each group presents their scene, improvising dialogue between the lines of narration. For example, in the "Jack and the Beanstalk" scene, Jack showed his beans to the audience as he addressed us directly, holding up each small bean and seeing how it reflected the light. The player added to the narration, saying, "Jack put the beans back into the velvet pouch and carefully stuffed the pouch into his pocket. Then he ran home, calling 'Mother! Mother!'" His mother took up the narration, saying, "'Jack's mother was kneading her bread for the day when she heard Jack calling for her. She put the dough aside, wiped her hands and went into the yard to greet him.'"

Mother

Jack, Jack, slow down. Here I am. What has gotten you so excited?

Jack

Mother, I can't wait to show you what I've got. I traded the cow for something really special. Let me show you.

Mother

You didn't get money for the cow? Jack, you know how important that was. Oh, my. What will we do? How will we live!?

Jack

Mother. Here. Look. In this pouch, I have these beautiful beans.

Mother

Beans!! Beans!!! How are we going to buy food with beans?

Jack

Wait! Wait! They are magic beans.

The scene continues with Jack explaining what the beans will do and his mother bemoaning his foolishness until she cannot take it anymore. She makes the transformation back to narration and says to the audience as she performs the actions, "Furious, Jack's mother threw the beans out of the window and ran, crying, into the house." Jack finishes the scene, narrating his shock and dismay at his mother's anger.

As in this example, each group explores and heightens the original texts, all the while staying true to the point of concentration – finding the transformation from narration to dialogue and from dialogue back to narration. Some groups draw on game calls like "Slow motion/double time," "full-body whisper," "tag," and even "constructs" to fulfill their task. The structure of relying on a predetermined beginning and ending line and a physical object helps the players understand the basic concept of story theatre performance.

Epilogue

Final thoughts

I take this opportunity to repeat that old saying "If you know where you are going, there are many ways to get there." The principles outlined in this book represent your destinations. Your point of concentration defines your choice of destination at any given moment. As in the game Interrupted Destination, you might change your mind on your way to one destination by taking a side trip toward another. This action requires a temporary shift in your point of concentration, while always keeping your eye on the ultimate goal. The class examples, games, and exercises offer you one way to achieve them. You could just as easily pick other games to achieve the same result or practice the same skills. The appendix of games offers you many options.

Our overarching goal is to open up possibilities for the actor. The games put the actors in touch with their intuitive selves, allowing for surprising discoveries that might not be available to the intellectual mind. In my estimation, the theatre experience should have a sense of danger, risk, the idea that "my cheeks are burning." Rote repetition of anything produces something that is dead unless the actor is able to find ways to make it fresh and alive. It is my hope that this book will illuminate one path toward making the theatre experience come alive.

Our journey to define and refine our work started with Byrne's vision of community – community as an aesthetic, as a process. And the most beautiful thing that comes from this work is the finding of one's own voice, one's own person, one's own creative domain. Byrne taught me to deal in principles, not in recipes. I've been thinking of late as to what was *the* most important principle of all and I was struck with an epiphany in the form of the famous title of Rollo May's book *The Courage to Create*. That's it, isn't it? The courage to create; the courage to stand in the face of the blank canvas and say, "I don't know what comes next," and let intuitive wisdom emerge … or not! It takes courage to be an artist in any walk of life. And everyone who has been in "The Work" and learned to be present and cross the abyss has something to transform their life. They have learned that it's fun to be brave. It's fun to risk.

Byrne's vision became ours. My son says that the work is "playing without the ball." My daughter, who mentored many students, had one who said, "It's training the impulse." We have found our voice through the "other," through the group, through ensemble – creating together and trusting ourselves and others. I have this little joke: I'm waiting for the White House to come to me for the solution to world peace. And I say, "Here it is: one creative workshop at a time – creating and building together – because the energy to build is greater and more courageous than to destroy."

Appendix

Alphabetical list of games

I. Format for game descriptions

For each game commonly played at the Piven Theatre Workshop between 1971 and 2012, I have provided the following information:

The name of the game as it is known at the Piven Theatre Workshop. When you read how a game is played, you may recognize it as a game you have played somewhere else or read in Spolin's book under a different name. If I know the connection, I will indicate the alternative name.

The dominant principle or principles underlying the game. All the games will be an expression of play by their very nature as games. THE CORE PRINCIPLE AND POINT OF CONCENTRATION FOR ALL GAMES: A FOCUS ON THE OTHER AND THE TASK AT HAND. Since the importance of the core principle is a given, I will not restate it in this section of the game description. However, other principles may have a dominant role in a particular game. We will indicate that principle. Many times a game will encompass several principles. That will be noted as well.

The specific point of concentration (POC) explains the focus for the players during the game. I repeat: in all games, the core principle is observed: Focus on the other and on the task at hand. In this section, I will be highlighting the specific task the game requires. Depending on how a game is used, a point of concentration may shift for a given game. The POC provided is for the basic game. It is up to the teacher to decide on the goal they are pursuing for a game or during a game and clearly communicate to the players what their point of concentration is at that moment. For example, if the players have lost impulse when a more heady call has been made, the teacher may shift the POC back to "impulse" to regain the spontaneity lost with the headier call before shifting back to pursue another objective.

Optimal group size applies to the optimal number or to a general recommendation. "Variable" means that the game can be played by small or large groups depending on the size of the space and the nature of the group.

Description explains how to play the game based on notes from actual classes taught at the Workshop. Most of the notes are from classes taught by Joyce Piven.

Calls refers to prompts from the teacher, words that help the players achieve play. Calls are the instructions given by the teacher to the players **during** the playing of the game. The teacher and the players are in a collaborative relationship with the goal of bringing the game or scene to life. Watching the game or exercise, the teacher senses what the players need to stay out of their heads – to play on impulse, and makes "calls" to keep the players "off-balance" or to move the players into more advanced stages of a game. The calls give the player an added "point of concentration" or shift the POC altogether. Viola Spolin uses the word "side-coaching" because the teacher is outside the playing, coaching the game or scene as it is being played.

The calls provided have been collected from actual class notes where the teacher was responding to something happening during the playing of a game or scene by a particular group of players. They are meant as suggestions and are to be used only as the situation requires. **By no means should all the calls listed be used in one playing of the game.** For further explanation on how to use "calls," see Chapter 4 on "Play."

The variations section of the game descriptions refers to different ways to play the same game, sometimes pointing to the development of the game during one playing and sometimes referring to totally different iterations of the game – variations that can be played as a game in and of itself. The "calls" that accompany the variations apply to the new point of concentration.

Commentary reflects ideas expressed by Joyce or Byrne Piven to students immediately after a game or ideas about the game developed later in interviews or notes to teachers.

Source refers to where Joyce or Byrne Piven first learned of the basic game.

Some games are so much a part of the vocabulary of actor training that it is difficult to identify an actual origin. And the game described as played at the Workshop may differ greatly from the original. The effort here is to give credit to the lineage of a given game where possible.

II. Games grouped by category

I have provided these groupings as a guide to help you search for a game to meet your point of concentration. Not all the games in the index are listed here. I've only included those games that are routinely played in the following categories.

Warm-ups: Space/Rhythms; Space Break; Machine (sound, word, transforming), Tag and all its variations; Yoga Sun Salutation; Mirror (Activity, Character, Scene Transformations); Activities in 2s (fold a blanket, put a leaf in a table); Give and Take; Fish; New York, Here I Come; Criss-Cross Sound and Movement Transformations; Streets and Alleys; Papa La Chaise; Who Started the Motion?; Red Light/Green Light; Simon Says; Four in a Moving Object; What Am I Seeing? Hearing? Eating?; Cat's Corner; Portraits; Yes game.

Mime: Stick, Ball, Wall; Earth Walk and Object Transformations (balloon, rope, bell, umbrella, leash); Portraits; 1-2 Decroux (Design of Bodies in Space/Levels, Slow Constructs, Who, What, Where); Impulse Constructs; Portraits (Slow/Fast/Character Calls); Hook-Up and Extend; Hook-Up and Twist; Hook-Up and Activate; Hook-Up with Story Narration.

Object games: Ball Toss; Make a Deal; Earth Walk with Objects; Four on a Heavy Object; Four in a Moving Object; Circle-Object Transformations; Mirror Object-Activity Transformations; Problem with a Small Object; Problem with a Large Object; Invested Object; Hook-Up and Twist (Object/Activities); Three on a Box; Add an Object Where; Where with Five Objects; Where Relay.

Character games: Swat Tag with Costumes; Mirror (Character Transformations); Neutral – One on a Bench; Neutral Scenes (1 in 3/3 in 1); Character Walks; Clothes Relay (Real and Imagined); Who Am I? (Waiting for a Bus); Character Layers; To Gets/Opposing Needs (transforming relationships); What's Between?; Papa La Chaise with Character; Hold It!; Portraits with Characters; Information Booth (Five Characters); Doppelganger.

Verbal games: Word Tag; Story Tag; Conversation While Eating; Three-Chair Conversation; Mirror with Simultaneous Speech; Simultaneous Rap; Four-Way

Telephone Conversation; Round-Robin Storytelling; Gibberish (Anecdote, Demo with Object, Translator, Scene); Poetry Workshops.

Impulse games: Papa La Chaise; Fingers; Constructs; Mirror Scene and Character Transformations; Entrances and Exits; Hold It!; Portraits; To Gets with Character Transformations.

Story games: Word Tag; Phrase Tag; Two-Deep Tag; Story Tag; Round-Robin Storytelling; Give-and-Take Storytelling; Hook-Up and Twist Storytelling.

Transformation games: Machine; Mirror Object-Activity Transformations; Mirror Scene Transformations; Criss-Cross Sound and Movement Transformations; Circle-Object Transformations; Fingers; Hook-Up and Twist; Portraits; Give and Take; Musical Transformations.

Where (scene) games: Where with Five Objects; Add an Object Where; Six-Sided Where; Where Scene Transformations; Where Relay.

The meaning of commonly used calls

Note that, in the following examples, many calls are paired with their opposite. Slow motion is always followed or alternated with double time, full-body whisper with hard of hearing, and so on. This pairing serves to keep the players "off-balance." When they are getting too comfortable in "slow motion" or they are beginning to lose focus, the call of "double time" instantly and dramatically shifts the point of concentration, putting the players back into their bodies and getting them out of their heads. It is the teacher's task to take from what the players need – to sense when to push them into a new space.

Slow motion/double time

"Slow motion" does not simply mean moving slowly. It means moving with the entire body as if through heavy space. The players should look as though a slow-motion camera is filming the scene – everyone must be moving at the same speed. To get to where they need to go, the players must reach with the body rather than speed up. Similarly, "double time" (silent film/Charlie Chaplin/shoelaces tied together) is not simply fast movement, but stylized fast movement.

The radical shift in tempo caused by going from slow motion to double time in an exercise or scene forces the players back into their bodies. The players must respond to the call instantly, on impulse, without thinking about it.

Full-body whisper/hard of hearing

"Full-body whisper" is not merely a whisper, but a "stage whisper" requiring the energy of the whole body. "Hard of hearing" forces the player to speak loudly. "Train overhead" accomplishes a similar end.

Explore and heighten

Explore and heighten is somewhat self-explanatory. The players must take a sound, a movement, or an idea and "explore" it as well "heighten" it – intensify it in some way. Making it faster, louder, adding more detail, softer, slower, heavier, lighter, and so on.

Objects must be used by all

Any imaginary object introduced into the scene by one player must be used by all. To accomplish this call, all the players must be focused on each other and what is happening in the space because the "object" introduced is invisible.

Help/hinder

When the call is "Help," players help each other make contact with the objects being used in the scene. When the call is "Hinder," players hinder or prevent each other from making contact with the objects.

Play strictly

This call alerts the players that they have strayed from the point of concentration and need to "play strictly," to play according to the rules of the game. For example, in Freeze Tag, all the players are to freeze when someone is tagged. The new "It" should wait until everyone is frozen before starting up the game again. In the playing, players often start to lose the crispness of the freeze or start to move without everyone's attention. "Play strictly" alerts them to what they are doing in an efficient way without being judgmental.

Calls derived from games

All of the following calls are based on individual games and exercises. See the game description in the alphabetical list for a more thorough explanation of the source game. Any game can become a call. Once the players have experienced a game in its pure form, the POC of that game becomes a language understood by all. That language can be used as a call to shift the point of concentration or to keep the players off-balance. For example, "Give and take" is often used as a call to make the players aware that they are all talking simultaneously and need to allow everyone to be heard individually.

Camera

"Camera" means an intensification of attention on another person. You can also call variations like "close-up," which would signal the player to move close to the subject, or "long shot," which would tell the player to intensify their attention but from a distant point across the space, including as many other players and as much of the space as possible.

Contact

Players must make some kind of physical contact with another player in a game or scene. The nature of the contact should change with each new thought. If the players are relying on their hands only for that contact, the teacher can call, "Hands are dead." Players must become more inventive by making contact with other parts of their body. The contact does not need to make sense in the context of the scene. The goal of the call is to get the players out of their heads and focused on the task – the contact – while the action and dialogue of the scene proceed.

Double scene

This call alerts the players in an improvisational scene that two scenes are happening simultaneously. The call suggests that they play Give and Take between the two scenes. That means the players in one scene would suspend or minimize their action to "give" the stage or focus to the other scene. The other scene can "take" back the stage by energizing their speech and action, thereby signaling the first scene to "give."

Entrances and exits

Players can make entrances and exits only if they have the full attention of everyone onstage. The entrance or exit must be grounded in the circumstances of the scene. Merely stamping one's foot or yelling out of context does not accomplish the goal.

Gibberish-English

On the teacher's calls, players alternate between speaking in gibberish (nonsense language) and in English. This call helps the players move from being "talking heads" into full-body commitment in support of what they are saying. It also discourages "playwriting" (the invention of all kinds of given circumstances and exposition) on the part of the players. Excessive playwriting in an improvised scene means the players are doing too much thinking and not enough interacting.

Give and take

Players in a scene are to "give and take" the stage. Played strictly, like the game, only one person can move and speak at a time. Everyone else must suspend, giving focus to the active player. Any movement on the part of another player "takes" back the stage. If played appropriately, no one should dominate for any length of time. The play should alternate fluidly between the players, with everyone participating.

Unacknowledged actions

This call prompts the players who are performing a scene improvisation or a scripted scene to begin to behave in ways that are outside the logic of the circumstances but to keep the dialogue going as if nothing unusual were happening. Players might stand on chairs, lie on the floor, jump into another player's lap, turn over the furniture, but no one in the scene is to acknowledge that anything odd is going on. They are to try to continue playing as if all were normal. This call shakes up the space, keeping the players off-balance, and gets the performers into a state of play. Often, the actors make surprising discoveries, especially with regard to the emotional life of the scene. The game Unacknowledged Actions was introduced to Shira Piven at Bennington College.

Interior dialogue

During an improvisational scene, the teacher can call, "Freeze!" and stop the action. The teacher would then call the game Interior Dialogue and identify the player who is to speak. That player would tell the audience what they are feeling and thinking at that moment. The other players remain frozen during this monologue. The teacher might resume the playing of the scene or identify someone else to speak.

Physicalize

This call asks the player/actor to get into their body. It prompts them to give physical expression to the meaning or emotion of a given moment or line.

Tag and its variations

Basically, the "It" must tag someone else, who becomes the new "It." In a scene, you do not have to worry about the logic of the movement. The idea is to get the players into play while they are saying the lines.

What's between?

This call refers to something that went on just prior to the scene that nobody is allowed to talk about during the scene, but that dominates the scene nonetheless. For example, someone just died, someone just got engaged, parents had an argument before the kids arrived, someone just got fired. The what's between? will inform the scene but should not be verbally addressed or telegraphed. The teacher might call, "What's between?" during an improvisational scene to reinforce the POC or to alert the players to a subtext that has come into the play improvisationally.

These calls are the ones most frequently used in the work, but many more exist. Once established, they become a shared language vital to the collaborative relationship between teacher and student at the center of this work.

Organic progression of session planning

The basic principle of organic flow applies to planning whole sessions. The early sessions involve establishing language, object work, verbal work, and simple Who, What, Where Scenes. More advanced work in character and transformation is interspersed as players develop basic skills.

In the generic sample for an eight-week session for children ages 9 through 12, the first four weeks are devoted to establishing language. The basic games played introduce players to the anchors for creative possibilities via play: Focus – on the body in space; on the other/outside self; on the object in space. In addition to focusing on the body in space and object work, early games develop group connectedness, giving and taking, agreement in movement and language. The second four weeks concentrate on steps in the story theatre process, going from teacher-directed to student-directed work on stories from the repertoire. This generic eight-week session traditionally ends with an Open Workshop for parents and friends. At the end of sixteen weeks, the Open Workshop generally involves the sharing of a story theatre piece.

III. Alphabetical list of games and game descriptions

Ages of Man – see Portraits

Ali Baba and the Forty Thieves
Principles: Group-Play, Agreement, Leader-Impulse.
Point of concentration: To copy the movement of the person to your right.
Optimal group size: Variable – large to small groups
Description: The players form a circle. This game is played like a "round." Player 1 leads a repeated chant – "Ali Baba and the forty thieves" – while creating a movement to the rhythm of the chant. Player 1 must create a new and different movement each time the chant repeats. The player to the left of Player 1 begins moving at the start of the second chant repetition, but he copies the *first* movement Player 1 created – like a round. Each player copies the movement of the player to his/her right, one step behind. The goal is to make it around the circle without dropping the pattern.
Calls: Keep the game going; focus only on the person next to you; energize the chant.
Commentary: Movements can be simple like clapping, tapping the head, bending both arms in front of you, kicking one foot out and in, but they have to be sufficiently different to be distinguishable by the followers. Being the leader is the most difficult task in this game because the leader has to find new movements "on impulse" without too much thinking or hesitation. The leader has to get a "motor" going or the game will bog down at the helm. Each time the game breaks down, pick a new leader so that many people get to experience both positions. This game is a good warm-up or introductory game for a group of new students.
Source: Unknown.

Amore – see Fingers

Balance the Stage
Principles: Impulse, Agreement.
Points of concentration: Balancing the stage picture so all parts of the stage are used and different levels and body positions are achieved. Starting and stopping as a group on your own.
Optimal group size: Variable

Description: Players move around the stage space rapidly – in and out – until the teacher calls, "Freeze" and all players suspend movement. The freeze is instantly followed by the call of "Balance" – all immediately make one move to adjust position to achieve a balanced stage picture. There is only a beat between "Freeze" and "Balance." Once the group has understood the rules and developed a sense of each other, the teacher instructs them to do a number of pictures (3–5) on their own, starting and stopping together as a group.

Calls: The stage needs balancing. Adjust.

Commentary: This game is an effective warm-up exercise, especially for advanced players. It is a way to get players immediately into connection, working on impulse, and using their whole body.

Source: Byrne Piven.

Ball Toss

Principles: Agreement, Specificity, Transformation.

Points of concentration: To take what's given. To respect the physical qualities of what's given – weight, shape, size.

Optimal group size: Variable.

Description: Players in a circle. Leader molds ball from space and begins to pass it around the circle. Every time it comes back to the leader, she will change the ball in terms of size, weight, etc. Whatever "ball" is passed from the leader must return to the leader with the same weight, size, shape, etc.

Variation: Players throw the ball with one part of the body and catch it with a different part of the body (e.g. throw it with your hip, next player catches it with their knee).

Variation: Players can transform the ball before they pass it along. Receivers must catch the "ball" they are thrown before they make their own transformation.

Calls: Slow motion/double time; hot potato.

Commentary: Hot Potato can lead into Machine. This game is basically a game of agreement. At the end of the game, the leader can point out moments where agreement was strong and a moment or two where there was agreement on one element but maybe not another, for example, the players may have agreed on the size of the ball but not on its weight.

Source: General.

Cat's Corner

Principles: Impulse, Risk-Taking, Explore and Heighten, Agreement.

Points of concentration: Cat: to get a corner; Others: to change places without losing a Corner.

Optimal group size: Variable.

Description: Players are standing or seated in a large circle on cubes. (Depending on the type of seating available, playing this game while standing is sometimes safer.) Each cube is a corner. The "Cat" is in the middle. Player 1 (the Cat) goes up to Player 2, one of the players in the circle, and says, "Cat wants a corner." Player 2 responds, "Go see my next-door neighbor" and points to the player on his left or right. The Cat follows that instruction and asks Player 3 for a corner. While the Cat is going from person to person requesting a corner, the other players can change places, by agreement (non-verbal contact between two players who then exchange seats). The Cat tries to claim the empty space. If unsuccessful, the Cat continues to ask for a corner. If the Cat is successful, whoever is left out becomes the new Cat and play continues.

Calls: Play fully but be aware of the safety of all concerned including yourself. If one player vacates their space or cube, everyone must change position. Slow motion/double time. Responders – mirror the style of the question, explore and heighten the energy you are getting from the Cat. Full-body whisper/hard of hearing.

Accents: Southern, British, Italian, German, Russian and so on.

Variations: This game can be developed into Who, What, Where Scenes. A place can be designated in a call that everyone will create through their body position, voice and intent. All players respond in character to the Where and the question.

Sample places for calls: Prison yard, Tea at the palace, Kindergarten recess, concert.

Variation: This game can also be turned into a series of To Gets with improvisational dialogue in place of the "corner/neighbor" exchange. For example, the situation can be given that the "Cat" has some emergency and needs to find a phone. The "Cat" as a character will "knock" on imaginary doors in an effort to be let in to use the phone.

Commentary: This game keeps the players in play because it asks them to focus on two things at once – the "scene" and the "game." In the To Gets version of this game, the player being appealed to by the "Cat" should engage, not dismiss because of the assigned role. Their resistance must come out of legitimate concerns.

Source: Paul Sills.

Character Layers

Principles: Play-Impulse, Transformation, Specificity.

Point of concentration: To describe physical traits in detail and find their expression in the body, adding on until the full character emerges.

Optimal group size: One performing; any number watching.

Description: Players sit in a circle. The teacher instructs them to think of someone they know, someone they can describe verbally in detail – a person with strong enough characteristics in terms of movement, physical details – "the most unforgettable person you've ever met." That person can be a real person or, for story theatre purposes, a fictional character.

One player volunteers to demonstrate their person to the rest of the group. The player begins in neutral. As the player describes their person, they will take on the characteristics, keeping each one and adding on to build a whole person. It is very important that every characteristic be held as the player moves to describe another characteristic. It is a process of layering to get to the transformation.

Calls: How tall is he/she? What does the face look like? Hair? What do their eyes look like? Take that on. Be as specific as possible – their head, shoulders, chest, knees, feet. How do they move? What does their voice sound like? How do they talk? Begin to take on that voice along with the thinness of the face, the squint of the eyes, the pursing of the lips. How would they walk? Describe it and take it on. How would the person relate to objects? People? Direct your attention specifically to things in the character's world – coat, shirt, shoes, personal objects. What would they say while using that object?

Commentary: Be aware that the player is demonstrating. It is more demanding because the actor must be very specific. The actor's job is not to impersonate but to present with everything at their command – voice, body, emotional instrument, craft, artistry.

It goes back to principle again. Everything is kept because we're working for a transformation. We want to see a new person emerge. The player will take on the character. The important part of this exercise is that, as the player details the physical traits, they must keep whatever they have described. For example, if a person talks like I'm talking now, they would keep that and then they might say, "She had long hair." Now what does that do to you when she has long hair? Or "She's very tall" – DETAIL. This is different than any other game. How do you hold and move your head if your hair is long? How do you look at the world if you are tall? Have the body connect with that. IT'S ABOUT TRANSFORMATION. It's about breaking down the process of transformation.

Source: Joyce Piven.

Character Walk

Principles: Explore and Heighten, Specificity.
Point of concentration: On letting the holding influence the movement.
Optimal group size: Variable – large to small groups.
Description: Players play Clown Tag (two tags per person). Players walk through space, holding the tagged spots from the Clown Tag. The players then walk without holding, working for normalcy, but letting the weight and rhythm of the walk come from the previously held position. The teacher spotlights one player. That player keeps walking; the other players stop moving and focus on the highlighted player. The teacher asks the other players to call out what they see with regard to occupation, age, intelligence, characteristics suggested by the player's walk.
Calls for the moving player: Trust more. Extend it. Don't go into character. Stay open and neutral. Release the holdings and continue to extend the walk. Find a different rhythm that is off your center. Lead with that new space you have found. Answer the door over on the other side of the room. Make it less. It's not a deformity. Don't tell. Keep to the new center, new rhythm. Put your attention somewhere else. Don't obligate yourself to a character. Count the white tiles on the floor. Count the lights in the ceiling.
Calls for the watching group: Where is the player holding the character? Is the player held or free? Occupation? Heavy or light? Romantic, poetic?
Variation: Start with Space Walk instead of Clown Tag. The teacher instructs players to push the space with different parts of their body – nose, chin, collarbone, stomach, hip, knees, feet.
Calls for the moving player: What animal does that suggest? Extend it. Exaggerate it. Now, lessen it. What kind of person does that suggest? Make sure you are pushing the space, not the space pushing you. Push so no one knows you are pushing with that part of the body. Explore for yourself the spectrum of a person moving this way. Play with it; see what it might give you.
Calls for the watching group: What animal does that suggest? What kind of person does that suggest?
Commentary: It is important to keep the highlighted player's focus outward, eyes on an imagined destination or an unrelated task, something that connects the player to the

environment. Sometimes looking down gives the walk a dimension or mood that can lock you into an attitude.

Source: General.

Circle-Object Transformations – see Object Transformations

Clothes Relay

Principles: Impulse, Specificity (Sense Memory), Agreement.

Point of concentration: To find the object through contact with the space substance, detail the object, let the object influence your movement, pass the object to another player who uses it in the same way as you did (agreement). Let it happen instead of making it happen.

Optimal group size: Variable – large to small.

Description: Players are in two teams facing an imaginary trunk containing imaginary pieces of clothing. The imaginary trunk is located on the opposite end of the room. The first players from each team go up to the trunk, find a piece of imaginary clothing in it, take a moment to non-verbally detail the clothing piece, then put it on. Players are to let the object do something to them and their walk. These two players bring back the object to the next two players on their respective teams. Those players receive the object, wear it back to the trunk, and find another object.

Calls: Don't anticipate what you are going to find in the trunk. Give yourself a moment to detail the object. Don't tell. Show how to use the object in a different way than you received it. Silent film. Slow motion.

Variation: This game can be played with real clothing pieces.

Commentary: Uta Hagen worked with the concrete and left the mystical out of it. She used real objects so the actors could discover how objects made them move as a concrete handle on character. The trap is the cliché – when you are so concerned with the item of clothing. If you know the hat and its details, then it is there, it has to be trusted. It makes you move in a particular rhythm, it changes your center. The object might make you feel stupid or regal or frivolous, but go with it. You must work on detail, but, once it's there, trust it. Another trap is deformities. You have to find what that change suggests in the body and how it changes your particular way of walking.

Character is the most difficult part of acting – the most clichéd. The problem is to relate to someone as though you were that character. We are a whole spectrum of characters throughout the day. You must continually find a new way of relating depending on who you are relating to. We fight clichés in our own relations with people every day. A lot of character is defined by who and what we are dealing with. We are many different people. In story theatre, you must make a transformation right to the essence of a character; there is no time for you to develop it.

Source: Joyce Piven; variation with real objects, Uta Hagen.

Conflicting Objectives – see **Three-Chair Conversation with Conflicting Objectives and To Gets**

Constructs (1–2 Decroux)

Principles: Impulse, Agreement.

Points of concentration: To create designs in space; to sense the movement of others using your peripheral vision and kinesthetic feeling.

Optimal group size: 5–7 players.

Description: The basic game proceeds as follows, but the entire sequence of this game has three parts: slow constructs with the focus on general designs in space; slow constructs in response to a noun called; fast impulse constructs to end the game.

Part One: Players begin in neutral (standing, no holding, weight on the balls of the feet), breaking up the space on the playing area. Each player is numbered, one through five or seven. When a player's number is called, he/she is to move in slow motion with the objective of making contact with another player. The teacher calls out the numbers. The player moves when his/her number is called and freezes when another number is called. The freeze is ideally a suspension of movement that will continue as if uninterrupted when that number is called again. Players move one at a time in slow motion to fulfill their objective of contact. Once contact has been established with one person, the player may break that contact and seek new contact with another person, *continuing to move until another number is called.*

Once everyone's number has been called, players move in a give-and-take fashion on their own to explore new designs. Same game, no numbers called, but the players still move one at a time.

Calls: Freeze (suspend) when another person's number is called. Only one person can move at a time. Move one at a time. Don't wait your turn, just move and the others have to suspend for you. Stay in contact. Find different levels and designs in space. Take stage, if you wish. The minute you see someone move, you must suspend. Get yourself seen. Freeze: small staccato moves – strong, tight, small, precise. See how little you can move and still be effective – how small and still take stage. Let anything come up.

Commentary: 1–2 Decroux is a mime game that focuses on creating designs in space with the body. Through mime the players can feel the connection viscerally and move toward true ensemble playing. The mime exercise is parallel to Spolin's Lone Wolf, which is more abstract and harder to get to. The mime exercise begins controlled, then the give and take, when uncalled, still has enormous definition. The rules give the players a frame of reference to connect with others.

Historical note: Joyce introduced this mime game into the Workshop before she was aware of Spolin's Give and Take game. Sheldon Patinkin introduced Joyce to Give and Take.

Source: Etienne Decroux; adapted by Joyce Piven.

Part Two: Slow word constructs

Playing 1–2 Decroux, players move one at a time in slow motion to create images or abstractions of nouns called by the leader. The game traditionally begins with one or more of the following basic structures: tree, bird, bridge, house. The leader does not call numbers in this variant. The object is not to be literal, but to go for the feel of the noun, the sculptural qualities – shape, line, space, mass, levels.

Sample calls (not to be used all in one playing): Orchid, sunglasses, grandfather clock, Japanese lantern, fire hydrant, zebra, neon sign, track meet, military industrial complex, bifocal lenses, car, castle, tiger, eagle, hut, bed, tower, bicycle, flower, chair, skyscraper. Explore and heighten a given noun – tree turns into oak tree, sapling, weeping willow, redwood; bird turns into hawk, dove, robin, eagle, stork, chicken; bridge turns into suspension bridge, covered bridge; house into cabin, mansion, ranch.

Additional variation (optional):
Add an Adjective Construct
Players, individually as they begin to move, call out an adjective to the noun and cause the whole construct to adjust to this new quality, for example, Player 1 – tree, Player 2 – oak tree, Player 3 – old oak tree, Player 4 – gnarled old oak tree, and so on. When the initial player moves and calls out the adjective, all the players in the construct move at the same time to adjust the design to reflect the feel of the adjective, and thus a whole new design is formed. Other examples: gate – old, strong, picket fence; paintings – Toulouse-Lautrec print, Bruegel oil painting, romantic English watercolor.

Part Three (pay-off/release for the slow sustained concentration):
Fast Impulse Constructs
Point of concentration: To keep the group responding on impulse with the first thing that comes to their minds rather than thinking about what they are going to do.
On impulse players respond all at once through sound and movement, in some kind of contact or connection, to the **sound, feel, or shape of a word**. Sounds can take the form of actual sounds or repeated words and phrases. For example, if telephone switchboard is called, players could respond verbally by repeating a buzzing sound, repeating the word "hello," or the phrase "one moment, please." Each sound, word, or phrase is accompanied by a physical action. The word must be embodied in the movement, so "one moment, please" might be accompanied by an "operator" pressing a hold button. This is not a scene or conversation, so the words and actions are short and repeatable. When the construct is fully formed, the teacher calls a freeze and gives a new word. The group moves around as they make a new response to the new call. If the group gets stuck in one place repeatedly, the teacher can call, "Scramble" before giving them the new word.
Calls: Get the word out. Throw the word into the space from the sounds that you have. Scramble. Be a part of the whole. Give and take the words and sounds. Collaborate!
(Ideas for calls taken from playing the game many times – not to be used all for one group: juicer, jukebox, merry-go-round, germ, prison search light, clock, washing machine, Xerox machine, a rose, eggbeater, water cooler, Model T Ford, X-ray machine, orange juice squeezer, refrigerator, head of wilted lettuce, mailbox, postage stamp machine, Monopoly game, medicine cabinet, carousel, pin-ball machine, telephone switchboard, Popsicle, phonograph, balloon, hair pin, car phone, football helmet, waterpik, remote control, beeper, motorcycle, brownie, microwave oven, paperback romance, dental floss, movie camera, carburetor, lawn mower, sprinkler, brooch, hair dryer, puppet, apple, curling iron, Alka Seltzer, butterfly, fire truck, dishwasher, traffic signals, typewriter, computer, toothpaste tube, peanut butter sandwich, puzzle, tonsils, clocks of all kinds, sushi, street signs, wrapping paper, stapler, diary.)

Commentary: Each phase of this game can be played individually. For example, you can play Impulse Constructs as an independent game.
Source: Slow Constructs: Etienne Decroux; Fast Constructs: Spolin, general.

Constructs to Explore Wheres
Begin by playing Part One of the above game with numbers first, moving to players designing the space without numbers – moving on their own. Next step is to shift into Where Improvisations: The teacher instructs players to build a Where together. The Where is a cooking school. Each player is to find an object in this space. Or the Where could be backstage at a theatre or in a costume shop. Once the Where is established, the players go into scene. They return to the mime game and end with a final frozen tableau.
Calls: Use those objects. Add dialogue. Slow motion, including speech/double-time. Take strongly so that everyone has to suspend. Stay in connection. Give and take both word and movement. Go into scene, giving and taking stage. Suspend. Find a final tableau.
Commentary: Usually when this game moves into a Where, the players lose their connection. One can return to the basic game (playing strictly) and then go back to construction for connection. Then games are called to bring the players back into contact. A return to the original game moves the scene back into the mime frame (one at a time) and finally into an ending tableau.

Focusing on a problem with an object can carry the players into verbal life easily. If you are in connection, which the mime game forces you to be, then that is real improvising.

Constructs to Explore Story – see Story Theatre
To use constructs to explore story elements, the calls are based on the needs of the story. For example, in preparation for work on the Greek myth "Arachne," players explored the following calls: water, water plants, fish, one fish, water nymphs, tree, spirits that live in trees – dryads, loom for weaving.

Constructs into Group Transformation of Scenes
Principles: Impulse, Transformation, Agreement.
Point of concentration: Designs in space, contact, part of a whole, give and take.
Optimal group size: 5–7 players.
Description:
1. Players begin 1–2 Decroux without calls to explore designs in space.
Calls: Take stage, if you wish. The minute you see someone move, you must suspend. Get yourself seen.
2. Players are then instructed to discover one object among them that they might find in a large office building.
Calls: Find it first. Then find out how it works. Still give and take, but not necessarily one at a time, slow motion. Once object is found, proceed normally and add dialogue. Freeze. Let that object change into another object you might find in a very old house. Right from where you are. Give and take, starting with Player A. Find the object. Connect with it.
3. Group transformation of scenes: Players go through a series of group transformations of scenes.

Calls: Freeze. New scene. Freeze. New scene. Continue from where you are. See if you can make the transformations by agreement without a call. Share with the audience.

Commentary: This game is for advanced players. It cannot be achieved without experience with previous exercises such as Mirror Transformation of Activities, Criss-Cross Sound and Movement Transformations into Mirror Scene Transformations, and Fingers. Ideally this game is like a mobile – there is no one person making the changes. Once the group is connected, energy increases and also the amount of risk-taking.

Source: Byrne and Joyce Piven.

Conversation While Eating

Principles: Impulse, Agreement, Specificity/Sense Memory.

Points of concentration: To discover the meal together. To focus on the taste, weight, temperature, texture, smell of the food. The players must accomplish two things at the same time – the meal and the conversation.

Optimal group size: Two players.

Description: Two chairs are placed onstage facing each other. Two players sit on the chairs as if at a table, eating a meal. First, the players discover together what kind of meal they are eating. They begin in silence – in mime. Players then begin a conversation on an unrelated topic while eating their imaginary meal.

Calls: Take from one another. Taste the food. Enjoy it. Be aware of the texture, temperature, taste. Add conversation about anything you want. Keep eating. Chew the food as you are talking. Allow the eating of the food its own space. Deal with your food. You must accomplish two things. Explore and heighten what is found in the space between you. Converse as you eat. Taste. Chew. Swallow the food. Taste the food – is it hot? Cold? Slippery? What is its texture? Chew at the same time you talk. Keep chewing. Keep tasting. No one may speak without imaginary food in their mouth. What is your partner doing? What is in your mouth? How does it taste? How much effort does it take to chew? What is in your hand? What have you just taken? What is its exact weight? Freeze. Continue. Freeze. Continue. Freeze. Continue.

Gibberish – English – Gibberish – English.

Commentary: The leader can give the players a topic of conversation. For example, she might call, "Harsh winter." If this game is being played to explore a scene in story theatre, the topic will come from the given circumstances of the beat. For example, the sisters in "Cinderella" could be plotting to keep Cinderella from going to the ball.

Source: Minnie Galatzer. Spolin calls this game Conversation with Involvement.

Criss-Cross Sound and Movement Transformations

Principles: Impulse, Transformation.

Points of concentration: To establish a repeatable sound and movement through physical exploration on your own. To "teach" this movement to your partner non-verbally through mirror. To let the sound and movement transform. To make a full-body commitment.

Optimal group size: 5–7 players in each line.

Description: The players stand in two lines facing each other with a generous amount of playing space between the lines. Player 1, someone at the end of one line, begins a sound and movement. The player brings that movement into the center. As she moves around the space, the player lets her sound and movement transform. It is important that the player accept the first change and then deepen it as she repeats it. When the transformation is complete, Player 1 moves toward the person diagonal to her original position, at the end of the other line. Players 1 and 2 go into mirror (Player 1 in essence "teaches" the sound and movement to Player 2 through mirror). When Player 2 feels secure with the learned movement and sound, he brings it into the center and lets the sound and movement transform, making it his own. Player 1 stays behind in Player 2's place in the line. Play continues diagonally between the lines until everyone has had a turn.

Calls: Mirror the arms, mirror the hips, mirror the feet. Get off your center. Risk it and find something ungraceful.

Variation: When the last players are in mirror, another pair goes into mirror and moves into a four-way relationship with the original pair. Each pair is in mirror only with their partners but they are working simultaneously to find a transformation of their sound and movement. Then the first pair, still in mirror, fades back to the line, staying in mirror until the last possible moment. Play continues until each pair has gone through the process.

Calls: Use the fullest extent of your energy. Get your full body into the mirror.

Commentary: Criss-Cross Sound and Movement Transformations can be played for its own value or it can serve as a lead into Mirror Scene Transformations (see Mirror variations for a full description of this game). In this sequence, once everyone has had a turn with the first game, players continue the Criss-Cross format but, instead of just transforming sound and movement, they explore scene transformations or poems.

Source: Criss-Cross Sound and Movement is a popular game that can be found in many actor training texts. Variants of the basic game were used extensively in the 1960s by a number of well-known experimental theatre groups working with collective creation techniques. Byrne and Joyce Piven adapted many different Mirror exercises, including this one, in their effort to find ways to help the player experience transformation and understand the true nature of play – impulse, flow, motor.

Doppelganger

Principle: Agreement.

Point of concentration: To express the thoughts of the scene player.

Optimal group size: 3–5 players.

Description: A group of players decides on a Who, What, Where Scene. For each player performing the scene, a "doppelganger" is assigned. The doppelganger shadows their scene player as the scene progresses. At points within the scene, the teacher points to a given doppelganger and everyone else freezes while the doppelganger speaks the thoughts of their partner at that moment.

Calls: Doppelganger. Speak your character's thoughts. Take from what is happening in the scene. Take from your partner. No playwriting.

Commentary: The call "Interior monologue" is based on the doppelganger concept but, with that call, the character speaks their own thoughts.

Source: General.

Earth Walk – see Mime Warm-Up

Exits and Entrances

Principle: Play-Impulse.

Points of concentration: To seize the moment. To take stage strongly.

Optimal group size: 2–5 players.

Description: During an improvised scene (Who, What, Where), a player may make an entrance or an exit only if they have the attention of all the rest of the players onstage. Players decide as a group the following elements: a situation in a Where; the location of four exit/entrances in the playing space; a very active What, e.g. a party; a Who based on an occupation so you don't end up with just a situation in a Where. The player who is making an exit must never announce where they are going, but your intention must be clear. Know generally where each exit/entrance leads.

Calls: At first, help each other make the entrance or exit. If you find yourself offstage with someone else, help each other enter together. Someone start making an exit. Now really work for your entrances and exits. Can't use words anymore, just sounds or silence. Now you all have to get back onstage and find an end to the scene.

Variations:

Taking an exit with objects

With the object that passed your way during the game Molding Space or Make a Deal, one at a time, use it before the group. If everyone guesses it, you've earned your exit. Exit with everyone's attention on you and surprise us by your exit.

Taking an exit with characters

Walk in space as the characters you just were in the Who, What, Where Scenes. Players may exit, one at a time, when they have the attention of the whole group, by narrating the exit or by delivering a line as the character.

Commentary: Onstage players can help a player make an entrance. There has to be a reason to enter or exit. There is always a What's Beyond. The task is to find a reason that would interest everyone onstage for a person to come back on. Offstage – need to listen to find hook-up to what's happening onstage.

Byrne's comments to an acting class, 20 October, 1997: "When the player has the attention of everyone, he/she has to find the rhythm of the exit. This is a rhythm game at its core. The player can't wait until the next beat begins in order to exit. We have to work for the interior timing of dancers and musicians. The game is about impulse, an understanding of the structure of the beat. You have to be the one to put the period/exclamation point on the beat. With kids, play it cooperatively first. Then play competitively."

Source: Sheldon Patinkin.

Fairy-Tale Moments (Story Theatre)

Principles: Transformation, Specificity.

Point of concentration: To start with the object and then to transform into scene (dialogue) using only one beat of the story.

Optimal group size: 6–8 pairs or groups of 4–5.

Description: Explore with a group or in pairs various moments from well-known fairy tales, using objects to transform into scene. Players are given "sides" taken from a story. The sides might include a description of a moment or a quoted passage from the story, the object to be detailed, a beginning line and an ending line. The sides are meant to give the players the general idea of the task. They are a starting place for the player's own version of the moment. The players then go off on their own to work on the beat. When ready, all the groups present their versions of the moment.

Sample moments:

1. SPINDLE (*Sleeping Beauty*): Player begins describing the spinning wheel and the action of the spindle the moment before the princess enters the tower room. The princess narrates herself into the room and the two characters move into dialogue: the princess is curious about the needle and the spinning process; the old woman draws her in until the moment is accomplished in the pricking of the finger.

Opening line: "The spindle was long and sharp as she slowly began to wind the soft brown thread around …"

Ending line: "And the princess slowly began to fall asleep" or "Just then the clock stopped and everyone fell suddenly asleep."

2. THE POISONED APPLE (*Snow White*): Player begins with an old woman describing the apple to the young princess while standing in the doorway of the cottage. The stranger (the Queen in disguise) needs to convince the princess to accept the apple.

Opening line: "The old woman held the bright red, shining apple up to the light and under the nose of young Snow White as she said …"

Ending line: "The young princess thanked the woman, and closed the door as she slowly began eating the delectable apple."

3. THE OVEN (*Hansel and Gretel*): Gretel details the oven and the actions of the witch. The scene: Gretel tricks the witch into showing her how to get into the oven. This scene involves conflicting objectives: each wants to get the other into the oven.

Opening line: "The oven was old and black and the witch motioned for Gretel to light the oven and climb in."

Ending line: "And as the witch climbed in … Bang! … Gretel shut the oven door."

4. MIRROR/QUEEN (*Snow White*): One or both players narrate the mirror: "The mirror hung on the vast wall. It was heavy, made of pewter or brass (whatever) …" and then the players who divide into the mirror and the Queen detail the ritual of the Queen in give and take. The Queen goes into Character Layer as well. They work slowly into the moment when the mirror tells the Queen she is no longer the fairest in the land. "Mirror, Mirror on the wall, tell me who is the fairest of them all."

Ending: Beat ends with the smashing of the mirror.

5. BEANS/MAGIC SEEDS (*Jack and the Beanstalk*): One player narrates into the scene by detailing the beans and transforming into Jack presenting the beans to his mother. Scene: Dialogue/argument with the mother.

Opening line: "The seeds were small and black in his hand, gleamed in the light, etc., etc., and he could hardly wait to show his mother the wonderful thing he had bought with the cow in the market."

Ending line: "And so, furious, the mother threw the beans out of the window."

6. MAGIC WAND (*Cinderella*): Begin with the godmother describing the wand (surely it's not an ordinary stick) and transforming into dialogue with Cinderella. Or start with the transformation moment.

Opening line for second option: "The godmother lifted her wand and transformed her rags into a beautiful ..." Detail the clothes until you can transform into scene, ending with the slippers: "But best of all, on her feet ..."

Commentary: None of these moments is sacrosanct. The Sleeping Beauty moment can also be narrated from the point of view of the princess using the winding staircase to the tower as the object you are narrating. You can use other moments in these stories – Cinderella has many – or other stories for this exercise. The samples here are only ONE WAY to transform into scene or dialogue, and so you must remind the class of this. It is whatever connects you into scene (like walking into a picture) – the time of day, the ticking of the clock, the sound of music, a strand of hair – virtually ANYTHING with specificity.

Source: Joyce Piven.

Fairy-Tale Object – see Invested Object

Fingers (Amore)

Principles: Play-Impulse, Agreement.

Points of concentration: To take from the space and from your partner to begin a beat, and, equally important, to sense when the beat is over. To find the scene on impulse from body position.

Optimal group size: Any number in pairs. (An entire class can work simultaneously. Individual pairs can then be highlighted.)

Description: Players work in pairs. Each finger is assigned an occupation. For example: "index – teacher, middle – worker, ring – judge, pinky – parent" or "index – doctor, middle – lawyer, ring – newsman, pinky – parent" or "index – servant, middle – princess/prince, ring – peasant, pinky – king or queen." The teacher can decide the names with the help of the class or the players can choose their own names as long as the names denote an occupation of some sort.

Players stand opposite each other and "throw" out fingers and say the appropriate names. Once in agreement – when they both say the same name, taking from where their bodies land – they immediately begin a scene from what's in the space between them – the occupation and their physical relationship at the time of the throw. In the two seconds that they may shift positions, impulse gets lost and they go into their heads. To play strictly, players must not shift and take time to think; they must start the scene from the landing position on impulse.

When they agree that the beat is over, the word-throwing is repeated. The agreement is not spoken; it is a non-verbal communication between the players when they sense/agree the beat is over. At that moment, they let the scene go and shift to "throwing" fingers again.

Calls: Find where and who you are by agreement. Don't playwrite. Let the moment happen. Don't be afraid of the time it takes to find your connection. Begin the beat from where you are in the space – from where you land. Don't move – begin from there.

Commentary: Players should avoid playwriting – exposition, seemingly clever plot twists and lines. The role of the teacher is to keep the players out of their heads – to help them focus on locating themselves in the Where and exploring the relationship. Players must end the scene by agreement. This game is related to Mirror Scene Transformations.

Source: Adapted by Byrne Piven from an Italian finger game called Bocci.

Fish

Principles: Play-Explore and Heighten, Agreement/Ensemble.

Point of concentration: To tag the tail without breaking the fish apart. Players are all part of a whole. The fish must stay together – it is one fish.

Optimal group size: 5–7 players.

Description: Players form a line by holding onto the waist of the player in front of them. The object of the game is for the head of the fish to tag the tail. The tail – the last person in the line – must be tagged below the head, on their shoulder or back. When this is accomplished, the head moves to the tail and the second person in line becomes the head. Play proceeds until all have had a turn as the head.

Calls: The head must move as a part of the whole. Have a sense of what's behind your head as you move.

Variations: The teacher can make calls to explore different rhythms and physical movement or even to explore characters from a story. For example: A "whale" moves differently from a "minnow." An "old" fish moves differently from a "teenage" fish. A "Russian" fish moves differently from a "French" fish or a "British Royal" fish. A "Samurai Warrior" fish moves differently from a "Businessman" fish. The calls are meant to stimulate physical and vocal play. The character calls based on different cultures are derived from work on specific stories. Pictures from various cultures can be used to stimulate ideas for movement.

Commentary: Two pitfalls – either the players are so into being "parts of the whole" that they never tag or the players are so intent on tagging that the whole fish falls apart. The goal is for the head to discover how the fish moves and use that to achieve the goal. The secret of the game: if the head gets into a weaving rhythm, the tail will virtually present itself to be tagged with very little effort. The players must discover this secret through playing the game. This game is a good warm-up for story work.

Source: Adapted by Joyce Piven from a Vietnamese children's game.

Four in a Moving Object

Principles: Play-Impulse, Specificity (Sense Memory), Transformation, Agreement.

Points of Concentration: To all be in the same moving object. To work together to communicate the movement, the experience of being in the same moving object as it starts and stops, turns and crosses different terrain.

Optimal group size: 3–4 players.

Description: Four players try, simply, to be in the same moving object. The teacher calls out the name of the moving object. Once the players respond, the teacher calls for the object to start and stop and turn. The players must respond together. Once that moving object is explored, the teacher calls out other objects, one at a time. The group must transform their movement to accommodate the new object.

Calls: Move immediately together. Go with your impulse. Sample objects: bus, old car, elevator, Ferris wheel, roller coaster, sail boat, train, Model T Ford, stagecoach, barge.
Source: This game originated with Spolin, who called it Object Moving Players. Byrne and Joyce Piven made their own adjustments to the original.

Four Moving a Heavy Object
Principle: Agreement.
Points of concentration: To establish together the physical qualities of an imaginary object. To all move the same object together.
Optimal group size: Four players.
Description: Players decide on a large, heavy object. They move the object from one side of the stage to the other, with a possible rest stop along the way.
Calls: Work together. Make the object real. Help. Hinder. Help.
Variation: Heavy Object with Independent Conversation on "Hot Button" Topic.
Players discuss controversial issues while dealing with a heavy object.
(Also see Problem with a Large Object.)
Calls: Focus on your task – move the object. Talk and move at the same time.
Commentary: Agreement is central to this game because, without it, the players won't make it across the room with the object intact. If the players are in agreement, the object will emerge.
Source: Spolin.

Four-Way Telephone Conversation
Principle: Play – Explore and Heighten/Give and Take.
Point of concentration: To converse and incorporate; to give and take the conversation.
Optimal group size: Four players.
Description: Players are arranged on the four corners of a square onstage – clockwise, corners are A, B, C, D. Player A calls Player C and begins a conversation. Once their conversation is established, Player B calls Player D and begins a conversation. Now there are two conversations happening at the same time. As they talk, the players try to incorporate as many words, phrases, and subjects as possible from the other conversation into theirs.
Calls: Try to give space for the other conversation. Give and take. Try to incorporate. Turn your backs to each other and continue. Slow motion. Hard of hearing.
Variation: The teacher gives each caller, Players A and B, an objective, for example, "A, you are trying to get C to volunteer for a local candidate's election push. B, you are trying to get a part in a musical. C already auditioned and got cast. You want to hear all the details."
Commentary: This game is related to Give and Take, Simultaneous Rap, and Three-Chair Conversation. It is about listening intently and focusing on your partner at the same time.
Source: Spolin.

Gibberish
Principles: Play-Off-Balance Moment, Anxiety of Not-Knowing, Agreement.
Point of concentration: To communicate through intent, physicalization, and melody.
Optimal group size: Any number – specific to each Gibberish variation.

General commentary: Gibberish is an exercise where normal English is abandoned in favor of nonsensical speech created by the player. It is the substitution of shaped sounds for recognizable words − a vocal utterance accompanying an action, not the word-for-word translation of an English phrase or sentence. In Gibberish, intention and melody are important. The "melody of intent" in speech is that intended meaning carried not by the actual words, but by the tone, rhythm, and feeling state (e.g. anger, sorrow, fury, joy, lament). Since the players don't have real words, they convey the meaning through the melody of the gibberish language used and the energy in their bodies. In Gibberish, it is important to have something real to say.

Values of Gibberish: It cuts out the extraneous. It gets the body involved. The effort is to communicate. You can't lie back. The nuances of language come through melodies, feelings. Gibberish frees you. You don't have to be a playwright. Gibberish loosens the actors when they get tight. It can be used to get in touch with the moment − what is really happening. It can be used to explore the story.

Source: Spolin.

Gibberish Practice (whole class simultaneously as warm-up)

Point of concentration: To communicate the anecdote through nonsense language.

Optimal group size: Variable − pairs playing simultaneously.

Description: In pairs, players share with their partners in gibberish a short anecdote or story of something that happened to them that day. When they finish, see if their partners got the gist of what they were trying to say. As a class, discuss responses, difficulties, types of gibberish that emerged.

Calls: Use as many different sounds as possible. Use consonants and vowels. Exaggerate your mouth movements. Vary the tone. Keep usual speech rhythms. Let the gibberish flow. Communicate to the other players. In this practice, don't expect them to interpret what you are telling them.

Gibberish Demonstration with Translator

Point of concentration: To sell a product.

Optimal group size: Two players.

Description: One player demonstrates a product in gibberish. The other player translates into English. If the English-speaking player is confused, he can ask the other player in his native language (gibberish) what was said.

Variation: One player demonstrates a product with no translator. Leader calls, "Gibberish." "English."

Calls: Try to get more vowels into your gibberish. Try not to repeat the same phrase. Keep connecting gibberish with English and with the objects. If you are stuck in one form of gibberish, change to another. Slow it down. Trust that you know what you are talking about and we will too.

Gibberish and Translation with a Story

Point of concentration: To tell a story in gibberish.

Optimal group size: Two players.

Description: Two players tell an original story. One player is speaking gibberish and one is the translator.

Calls: Don't be afraid of putting the body into it, but don't charade. Begin with the phrase "Once upon a time …" *Switch roles,* again, again, again … Pick it up right away.

Gibberish Translation in Threes

Point of concentration: To translate by taking from the other.

Optimal group size: Three players.

Description: Three players sit in a row of three chairs. The player in the middle is the translator for both of the end players, who presumably speak two different languages but are having a conversation with each other.

Gibberish Who, What, Wheres

Point of concentration: To teach a skill.

Optimal group size: 3–5 players.

Description: Players are divided into groups. Each group decides on who the teacher is, what they are learning, and where they are. The teacher will teach in English; the students speak the same gibberish so they understand each other. Sample situations: how to ski, how to plant a garden, how to cook a fancy meal, how to play tennis.

Calls: The class doesn't understand the teacher but they all understand each other. Teacher – gibberish. Students – English. Teach names of objects.

Gibberish with Contentless Scenes

Point of concentration: To find the melody of the event.

Optimal group size: Any number in pairs.

Description: Take six sentences from a favorite advertisement and use them as the dialogue for a "Contentless Scene." Assign a scenario and a relationship. Sample scenarios: seduction, firing, scolding, first date, marital spat, teacher conference.

Calls: Gibberish – English – gibberish – English. Find the melody of that event.

Give and Take

Principles: Play – Impulse/Explore and Heighten, Transformation, Agreement.

Point of concentration: To give and take stage with sound and movement.

Optimal group size: 5–6 players.

Description: Players begin in a state of suspension, stillness, with the stage balanced, each in their own starting position (can use a cube or two or not). Players may not speak but can make sounds.

Player 1 takes the stage with a sound and movement. That player must continue to move until someone else takes the stage or until Player 1 stands directly in front of another player and "gives" to them. "Giving" means that the moving player suspends movement with the intent of transferring energy to the still player. Suspend is a more accurate word than freeze, because the player in a suspended state is ready to take, ready to respond, immediately ready to take back the stage.

Ideally, the frozen player will "take" what was "given" and explore and heighten it or let it transform. The player is responding on impulse to what is given rather than "making up" something new. The player "given the stage" must then begin to move/make sound. That moment is the new player's moment and supersedes another player's impulse to take stage. In other words, if someone tries to "take" stage at the same moment of a "give," the "give" has the right of way. When not moving, the player is suspended and ready to move again. If relationships, situations, or character occurs, players can respond to it.

Use no words in the initial phase of this game. Only sounds and movements are allowed. The teacher helps the players get connected to impulse by keeping them off-balance, calling, "Only giving," "Only taking," "Give and take." *There should be no physical contact in this game.* When the game moves into themes or environments, players should continue to use sounds unless compelled to utter words.

Calls: Balance yourselves so each of you can be seen and the stage is balanced. You can take anytime you want. No contact. No touching. You must keep moving unless you give or someone else takes. Now only giving. Now only taking. Now give and take. One person moves at a time. Take strongly. Give clearly. If character or situation comes up, explore it. Keep to strict discipline of the game – give only/take only. Bounce off what you are given.

Start in absolute stillness. Game is take – how many times can you take? How many times can you take legitimately? Good – hang in there. Only giving. You can't side-give. Begin to take what's given to you. Don't make it up each time. Take that energy and bounce off it. No contact in this game. Give and take. You don't have to invent the wheel each time.

Comments: You must take strongly. In order to take effectively, there must be agreement – everyone else must give.

Source: Sheldon Patinkin and Spolin.

Variation: Give-and-Take Environments

Calls for environments to explore include: Zoo, hospital ward, ocean beach (5 a.m.), hairdressers, movie set – horror film/Disney film/foreign film, Sunday in the park, auditions, doctoral exams, opening night backstage, Hansel and Gretel in the forest, Cinderella's kitchen, Lovers' Lane, SAT exams, school hallways between classes, beach in the Bahamas, movie styles: horror, Shirley Temple, gangster, Ingmar Bergman in Swedish, spaghetti western, slow-motion fight, melodrama, death scene in *Hamlet*.

Calls on themes: Go into that space slowly – sounds of early morning. You can move. Don't take turns – Sunday in the park; hospital intensive care in the middle of the night. Leader lets them talk and then reminds them of the no-speech rule by telling them to explore the sounds – whispering. Explore slow motion. Explore double time.

Variation: Give-and-Take Storytelling

Players tell a story (known or improvised) in give-and-take framework.

Commentary: This game is often used in story theatre classes or rehearsals as a way for the group to retell a story they've read or been told by the leader. Joyce is also exploring this game as a way to experience "encounter."

Source: Sheldon Patinkin introduced this way of approaching give and take to Joyce and Byrne. Spolin's basic Give and Take game is a give and take between two scenes and then she extends the principle of give and take to reading as a group and other games.

Hidden Problem

Principle: Specificity.

Point of concentration: To let the problem inform the situation but remain unknown to the audience.

Optimal group size: Any number, one at a time.

Description: A player relates a story or gives a speech while having an unspoken, unmentioned problem, for example, toothache, headache, itch.

Calls: Fix the problem. Deal with it as an obstacle.

Variation: Two players set up a scene about a job interview. One player is the interviewer, the other the applicant. Each has an unmentioned, unspoken problem.

Calls: Play the scene, not the problem.

Commentary: This game is related to What's Between?

Source: Spolin.

Hold It!

Principles: Play-Impulse, Transformation, Specificity.

Points of concentration: To get into the space of your line, to pinpoint in the body, and then "hold it" throughout the exercise. To focus on keeping and communicating the point of view of the line — the character's "center" — through all the transformations in time and space. The player's whole body should reflect the thought.

Optimal group size: 5–7 players.

Description: Each player thinks of a different line, something off their own center, something that they would like to explore. The line must have a definite space; a simple line — nothing creative. Lines should be distributed so that there is a range of both positive and negative spectrums. Players try out their lines. Examples: "Nobody understands me." "Oh, that feels so good."

Calls: Fill the whole line. Get it in the whole body. Deepen it in the body. We don't even need to hear the words. Your whole body reflects the thought.

Once the players have gotten the spirit of their line into their bodies, they begin a scene — It's your first day of kindergarten. Have your line in mind. That shows how you feel about the world. You can say the line to each other at the appropriate time.

The players are led through a series of scenes by the teacher to discover how they react in different situations. For example, it's your eighth-grade graduation. You are receiving your diplomas from the principal (an outside player). Same adjustments apply. The teacher can continue to change the age and situation of the players, but they must keep their same point of view on life in each new situation. Play can end with the players in a retirement home playing cards. At the end of the exercise, players repeat their original line.

Calls: Don't be so literal. Give and take. Remember your line. Get your line back into your body.

Source: Spolin.

Hook-Up and Twist

Principles: Play-Impulse, Transformation, Specificity.

Points of concentration: To transform the space, on impulse, from the position of the body. To precisely observe and physically copy the stance of another player.

Optimal group size: Any number.

Description:

Step One: Hook-Up and Extend

Player 1 starts an activity in a Where (like breaking an egg and adding it to a cake mix or throwing a bowling ball), and when that one activity is clearly underway Player 1 freezes. Player 2 goes onstage and tries to get into the exact position of Player 1 (copying the stance, angles of the arms, head, etc.). When Player 2 has duplicated the position of Player 1, Player 2 starts to move while Player 1 unobtrusively and slowly leaves the stage. Player 2 continues or *extends* the activity in the Where set up by Player 1, adding something of their own and then freezing. Play continues as more people flesh out the activity in the Where. The game at this stage is similar to Add an Object Where (see Where games) except for the transfer of exact position between players.

Calls: Take your time to exactly duplicate Player 1. Player 1 – have patience to wait until 2 has started moving and then fade out of the scene. Player 2 – continue the activity so that you extend it by adding more objects. Try to freeze at the height of the activity, the moment when the body is most involved.

Step Two: Hook-Up and Twist (Transform)

Players "hook up" and "twist" or transform to a new activity in a new Where as a new character. Each time a player hooks up, they let their physical position suggest a new space – a new Who, What, Where. To give the next player a strong physical position for the transformation, the initial players must freeze at the height of the activity (just before the bat is to hit the ball, just before the arrow is released and the bow is drawn to the maximum).

Step Three: Hook-Up and Activate into Scene

In this variation, Player A stays onstage while Player B hooks up and then activates Player A into a Who, What, Where Scene with dialogue. When the beat is over, they freeze or Player C from the audience calls the freeze. Player C hooks up with Player A (who leaves) and C activates B into a new scene. Players continue creating new two-person scenes, always releasing the player who has been onstage the longest.

Step Four: Hook-Up Scene-Add On

Now instead of releasing old players, all players stay onstage in a freeze, while, one at a time, subsequent players hook up with one person in the onstage group and activate all the players onstage into a new Who, What, Where. The teacher calls the freezes. Two-person scenes become 3, 4, 5, 6-person scenes. The new player looks at the frozen group and tries to find the most dramatic event suggested by the players' positions, then hooks up physically with one player to define the new scene. As the group gets bigger, the trick is to find the focus of the new scene, the most interesting physical relationship. Once the scene is activated, all the players adapt and adjust to the new circumstances.

Commentary: The "hook-up" or "duplication of physical position" is the most critical aspect of this exercise. It keeps the players out of their heads and focused on the other player. It gives the players a dynamic position to use as a transforming anchor. When freezes are called from outside the scene, the call should catch the players at a moment when their bodies are most involved. The goal is to find a real scene to be played and to avoid the trap of the new player activating by "teaching dancing" or anything else. What you are seeking here is character relationship in service of some event or activity.

Source: Some improv groups play a similar game called Freeze.

Hook-Up and Twist Narration

Principles: Play – Impulse, Explore and Heighten, Transformation.

Point of concentration: To find the story in the physical life of the players.

Optimal group size: Variable.

Description: This game is played the same as Hook-Up and Extend but storytelling is added. Player 1 begins a story in the third person with an object activity. When the moment is right, Player 1 freezes. Player 2 hooks up and begins to move, continuing the story – exploring and heightening the narrative.

Calls: You can pick up the story from your chair and then hook up, talking all the time you duplicate the position, or you can run up and take the position and then continue the story. The Round-Robin principles hold – no backtracking, keep in narration, freeze mid-sentence (see Round-Robin Storytelling).

Variation: You can make a transformation into dialogue and scene. For example, Player 4 freezes; Player 5 goes in and they both stay in scene, giving and taking the story.

Commentary: It is important for everyone to stay grounded in the objects and the Where so that no "little green men" appear in the story. The person who is freezing should stay onstage so the new person can take the time to hook up.

Source: Joyce and Byrne Piven.

Information Booth: Five Characters

Principles: Play-Impulse, Transformation, Specificity.

Point of concentration: To transform character on impulse.

Optimal group size: Pairs.

Description: Players are divided into pairs. They go off by themselves to rehearse. One player is an information clerk in a department store. The other player is to come in as a different character five times and ask where certain things are. That player must decide where their "corridor of change" is going to be, for example, go around in a circle and make change of character while re-entering the scene. Players are told not to do accents or to play very young or very old.

System for pairing: Count off in 2s. 1s are a group and the 2s will play opposite them. One of the 1s and one of the 2s are paired down the line. This pairing is for rehearsal only (10 minutes). In performance, the pairing is changed.

Performance: After the player has finished all five characters, they are asked to stay onstage while their performance is fresh in everyone's mind. Feedback includes a discussion of which character was the most successful.

Commentary: Try to make specific choices with your body – as specific as possible, for example, high-class lady – general; why does she hold her head that way? – specific. Students were assigned to bring five more characters to class the following week and to use the critique in developing their new characters. The teacher suggested that players try to think of five different characters that they make specific – they should try to use articles of clothing so, when they walk out, they've pinpointed the character, for example, a large hat with a veil, a long silk scarf, a long woolen scarf, etc.

Walk away in character and then drop it in corridor of change. The info clerk remains the same character throughout. Work for different vocal rhythms/light-heavy – not whole big speech changes. Avoid "the problem" – e.g. need to go to the bathroom, lost child. The trap is that the "problem" overshadows the illumination of character. Problem – showing vs. telling. When we feel onstage that we don't know who we are, we feel the need to tell.

Trust more. You don't need a whole scenario. You could actually come up and ask one question and leave and we would get the character. Trust that it will all be there. When not trusting, subtle telling can occur with the player continually reaffirming character through scenario.

An elegant lady – instead of coming in and asking for "the Elegance Department," ask for the "imported jam," "the monogrammed handkerchiefs," whatever. Your objective: the dimensional specific character, not the cliché.

Technical point: When the playing is too much into the body – a subtle form of telling happens. You need an outward focus (answer the phone, count tiles, etc.); make your choices, trust them, and then go after the objective (to walk to the info booth). Worry less about what you are saying (plotting) and make more specific body choices.

Source: Second City audition exercise.

Invested Object

Principles: Specificity, Transformation.

Point of concentration: To detail the object and transform into character and scene.

Optimal group size: Any number – one player at a time demonstrates for group sitting in a circle.

Description: A player is to think of a real object, something that belonged to someone else but that the player now has. Preferably, the object should have some meaning for the player. For example, the player could choose a "hot" object like their grandfather's watch given to them before he died. The player is to share the object (now imaginary) by describing its physical qualities – weight, shape, size, color, texture, smell, temperature – until the imaginary space transforms into the object that the player is holding and showing to the class.

The player then begins to describe and communicate the history of the object now to one person instead of the group. The other player can ask questions, can hold the object, and share the activity of using it. Next, the player has a scene with their partner, cleaning and using the object but no longer talking about it. The players let the object be present in the scene as subtext to the independent conversation with Player 2.

Calls: Be specific. How does the object feel? What size is it? What shape? How heavy?

Variation: Instead of developing a scene with another player, the original player adds a Character Layer exercise to this one. As the player uses the object – cleans it, handles it – he/she describes physically the person who gave it to him/her. The player is to begin to take on those qualities of the person described.

Calls: Who gave it to you? How tall is he? Keep handling that object. What does his voice sound like? Begin to take on that voice, his thinness of face. What do his eyes look like? Take that on. How would he walk? Describe it. What would he say if he were using that object?

Variation: Invested Fairy-Tale Object

Think of an object connected with a classic fairy tale (e.g. apple, slipper, spinning wheel, etc.). Describe that object to the other players, being real and specific. Find the moment of the story when the object becomes real. Find the beat of the story and go into telling.

Calls: The jump into the story doesn't have to be logical. If needed in the beat, another player can pick up the conversation within the tale.

Source: Byrne and Joyce Piven.

Machine (parts of a whole)

Principles: Agreement, Play-Impulse, Explore and Heighten.

Point of concentration: To be part of a whole.

Optimal group size: 5–8 players.

Description: Create a "machine" by building it one at a time. One person starts a repeatable movement and sound as part of a "machine." Other players join in one at a time, adding their own sound and movement pattern in relation to another person in the machine. Machine can be started by a game of Space Break or Hot Potato to generate energy. Once all the players have joined the machine and are fully committed to their sounds and move-ment, the teacher asks them to wind the machine down, by agreement, until it comes to a stop. Telling them to breathe together, the teacher instructs them to begin again on the breath, by agreement, to accelerate and stop – to find their own freeze.

Calls: Don't all play to one spot on the floor. Try to open it up and not be held to one point of focus. Move the space. Really carry the space and push the space. See how much of the body you can involve. Push the space with your hands. Commit your whole body. Make the movement more efficient. Don't hang up the leader. Move the space as if you did this for a living and could get fired at any moment.

Byrne Piven's suggestions for calls that help the players understand Machine as a meta-phor for all the work, as a way to understand through doing the core principle of "focus on the other and the task at hand" without a theoretical discussion. Calls: "Build the machine on impulse." "Find your unique contribution to the whole." "Take the positive." "Find the group!" "Find the rhythm!" "Commit." "Trust yourself!" "Trust each other!" "Find the center of the energy!" "Follow the follower!" "Everything counts!" "The pull is as important as the push!" "Move the space!"

Commentary: In the machine, if you find, privately, that you are bored or the game is a struggle, then you are not connected, not focused. The stronger a movement is, the easier it is to hook into. A movement that is too general is harder to hook into.

Source: Spolin's "Parts of a Whole", adapted by Byrne and Joyce Piven.

Variation: Word Machine

Same as basic machine game, but each player must say a word connected with their movement (e.g. slice, punch, push, pull).

Calls: Let the body help the word and the word help the body. Get the action going and add the word. Give and take the word and throw it out into the space. You don't have to say the word every time you make a movement.

Variation: Poetry Machine

Each player is given a phrase from a poem and they create a machine. For example: #1 – The earth; #2 – voomed out, #3 – like a baseball, #4 – CREATION! The phrases do not have to be said in order.

Calls: Give and take the word. Slow down. Find that space to say your word. Keep the motion going.

Commentary: This game is usually played as part of the Poetry Workshop developed by Joyce Piven. It is part of a sequence of games that explore poetry.

Variation: Transforming Machine

Same as basic Machine game, but the teacher calls a freeze and then calls a new type of machine. The players must make the adjustment together on impulse by transforming their sound and movement. This game can be used to explore elements of a story in story theatre rehearsal and performance.

Sample calls: Forest machine, bird machine, storm machine, killing machine, carnival machine, boardwalk machine, circus machine, bakery machine, knitting machine, fountain machine.

Commentary: The transformation can also be made on the start-up section of the game. The players find a new movement and sound in relation to everyone else together.

Make a Deal

Principles: Agreement, Specificity.

Point of concentration: To communicate the physical qualities of the object clearly and precisely.

Optimal group size: Any number.

Description: Play begins with molding space. Players shake the space up with their whole bodies, not just with their hands – with their hips, stomach, back. They mold the space in front of them into an object. The teacher instructs players to begin to shape the space with their whole body until an object emerges (no balls or toothbrushes). They are to use the object as it is ordinarily used – sweep with a broom, roll dough with the rolling pin, etc. Then the teacher tells the players to use the object that they've "found" in the space in an extraordinary way, i.e. in a way the object would not ordinarily be used – balanced on the head, touching the cheek, etc. The players return to using the object as it is ordinarily used.

Players are told to begin to trade their objects. They are to find a partner and demonstrate their object to the partner silently or using gibberish. If the object is successfully communicated on both sides, a trade is made. If your partner's object is not clear, don't make the exchange but move on to someone else. The group is instructed to make as many trades as possible. After five or so trades, the players take the last object they received into the circle and demonstrate it to the group.

Variation: Taking an Exit

Each player takes an exit with the last object they received. One at a time, players use their object for the group. If everyone guesses what it is, the player has earned the right to make an exit. The player needs to exit with everyone's attention.

Calls: Surprise us by your exit. (See Exits and Entrances.)

Source: Spolin.

Mime Warm-Up
Principles: Specificity, Transformation.
Point of concentration: To endow imaginary objects with weight, shape, size, texture, movement.
Optimal group size: Variable.
Description:
Earth Walk
Players walk in place – toe-heel/right-left. Use the foot to release into the ground, like you are crunching snow. The foot is contracting. Best played in slow motion.
Calls: Feel the ground beneath your feet. Focus up and out. Permit help of arms. Reach out and find a string with a big balloon at the end. The pull of feet keeps you grounded. Balloon changes to kite – pull and freeze/wind change/blowing against back – free-flowing kite – play with kite. Kite changes to a large umbrella – wind in front/in back. Umbrella changes to dog leash – dog in control/you in control/dog runs away.
Source: Etienne Decroux.

Variation: Mime Object Transformations
Players mirror teacher making object transformations while walking around the space.
Picking up/putting down a very heavy sack.
Sack changes to a fishing pole with a fish on the line.
Fishing pole changes to balloon on a string.
Balloon string changes to kite string/wind changes.
Kite string changes to a leash.
Dog on leash has control/you have control.
Dog leads you to a partner for mirror.
Commentary: Mime work with imaginary objects gives a concrete connection with the space. It prescribes a way to deal with space. One is constantly connecting with the space in story theatre and scene: 1) props are never the real thing onstage, but we must deal with them as if they are; 2) in teaching children, mime allows one to deal with their non-verbal life. When a child is comfortable in space, he/she can speak up; 3) mime helps to create the particular Where of the moment, opens up the space of the creativity, enhances one's whole stage life.
Source: Sequences developed by Joyce Piven from study with students of Etienne Decroux.

Mirror and its variations
Principles: Play, Transformation, Specificity, Agreement.
Point of concentration: To mirror the movement of your partner precisely; to follow the follower.
Optimal group size: Variable – can be played in pairs, groups of 4, 6, 8, up to a whole class.
Description:
Basic Mirror
In pairs – the players decide who is A and who is B. A leads as B follows in mirror image; B leads and A follows.

Calls: Slow down for your partner. Move out into the space. The teacher calls changes quickly from A to B to A and so on until both are leading/both following. When "Follow the Follower" is achieved, the teacher calls, "Freeze." Take that energy and find a new partner. Go into mirror right from there. Freeze. Find a new partner.

Commentary: This game is a combination of thrusting and trusting.

Source: Spolin and many other sources.

Variation: Mirror Transformation of Activities

Players in pairs, beginning in mirror, are to find an activity between them. Once the activity is explored in mirror, they are to let it change/transform into another activity.

Calls: Find an activity in the space. Stay away from just movement. What is between you? What activity? Get it in your body. What's in the space between you? Try to stay away from yourself (movements that involve the self). Get into the space between you. Extend it. It needs to go somewhere. Come to a rest. Commit yourself to the object – deal with the object. Grab it. Extend it. Make a full-body commitment. Explore quietly each change; let it find its last moment.

Variation: Mirror Scene Transformations

Two players begin in mirror. The players work to find a change together in both sound and movement. Once they have a motor going, players can go into give-and-take dialogue (play a scene). Once the beat is over, players make a new transformation. Play continues going from scene to mirror to scene and back to mirror. The next step is to make a transformation without returning to mirror between each beat. Anything can spark a change – a sound, a move, a sense of character, place, or emotional connection.

Calls: Right from there, find a new scene, a new transformation. Change.

Commentary: The scene transformation focuses on the change rather than the framework. Anything goes. Anything constitutes a change. It means real give and take. This game can also develop out of Criss-Cross Sound and Movement Transformations.

Variation: Mirror/Simultaneous Speech

Players in pairs decide who is A and who is B. Go immediately into mirror, both following/both leading. When players feel connected, A begins to tell a story.

Calls: Start the story from what the space is between you. A – speak slowly enough so B can follow along. Mirror the speech as you tell the story. Take your story from what you find between you. Make sure your partner is following you. Help your partner follow you. B – Continue the story right from that point and let A follow. A lead; B lead; A lead, etc. (quicker and quicker). You're at simultaneous speech. Go with it.

Variation: Three-Way Mirror

Three players form a three-way mirror for the fourth player. The fourth player puts on and takes off imaginary articles of clothing in front of the "mirror."

Transforming characters: a four-year old, a teenager, an old person.

Transforming places: an army/navy surplus store, a Paris boutique, a theatrical costume shop.

Musical Transformations

Principles: Play – Impulse, Explore and Heighten, Transformation, Agreement.

Point of concentration: To transform musical styles as a group.

Optimal group size: 4–7 players to larger groups.

Description: Begin with a small group of players onstage. The players are assigned a simple song that can be repeated continually, for example, "Mary Had a Little Lamb," "Row, Row, Row Your Boat," or one the group chooses. As the players sing the song, the teacher will call out different song styles or character prompts. The players transform their singing style in response to the calls. When they have a motor going, the teacher tells them to find their own transformations as a group.

Calls (not necessarily in this order or number): Lullaby, nursery rhyme, jazz, opera, country and western, ballad, rock, hymn, gospel, barbershop quartet, Gregorian chant, Call and response, Recitation, Oration. Cultural styles such as Japanese, Russian, Italian, British. Character types like ghosts, witches, children, cowboys, geishas, samurai warriors, drunken sailors, square dancers, Shakespearean actors. Time periods like Gay 90s, sixties.

Source: Unknown.

Neutral games

Principles: Play-Anxiety of Not Knowing, Specificity, Agreement.

Point of concentration: To help the neutral know who he/she is by relating to the Where and by relating to the neutral as a specific character in that space.

Optimal group size: Variable, pairs to full groups.

Description:

Neutral games are "Who" games adding "Where," and "What."

One player in a Who, What, Where situation begins the game in neutral. The player does not know who he/she is. Throughout the course of the game, other players who know who they are and who the neutral is relate to the neutral player. As the neutral player comes to know his/her identity, that player begins to take on the character assigned to him/her by the group. The scene comes to an end when the neutral knows his/her identity and joins the action fully.

Calls: Keep the verbal clues to a minimum. Leave it open. Neutral – adjust your body to the clues you pick up. Leave a space for a response from the neutral player. Give and take to create the scene. Take a chance. Let time go by.

Commentary: This game focuses on listening and seeing, because the neutral must get his/her identity from given clues. This listening must be extended even after you know who you are. Without objects and without a sense of Where, the neutral's clues are limited.

Source: Spolin.

Neutral Warm-Up/whole class

One player leaves the room. The rest of the players decide who he is by assigning an occupation to the neutral (e.g. policeperson, nun). The scene is set in a park. Alone or in pairs, the players enter the scene and relate to the neutral. When the neutral knows who he is, he begins to act the part. The teacher calls a freeze and asks the neutral who he thinks he is. If correct, the scene ends. The game can be played over with a new neutral.

Variation: Players can enter the scene at any time. They do not have to wait for the preceding player(s) to exit.

Traditional Neutral Game

Set up two chairs on the stage, side by side. Player A sits on "bench" and is neutral. Player B decides who he/she is and who Player A is and what their relationship is. Player B enters the space and through his/her behavior communicates to Player A the above information. The scene ends when Player A guesses who he/she is and behaves accordingly.

Calls: Go with what's given to you. Help your neutral. Give her more identity. Communicate specifics. Deal with the objects. Don't lean on verbal cues. Help the others know. Keep listening – don't make assumptions. Detail exactly what she's wearing. Make sure she knows exactly who she is.

Source: Spolin.

Neutral Activity

One player begins an activity in neutral, in that she does not have a specific identity – anyone could be doing that activity, for example, fixing a pipe, hanging curtains, sewing a dress. Player 2 enters the scene knowing both who he is and who the neutral is. Succeeding players enter the space knowing who they are and building on the characters that have come before them. Build the Where as the scene progresses. Players can enter and exit.

Neutral in Teams

Players in groups of four. Three players decide on who they are, where they are, and what they are doing. The fourth player will begin the scene along with the others, but will be in neutral. The player will acquire her identity as the others relate to her.

Calls: Help your neutral. Give her more identity. Communicate specifics. Deal with the objects. Don't lean on verbal cues. Get them into action. Share with us. Help the others know. Keep listening – don't make assumptions. Detail exactly what she's wearing. Make sure she knows exactly who she is.

Variation: Three players are neutral and the fourth player knows the Who, What, Where.

Example situation: A non-traditional wedding – Player 1 is the mother of the bride. The other players are the bride, the younger sister of the bride, the maid of honor, and the mother's sister.

New York, Here I Come

Principles: Play – Impulse, Explore and Heighten, Specificity, Agreement.

Points of concentration: To communicate an occupation through movement and sound. To guess the trade.

Optimal group size: Two teams – variable sizes/space dependent.

Description: Two teams of players face each other on opposite sides of the room. Each team decides on a trade or occupation to perform.

The teams approach each other saying this rhyme:

Team A: Here we come.
Team B: Where from?

Team A: New York.
Team B: What's your trade?
Team A: Lemonade.
Team B: Give us some (if you're not afraid).

The teams stop an arm's length apart. Each player on Team A pantomimes an activity of its trade. Team B guesses out loud. When Team B guesses the correct trade, Team A runs home. Team B tries to tag as many Team A players as they can. The tagged players become part of Team B and the game is played with Team B demonstrating the occupation.
Variation: Each team can portray the trade or occupation in a group construct with movement or as a machine. Starting at one end, the first player begins their movement (maybe with a sound). One by one, the players add on, performing their movements and sounds, until all the players are working at once. The teacher then gives the okay for the other team to start guessing.
Variation: The rhyme can be done in character, for example, Confederate soldiers, New York gang members, school kids, tough football players.
Calls: Establish the activity one person at a time until all are in action. Hold off guessing until everyone is performing their activity.
Commentary: This game is fun for all ages.
Source: General.

Object Transformations
Principles: Play – Anxiety of Not Knowing, Transformation, Specificity.
Point of concentration: To transform the space object.
Optimal group size: Variable.
Description: Players are seated in a circle. Leader establishes an imaginary object and transforms it once, then passes it on. The next player continues the movement and the handling of the object and transforms it once. Extend or compress the activity, then make a transformation. The object does not have to be tremendous or terrific.
Calls: You don't have to be able to name it. Even if it's mundane, if the transformation is honest, it will be exciting. There is no fast or slow. Go for the discipline of the first transformation and hold yourself to that.
Commentary: This game is also known as Circle-Object Transformations. It forces you to submit to the creative process and something will emerge. Go into the space and it will emerge. Once the transformation is made, you must be committed to it – you must know what it is even if others can't name it.
Source: Spolin, general.

1–2 Decroux – see Constructs

Papa/Mama La Chaise
Principle: Play – Impulse, Off-Balance Moment.
Point of concentration: To play the game.
Optimal group size: Variable.

Description: Players stand in a circle. One player is "It." The "It" walks around the circle and taps another player on the shoulder. Player 2 walks around the circle the opposite way to Player 1 until they meet at a place equidistant from where they started. Player 1, the It, then says, "Good Evening, Papa La Chaise. And how are you?" Player 2 says, "Fine." Player 1 responds, "And what shall I say when I get home? Shall I say, 'How are you?'" Once these words are repeated, the two race around their half of the circle to home base (the space left by Player 2). Whoever gets to home base first is safe. The player who reaches there last is the "It" and play continues.

Variation: Once Player 2 has been tapped, the leader gives her a line to say. That line becomes the first line in a little beat or scene between the two players. When the It finds occasion to repeat that first line, the two run for home base. Examples of lines – "You plug the first hoochamagigger here to make the first connection;" "You hold the fork like this and wrap the noodles around it;" "You make-a da salad-a this way!"

Source: Joyce Piven found this game and transformed it into a theatre game. A Haitian children's game.

Polymorph

Principles: Agreement, Transformation.

Point of concentration: To let the game change into another game by group agreement.

Optimal group size: Variable.

Description: The players decide on a set of games. They begin playing one game and let it "morph" into another, then another, until they have played all the games named.

Calls: Play strictly. Commit your whole body. Morph into another game.

Variation: The players decide on an opening game only. The transformations during the play determine what games are played.

Commentary: In order to play this game, all the players have to have experience playing the games named prior to this game. The game is dependent to some extent on a common language shared by all players.

Source: Byrne Piven.

Portraits

Principles: Play-Impulse, Agreement/Ensemble, Specificity.

Points of concentration: To build a group pose or "portrait" for an imaginary camera by getting yourself seen, being in contact and maintaining an outward focus. To find changes, new poses, together.

Optimal group size: 5–7 players, but can be done with larger groups.

Description:

Part One: Players in groups of five to seven build a "portrait," one at a time, in contact. Players all stand upstage. The first player comes forward to a predetermined mark and strikes a pose facing the audience. Player 1's focus is on a spot (the "camera") above the audience's heads. The next player comes forward and strikes a pose in relation to the first, making some kind of contact (touching with an elbow, toe, hip, etc.). Player 2's focus is also on the "camera." The next player adds on, and so on, until the whole group has created a group portrait. Players come forward one at a time, on impulse, with no predetermined order. Once a portrait is made, the players go back to upstage and start again to make a new portrait. The POC at this point is to get a motor going – players running in with energy and striking a forceful pose, one at a time, on impulse, getting their faces seen and making contact. They are learning the rules and making a full-body commitment to the game.

Calls: Get your face seen. Make contact. Use levels. Support your own weight.

Part Two: Working as a group to change the picture. Players build a portrait without returning upstage. They play as before, but now the players make new portraits on impulse – on their own, beginning and ending as one.

Calls: In slow motion, on my handclap or when I say, "Change," make a change in the portrait ending at the same time and in contact. Make the adjustment in really heavy space, slow motion, but keep the space buoyant. It's almost like taking one slow-motion breath as a group. All change position simultaneously. If you are right, go left. Left, go right; up, go down; down, go up. Use levels.

Now small, fast changes. You don't always need to make large adjustments. Small changes like the tilt of a head, change of hand, attitude, etc. Now on your own, make three changes, beginning and ending in agreement.

Commentary: Note that players are not assigned an order to joining the "Portrait." It is important that they "take a chance," that they move in a give-and-take fashion, one at a time. This opening puts them in touch with each other in a non-verbal way. Assigning numbers and an order undermines the point of concentration of the game – impulse and agreement.

Variation: Portraits using characters
Calls: Peasants, maids, kings, rock group, accountants, teachers, actors. Explore how they are different.

Variation: Portraits with a theme
Players make new portraits in response to a "caption" called by the leader (e.g. "Why Me?" or "I Won!!!").

Variation: Ages of Man
Players change the portrait in response to the calls, progressing from young to old and ending where they began.

Calls: First day of life, first day of kindergarten, parents of first-day kindergartners, junior high, first day of high school, driver's license, first accident, high-school graduation, first date, first finals week, first job, marriage, first child, fifth child, bowling league, old people's home card party, first day of life. Explorations can be made within age calls (e.g. junior high – first dance, field trip).

Commentary: This game is similar to Spolin's Hold It!

Variation: Portraits of people seeing and hearing things
Calls for people watching events: A baby nursery, a car accident, horror movie, your baby's first step, the school talent show, a biology lecture on a dissection, a fiery red sunset, a spring sunrise, a rainy day out the window, a modern art exhibit, the keynote speech at a political convention, the wedding of a relative, a baseball game – bases loaded, a pop-up hit, the Bears-49ers game, your grandma getting off the plane for a visit, a soap opera, Saturday morning cartoons, the opera, the present you wanted for Christmas under the tree,

an oral report in history, people coming into the prom, your girlfriend/boyfriend out with another girl/boy, your parents fighting/hugging, a tornado, Halley's Comet, an overnight camp campfire, a bank robbery, a funeral, video games.

Calls for people hearing things: Gossip, you won the lottery, someone close has died, a wedding proposal, asked to go steady, told you just failed your final, your best friend is moving, your kid sister is going to throw up, your mother has just told the family your secret, the nurse announces your weight, the president declares war, a lecture on quantum physics, a school debate, a pep rally, the principal over the loudspeaker, a rock concert, chalk scraping on a blackboard, a morning wake-up alarm, Christmas carols, a lullaby, a Shakespearean monologue, your mother yelling at you, teacher conferences, compliments/ praise from a special teacher.

Commentary: This variant is related to the game What Am I Seeing? Hearing? Eating? Note that the calls all imply a subtext or emotional point of view to be communicated.

Poetry Portraits

Principles: Play – Impulse, Explore and Heighten, Agreement.

Point of concentration: To build a poem portrait physically and through words by adding on to what is being created in the space.

Optimal group size: 4–7 players.

Description: Players build a portrait with their bodies and words, one at a time, in contact.

Step One: No subject is given. Players start by building a portrait with each player saying ONE WORD as they strike their pose.

Step Two: TWO-WORD LIMIT.

Step Three: THREE-WORD LIMIT.

Step Four: Using themes. Can get suggestions from the audience. Sample subjects: thunderstorms, garbage, lighthouse.

Sample poems that resulted from one class:

ONE WORD:	Fountains	TWO WORDS:	My mother
	Are		Is so
	Amazing		Juicy
	When		That I
	Water		Am Really
	Sprinkles		Happy!
THREE WORDS:	So I turned	THUNDERSTORMS:	Boom, Boom, Boom
	The big big		Siss, Boom, Bah
	Channel		Crash Crash Crash
	And watched		Wack Wack Wack
	My TV		Rah Rah Rah
	And then		It's Cold
	It Blew up!		I'm Scared
GARBAGE:	My Sister	LIGHTHOUSE:	A Promontory
	Loves the Trash		Amongst Swirling
	She plays with it everyday		Things that
	Those Big green dumpsters		Go about

The Switches	Seas with
The smell	Green
I don't know why	Waves

Commentary: The POC of this game is for the group to work together to build on what is in the space, but to do that on impulse and not in the head. The goal is not necessarily to create great poetry. This game has also been used to develop song lyrics. Have someone write down the poems so that they can be read as poems after the exercise.
Source: Shira Piven.

Poetry Workshops
Sample plan: Ball Toss/Word Toss, Word Machine, Poetry Circle Transformations, Mirror Transformations, Poetry Machine, Musical Transformations, groups devise Ariel's speech from *The Tempest*.

Problem with a Large Object
Principles: Agreement, Specificity.
Point of concentration: To agree on the weight, shape, and size of the object as it is handled and to solve the problem.
Optimal group size: 2–5 players.
Description: The group decides on a large object and a problem with that object (e.g. Christmas tree too large for a room, couch too wide for a doorway). The group deals with the problem, trying to solve it a number of ways, and they finally solve the problem (e.g. making it up a narrow staircase with a large, heavy sofa).
Calls: Help. Hinder. Agree on the weight, the size, the shape. Solve the problem. No playwriting. Focus on the object.
Commentary: Keep the players focused on the task of solving the problem – the doing of it rather than the talking about how to solve the problem. Remember that, as players, you really don't have anything to play off of except the other players, which is all you'll need. The life of any game and/or scene is in the agreement of the players. By using large, full objects, the players are compelled to agree, lest chaos reign. And it's wonderful to watch players in full and total agreement using and moving things like imaginary cars or couches. By agreeing to the object's size and mass and weight or bulk and every other possible detail about that object, it becomes real for the players and for the audience. The alternative is like the Five Blind Men and the Elephant. Each individual knows what he or she has got, but nobody knows what anyone else is about. For example: "Grab this wheel here," "You mean the pillow here." Aaargh!
Source: Spolin.

Problem with a Small Object
Principle: Specificity.
Point of concentration: To give weight, shape, size to' the object and then solve the problem.
Optimal group size: One player at a time.
Description: Players must think of a small object that one could have a problem with (e.g. open a bottle, caught zipper, jammed drawer, tight boots, hook of necklace). One player

shows their object by how they handle it. The player shares the problem they are having with the object and then shares three different ways that the problem could be solved. The player solves it on the fourth try.

Calls: Respect the size, shape, weight, texture, temperature of the object you are working with.

Commentary: It is important that the player treat the objects and the situation "as if" it were real.

Source: Spolin.

Queen's Trunk

Principles: Specificity, Transformation (Story Theatre Narration into Scene).

Points of concentration: To detail the character and object through action and narration. To find the transformation into scene and out again.

Optimal group size: Variable.

Description: Players form two straight lines facing each other, either sitting or standing. The Where is a castle and all the players are going to be people who inhabit the castle. On one end of the playing space, there is an imaginary trunk with two players guarding it. The premise of the game is that it is the Queen's birthday and the trunk contains presents for all the people in the castle.

The game starts with one player at the opposite end of one of the lines. Player 1 briefly describes a person who lives in the castle until they have made a transformation into that character (see Character Layers game). That character will then narrate themselves down the aisle (through the castle) to the trunk. They will reach in, find and detail an object, and return to their place in one of the lines.

On the way, Player 1 may stop to talk to one person, assigning them a role (e.g. the cook). The "cook" will quickly detail that character, ending with the line "Then she said," and have a beat of scene with Player 1 who will end the beat by saying, "Well, I'm going to the Queen's trunk."

At the trunk, Player 1 might have a short interchange with the players guarding the trunk. And on the way back to their place in the line, Player 1 may stop and show what they got from the trunk.

The teacher illustrates the first journey.

Calls: Get the details in your body. In your voice. Find a way out of scene and back to narration. Get to the trunk. Detail the object you find before you name it. What does it look like? How big is it? What color is it? Is it heavy? Light? Do you like it?

Commentary: This game is particularly effective for younger students. It introduces them to the use of narration and character transformation in story theatre and gives them practice in going from narration to scene and back to narration. It combines the games of Character Layers, Three on a Box, and Round-Robin Storytelling.

The "character layers" should be short and efficient – one or two traits to define the character, for example, "The cook was a chubby, jolly old woman who giggled a lot." The player "Cook" would then move as a large woman and giggle as she spoke.

Source: Joyce Piven.

Rap Song game

Principle: Agreement.

Point of concentration: To communicate and connect with the group.

Optimal group size: Variable.

Description: The whole group is in a huddle. The players softly sing a song over and over as individual players "rap" on a pre-decided theme, one at a time. The leader touches the back of a player gently to signal that they should begin their rap. When the leader touches that player's back again, the player stops talking and returns to the song. The leader then moves on to another player until everyone has had a turn.

Commentary: This game is a nice end to a very intense class. It quiets everyone down and sets up a structure for connection. It functions like a "cooling-off" period after intense exertion. It is also good for bringing closure to a series of classes. It's a nice way to say goodbye to fellow players at the end of a term.

Source: David Shepherd.

Red Light/Green Light

Principle: Play – Impulse.

Point of concentration: To tag the king of the hill without getting caught moving.

Optimal group size: Variable and space-dependent.

Description: Player 1 stands on one side of the room facing the other players who are in a horizontal line on the opposite side. When Player 1 turns his back to the group and says, "Green Light," the group can move to try to tag Player 1. When Player 1 says, "Red Light," he turns to face the group and tries to catch anyone moving. If he does, Player 1 sends the moving player back to the wall to start again. The object of the game is to tag Player 1 and take his place. The game begins again with a new Player 1.

Calls: Slow motion, walk with a basket of fruit on your head, heavy boots, in Elizabethan dress, carrying two heavy suitcases, shoelaces tied together, long tight skirt, hot sand, rain storm. Look around and see the other movement and strategies; Elizabethan costume – be specific. Detail it. What kind of hat? What material? What are you wearing on your feet? Two heavy suitcases – what muscles are involved? Gravity would pull you down if you did not work to pull yourself up. Holding tea cups; carrying a bowl of hot soup; carrying red wine across a white carpet to the Queen.

Commentary: This is a game of focus and attention; of developing the discipline of the freeze as more than simply the cessation of movement. This game can be played simply as a game to encourage concentration and total commitment to a freeze. When objects or environments are added through calls, the POC shifts and the game becomes a useful warm-up for an object class, a character class, or a story class.

Source: Children's games.

Repeating game (Echo)

Principle: Play – Impulse, Explore and Heighten.

Point of concentration: To repeat the previous player's last word or phrase as the beginning of new dialogue.

Optimal group size: Variable.

Description: Players decide on a Who, What, Where and begin to play the scene. When "Repeating game" is called, the players repeat the last phrase or word of the previous player's dialogue as they begin to speak.

Calls: Repetition doesn't mean sameness. Try a new way to say the words.

Commentary: This game is a useful call for any scene. It immediately gets the players focused on a task and away from playwriting. It keeps them off-balance and focused on the other, listening for the words they will need to continue the scene.

Source: Spolin.

Round-Robin Storytelling

Principles: Play-impulse, Explore and Heighten, Specificity.

General point of concentration: To tell a story in give and take.

Shifting points of concentration: Getting the word out, to remember detail from a known story, to handle objects, to transform.

Optimal group size: Variable.

Description:

Rules: Tell the story in third person.

Pick up the story in midsentence.

No backtracking.

Players are seated on the floor in a circle. The teacher begins a story and then points to another player who picks up the story at the exact instant, mid-sentence, without repetition or "backtracking." Eventually, the teacher stops pointing to players and the players continue telling the story in a give-and-take fashion. The story is told in third person. It can be an invented story or a retelling of an existing story – fairy tale, folklore, literary story.

Calls: Speak in full-body whisper, slow-motion speech, double time, shout it, sing it. Keep it in third person. Stay in narration. You must earn the right to become that character. Try to get the story out into the space – so no thinking ahead or playwriting.

Variation: Players handle and transform objects as they pass the story along.

Variation: Player, mid-story, assumes the character or Who in the story and they give and take the action in a scene. The scene can take place in the middle of the circle and, when the beat is over, the tellers return to third-person narration, move back into the circle, and other players can pick up the story and continue.

Variation: The teacher tells the group a story (e.g. fairy tale or folk tale). The group re-tells the story in round robin, expanding the details. Then players "act out" the story, mixing narration and scene (dialogue).

Commentary: This game lays the groundwork for story transformation. We must first learn to exercise the discipline of detail. Questions to focus on: When do we go into the story? When do we step out? Can you go in and come back? Can you make a transformation and still keep in narration?

Source: Paul Sills.

Variation: Round-Robin Narration into Story

Point of concentration: Earning the right to transform from narration into the story.

Description: Players in groups create a beat of a well-known fairy tale, for example, Cinderella – preparing for the ball, returning from the ball, the prince arrives. Each group will create the Who, What, Where with a focus on the detail of Who and Where.

Players begin by narrating and detailing the who and where as they play the scene (see Verbalizing the Who, What, Where, and Fairy-Tale Moments).

Calls: You must earn the right to speak in dialogue. Now that you have earned the right to be the stepmother, back away from it. Find that moment when you transform. Maybe it won't come until miles into the dialogue. Take the moment to detail Cinderella.

Variation: Round-Robin Story with an Object Hook-Up
Players share an original story round-robin style with an object hook-up. When the story passes to another player, the second player must get into the first player's space (see Hook-Up and Twist).

Calls: Stay with the object. Detail it. Work with it. Earn the right to leave.
Source: Joyce and Byrne Piven.

Simon Says
Principle: Play.
Point of concentration: To do as the leader says.
Optimal group size: Any number of players.
Description: Players stand in a circle. When the leader prefaces a command with "Simon says," players must follow. When the leader says only the command without saying "Simon says," players are not to follow. Those that do are out.
Variation: If the leader says, "Simon says put your hands on your nose," and then the leader puts her hands on her stomach, those players that do not put their hands on their noses are out. Do as the leader says, not what the leader does.
Variation: Instead of saying, "Simon says," the leader uses a signal to start a movement, for example, a hand-clap. Same rules apply, i.e. if the hand-clap is not done, players should not do the movement.
Commentary: When the leader is totally focused on getting the players out, the game does not work and the connection is lost. The goal cannot be to trick or win alone, to win you must really play the game. This game can be used as a warm-up for a Gibberish class.
Sample sequence: Simon Says, Phrase Tag with Gibberish, Mirror into Simultaneous Speech, Conversation While Eating, Gibberish Warm-Up with Anecdote, Gibberish Activity, Simultaneous Rap, Gibberish and Translation with an Object, Gibberish and Translation with a Story, Who, What, Where in Gibberish.
Source: Children's game.

Simultaneous Rap
Principle: Play – Impulse, Explore and Heighten.
Point of concentration: To "rap" on a theme; to fight to win.
Optimal group size: Any number played in pairs.
Description: Players in pairs, facing each other (seated on floor or on chairs). The audience is asked to come up with sets of opposites (e.g. hot/cold, tall/short, winter/summer). The players settle on the opposites they like best. Each player takes one side of the subject. Players talk at the same time about their subject in "rap" fashion. Rules: Players cannot use the first-person pronoun "I" or any negatives. The "rap" must be a third-person, objective essay-style talk.

Phase 1: Players begin to talk simultaneously on their subjects.

Phase 2: Same rules apply, but players now incorporate words and phrases heard from their partner into their own rap.

Phase 3: Same as above, but players are told to switch subjects.

Phase 4: All rules are suspended and players are instructed "to fight to win."

Calls: Keep the game going. No negatives. Fight to win.

Variation: HOT TOPICS. Played similarly to the above game, but the emphasis is on the give and take and changing relationships.

Hot Issues:

◆ Death penalty vs. life imprisonment
◆ Women on the front line in war vs. not
◆ Pro-Choice vs. Pro-Life
◆ Grounding vs. no grounding
◆ Curfew vs. no curfew
◆ Gender – restrictive dates vs. no restriction/or allowed to go to prom
◆ Boy/girl parties with parents or without
◆ Report cards vs. progress reports
◆ No summer school vs. year-round school.

Source: Original game, Spolin. Variation, Byrne Piven.

Six-Sided Where – see Where games

Space Break

Principles: Play – Impulse, Explore and Heighten, Agreement.

Point of concentration: To "break the space" with a contrasting sound/movement.

Optimal group size: Variable.

Description: Players walk through the space in slow motion. One player "breaks the space" by initiating a *contrasting* sound and movement. Players slowly pick up the new sound and movement until everyone is doing the same thing. Once all have joined the new sound and movement, a new player "breaks the space." Play continues until a motor gets going.

Calls: Hold on to the old space until you have to give it up. The old space and the new space should overlap each other. Break the space with a contrast – slow to fast, light to heavy, loud to soft.

Commentary: Space Break is often part of a sequence: Space Walk into Space Break into Machine.

Source: Joyce and Byrne Piven.

Space Walk

Principle: Agreement.

Point of concentration: To focus on the other players and the space around you.

Optimal group size: Variable

Description: Players walk through the space, feel it around them, see the other people in the space. The leader directs the players: Begin to see: colors and designs (the leader calls colors and designs in clothes of group). Freeze. Take a picture with your eyes of what is immediately in front of you. Close your eyes. See if you can see the picture in your mind's eye. Open your eyes and see what you missed. (This freeze-picture-check sequence is repeated several times with the objective of keeping as many people in sight as possible. Sometimes the leader asks players to count the number of people they see when they freeze and then to try to see more the next time.)

The space begins to become heavy by agreement. Cut through the heavy space with the angles of the body – elbows, knees, hips. Mirror other players to discover how heavy the space becomes. When the space becomes so heavy that the group is barely moving, the leader notes that the space is becoming lighter and lighter until everyone is jumping through the air.

Variation: Letting space in behind and around different parts of the body; leading with different parts of the body; slow motion. Let space in around the mouth. Don't move the mouth, just feel the space around it. Let space in under the arms, behind the knees, behind the eyes, behind the neck. Let us agree that the space is heavy, but it is fluid. Push the space with your forehead, with your chin. Freeze. Look at how the bodies of the players around you are shaped.

Variation leads into Character Walk: Push the space with the collarbone, stomach, hips, knees, toes. What character could be suggested?

Source: Spolin and other movement practices for the actor. Shira Piven talks about Paul Sills doing Space Walk like a meditation.

Stick, Ball, Wall
Principle: Specificity.
Point of concentration: To give weight, shape, size to an imaginary object and use it as if it were real; to be precise.
Optimal group size: Variable.
Description:

Ball: with weight on left leg – focus on where you want to throw ball. "Mitt" in right hand – baseball mitt – feel it. "Ball" – never take eyes off tip of finger. Throw ball and slowly move back into place with left leg next to right – move back – throw – watch – return to neutral. Make one complete arc – a beginning, middle, and end.

Prolong last moment – beat, beat – as long as it takes to complete the action. Notice how you balance and focus – still looking at the ball. Appreciate the arc: beginning – middle – end. Concentration remains throughout – body cooperates to create arc.

Do it in a round: Everyone in a circle in neutral with weight a little forward.
As one player goes back (right after they throw the ball), the next begins.
WHEN YOU TEACH IT, YOU HAVE TO BE THIS PRECISE.
Kids love that – it's a discipline and it increases concentration.
1. Neutral; 2. Mark point at tip of finger – see point; 3. Right hand – ball (baseball mitt); 4. Step forward and throw ball – watch ball as slowly return to neutral.
Throughout whole thing focus always on the ball until the last.
SEQUENCE:
1. Throw ball; 2. Catch ball.

Catching Ball: Catch ball from ceiling and let it go – drop to floor. The release takes care of itself. You don't have to flatten the hand. Baseball – middle of the hand. Throw it into the other hand – then back and forth. Every time it hits the hand, say, "Duck!" or "Bing!" (brings your hands alive – you are handling weight. You don't have to help it – isolating part of the body). Let it come from top – someone is throwing you a ball: the object comes from somewhere. POC – Seeing the imaginary object. Shifting point of concentration: One thing at a time. Primary POC – following through with concentration. Shift to "weight."

Stick: Hold the stick parallel to floor in as open a position as possible – avoid holding it too tight (hands too close together). Left hand on top/right hand under.

Call: You are the owner of the stick (of space – because there is nothing there). Don't let the space boss you. You own this space. Don't let it push you around. TURNING THE STICK: Turn to the right – let go – go down as far as you can go and return the stick to starting position (parallel with floor). Work for a wide grip. Continually remind them to own the space – a mime principle. Your hands will hurt for a bit. The stick is just the right weight – not too heavy/not too light. Each time – center yourself. Turn the stick first to left, then to the right. Experiment with weight: First the stick is going to get heavier and heavier – in your own good time. Keep a wide grip – heavier and heavier – more of body involved, as it gets heavier – as heavy as you can manage it and then stop. Your body will tell us how heavy it is – not about creating tension. When it is at its heaviest, start releasing the weight until it becomes light. Light – light – light until you come to a stop. Notice how wide your grip is – quickly correct it. Leave space for shape of stick – don't want a fist.

Wall: Put hand on wall and just release it imperceptibly – more subtle. Same with traveling wall. MOVE THE BODY FORWARD WITH HANDS PLACED THERE. It's hard – move hands – next step. Stop in the middle and shake out if necessary. Direct the students' attention to the POC. As long as you do it with authority – if it has weight-shape – everyone will be with you. Trust – OWN IT.

Source: Joyce Piven – History of Stick Wall Ball – Mime link to 1–2 Decroux.

Streets and Alleys

Principles: Play – Impulse, Off-Balance Moment, Agreement.
Points of concentration: To catch the robber. To move as a group.
Optimal group size: Variable.
Description: All the players except three form a number of lines so that, when they stand facing front in a line across the stage or when each line faces the wings, their extended hands make contact with the extended arms and hands of the adjacent players. When the

line faces the audience, the players are forming the "streets." When the line faces the wings (decide ahead of time whether you will always face left or right), the players are forming the "alleys." To play the game, you need enough players to make three or four lines.

The other three players: one is a "cop," one is a "robber," and one is the "caller." As the cop pursues the robber, the caller calls either "streets" or "alleys" and the line players respond immediately by turning to one position or the other, thus cutting off the routes of the running players. The caller tries to help the cop catch the robber while they run through the paths formed by the line players. The robber cannot duck under the arms of the line players. The line players form a barrier, forcing the runners to stay in the paths delineated by the lines.

Calls: "Streets." "Alleys." Move as a group. Slow motion. Double time.

Commentary: Joyce Piven used this game very effectively in performance to create the opening moment in the Greek myth "Persephone" where Demeter and Persephone are playing in the garden at the beginning of the story. Instead of using "streets" and "alleys" as the call, she used "spring" and "summer."

Source: Children's game.

Structures and Movers

Principle: Play.

Point of concentration: To be aware of space – levels and relationships.

Optimal group size: 10–20 players.

Description: Players are divided up into two teams – Team A and Team B. All players begin to move about the space exploring levels and closeness and separation. The leader calls "Freeze". For the next sixteen counts (leader keeping rhythm on a drum), Team A becomes the Movers and Team B remains frozen as the Structures. Only the Movers move – in and over and around and under the frozen Structures. The leader calls, "Change," and for the next sixteen counts Team A becomes the Structures and Team B the Movers. Play continues alternately as the players explore the positive and negative space created.

Calls: Explore the negative space. Crawl under legs. Explore the space between figures. Explore openings created by body parts. Change. Slow motion. Double time/silent film.

Commentary: This exercise comes out of a modern dance framework but it relates directly to many of the space and mime exercises used at the Workshop to design and explore space and body relationships.

Source: Modern Dance Workshop of Kasia Mistek.

Sun Salutation

A physical warm-up for stretching and centering drawn from yoga practice. The Sun Salutation begins many classes, especially those for teens and adults.

Tag and all its variations

Principle: Play.

Point of concentration: To play the game.

Optimal group size: Variable (can accommodate large groups if you have the space).

Description:
Basic Tag game: Freeze Tag
Players play Tag. Player 1 is It and tries to tag someone else in the group. Players in the group try not to get tagged. In Freeze Tag, when Player 1 tags another player, they both freeze and then wait until everyone else freezes too. When everyone is frozen, the new It begins to move, signaling everyone else to move and play Tag again.
Calls: Slow motion, double time, heavy boots, shoelaces tied together.
Source: Children's games.

Variation: Clown Tag
Game of Tag where the player must hold the spot where they were tagged throughout. This game leads to Character Walk.

Variation: Death Tag
When tagged, the new It "dies" a magnificent death, then gets up to tag another player. The means of "death" should be clear and specific (e.g. stabbed, shot, stung by bees, poisoned, etc.).

Variation: Hug Tag
Players play Freeze Tag. Person cannot be tagged if she is hugging (in physical contact) with someone else. When about to be tagged, the player will hug another player and say, "One elephant, two elephant, three elephant" directly to the player who is the It, thereby remaining safe for that duration. Player must then release hug and play continues. The It must let group disperse before trying to tag.

Variation: Impulse Tag (Touch-and-Go Tag)
Like Clown Tag, but, instead of holding the tagged spot, the player feels the impulse in the body and goes with the feeling of off-centeredness. The It keeps the new rhythm until they tag someone else. The new It goes with a new impulse. This game can lead into Character Walk.

Variation: Explosion Tag
When the new It is tagged, that player makes an explosive physical and vocal response to the tag on impulse.

Variation: Name Tag
Played similarly to Word Tag but, in this variant, the tagger says his name and subsequent players "add on" their own names. By the end, the last person tagged will be repeating all the names of the group.

Variation: Phrase Tag – see Word Tag

Variation: Scene Tag
The tagger and the taggee go into a beat of scene after the tag. The leader calls the relationships for each scene.

Variation: Story Tag
Players tell a story phrase by phrase on each tag. Similar to Word and Phrase Tag, but here the players strive for a continuous narrative. The phrase should not end the sentence. The story starts with the traditional "Once upon a time …"

Variation: Style Tag

Players begin playing Freeze Tag. Leader calls various contrasting rhythms each time a new It begins to move (slow motion, double time, heavy boots, shoelaces tied together, tip-toe tag) to get the players accustomed to changing styles. Once a motor is going, the leader tells the players to find their own styles of movement. The new It will begin to move in a style and everyone else must begin moving in that style. When everyone is moving in the same style, the It can tag another player. Players keep exploring their own movement ideas. This game can lead to Group Transformation of Sound and Movement.

Variation: Swat Tag (Good warm-up for a new group)

POC: To fake out the other player.

The players sit in a line at one end of the room. Facing them in the center of the room is a "home base" – a cube or chair. One player is It. A soft "swatter" of some kind (e.g. a rolled-up newspaper) is placed on the home base. The It takes the swatter off home base and walks around the room to where the other players are sitting. The It tags another player (below the shoulders) and must return the swatter to home base and then return to the space left by the tagged player before being tagged themselves.

Calls: Slow motion. Double time. Deepen the fake-out. Silent film. Double time. Normal. Heavy boots. Velvet slippers. Sword and cape. Bucket on head. Elizabethan costume. Get to where you are going by reaching forward instead of increasing your speed. Try to be in the same camera frame.

Commentary: Players are given two things to focus on, for example, slow motion and tagging someone. To win/to tag – to do character – creates theatrical tension. These conflicting foci are parallel to the problem of acting where one must focus on the character one is playing, on the other player, and on the audience. Each must be given attention without ignoring the other.

Variation: Two-Deep Tag

Players form two circles, one inside the other, with each player standing behind another as if paired. One player is It; one player is being chased. When the player being chased runs in front of a player in the inner circle, the outer player is released and becomes the player being chased. The It tries to tag the other player as they run around the circle. If the It tags the other player, the roles are reversed.

The player being pursued sings a song like "Row, Row, Row Your Boat." The singing player is safe when she runs in front of an inner circle person, releasing the outer player behind who becomes the one being chased and who also picks up the song. If the It tags the singing player while they are running around the circle, they switch roles. The singer becomes the It and the It becomes the new singer being pursued. The song must be passed mid-sentence with no backtracking.

Variation of Two-Deep Tag: Instead of using a song, the players can create an original story. The same rule applies. The story must be passed mid-sentence. The storyteller is the player being chased.

Variation: Word Tag

Players play Tag. When the It tags another, all freeze and the It says a word on impulse. All move again. The new It tags another player, all freeze and the new It says the word given to him, plus one of his own. Play continues, adding on words until the list becomes too long to repeat.

Calls: Get into the space of each word; say the words from your own center. Whisper. Slow-motion speech. Double time/shoelaces tied together. Sing it. Try to fill the space of the word; give each word its own values. You are sending the word to the person you tagged. Energize it. Don't get it in your throat. Sing it. If you can't sing, give it a rhythm. Get to where you are going. Don't think too much. You are passing the word to your partner.

Variation: Use a theme to explore with words, e.g. favorite foods, Halloween, winter.

Variation: Sometimes called Phrase Tag. When the It tags another player, everyone must freeze. The It begins a sentence with a phrase (two-word minimum). The new It tags another and continues the sentence with their own phrase. The object is *not* to end the sentence as the phrases are passed on. The phrases are given a theme, for example, twilight, winter, quiet, noise, about an old man. Play continues with each player adding a phrase.

Calls: Slow-motion speech. Full-body whisper. Keep the contact while saying the phrase. A phrase does not end the sentence. If the sentence is ended, the game is over.

Commentary: From Kenneth Koch – the more personal the theme, the more specific the ideas. A general theme leads to attitude.

Three-Chair Conversation

Principle: Play.

Point of concentration: To focus on and communicate to your scene partner as if you were alone.

Optimal group size: Three players at a time (can involve the whole class).

Description: Three chairs face the audience in a row. Player A sits in chair 1 and plays a character with an occupation in conversation with Player B who sits in the middle chair. Player C sits in chair 3 and plays herself in a conversation with Player B in the middle chair. The two scenes occur simultaneously with the center person attempting to be an active participant in both scenes. Player A and Player C do not acknowledge the presence of the other. When the teacher claps, the players move down one chair and start a new scene. Play continues until the entire class has had a chance to play each chair.

Calls: In this game, the teacher claps or says, "Change" to have the players move along to the next chair, join, or exit the game.

Commentary: Byrne wrote: "Though Joyce and I agree fully on the principle and the goal, I have found that the game Three-Chair Conversation (in open workshops, in classes observed, and in my own experiments) tends to encourage pettiness, bickering, and the least common denominator in the players. On the other hand, Joyce assures me that she has had some wonderful results with players of all ages. So it must be in how the game is defined and sequenced.

"Let me suggest ... this is really a double-scene game with the player in the center (Player C) maintaining a scene with Player A to her left and Player B to her right. I sometimes dramatize the separateness of the scenes by asking the players to imagine a camera on either side of the stage filming each scene (A and C), (B and C). Each scene should have its own integrity at all times. Go further if necessary – place players in the down right and down left positions as 'camera operators.' The 'camera' players can call 'cut.' By 'integrity,' it is meant that Player C (center player) stays in touch with each of her partners to the extent that were each scene viewed separately, that scene could be accepted as a valid entity. (Note: constant eye contact is neither necessary nor natural.)

"This is a very demanding game. It probably can't be solved without resorting to a very passive (therapist-like or Zen guru, perhaps) role being assumed by the center player. I've seen it done many times where it becomes an exercise in verbal virtuosity but still doesn't do the job. The game can have great value, though, in driving the center player toward concentration and the players on the sides toward verbal freedom. Variations: Players A & B: one can be neutral, a friend talking about her day, the other a Who with a mission. Both can be neutral, each can have a relationship to C, separate objectives, etc.

"'Simultaneous Rap' should not be encouraged. Every conversation has its rhythm. The game could yield to 'give-and-take' calls if the players are merely in competition in order to demonstrate verbal adroitness. Encourage 'natural' conversation vs. manic competition and showing off."

Three-Chair Conversation with Conflicting Objectives
Principle: Specificity.
Point of concentration: To find the "Action" (Stanislavski term – the ways in which we go about trying to achieve our objectives).
Optimal group size: Three players.
Description: Played similarly to Three-Chair Conversation but with the addition of conflicting objectives given to Players A and C.
Commentary: Byrne wrote: "Try to avoid objectives that will elicit petty bickering (Get her to clean her room, get her to raise your allowance, etc.). Try something like 'You need to tell her this great dream you had last night,' or 'Get her to tell you about her date last night,' and here you can indeed begin transforming ages. These are merely opening suggestions. Get her to vote for a certain person for class president, Get her to forgive you would be some others – find your own. Look for objectives that will elicit a focus on the other person rather than on the indulgence of your need. If you must do the "allowance", situation, help the mother feel badly about not being able to raise their allowance, or something like that. Give and take should be the mode here.

"Maybe we ripped this concept (like Macduff) 'untimely from its mother's womb.' Maybe the problem is that we use scene and, in fact, Beat Objectives without the grounding of Life Objectives. So give each player a balancing Life Objective. For example, if you're using 'to raise your allowance', A's Life Objective could be 'to be an artist,' B's 'to be like Mother Theresa,' C's 'to give my children a better life than the one I've had.' (If you don't know Life Objectives, sometimes called Overall Objectives, too bad. You should read Uta Hagen or Stanislavski's *An Actor Prepares* or *Building a Character*.) But it should be self-explanatory. Our daily encounters are informed by the context of who we are (obviously). One of the key markers in that conundrum is 'What do I want most from life?' I may, for example, want an electric train more than anything right now but I really want every day on the Earth for 'people to love me' or 'to be like ...'

"So this is basically the scheme:

Given: Overall objective, Scene objective, Beat objective.
POC: To find the action.
Game: Three-Chair Conflicting Objectives.
   "When they begin to play BELIEVABLY you may add transforming ages – this begins the introduction of 'To Gets.'"
Source: Byrne Piven based on Uta Hagen – conflict and objectives.

Three on a Box

Principle: Play-Explore and Heighten, Specificity, Agreement.
Point of concentration: To detail the physical qualities of an imaginary object together.
Optimal group size: Three players.
Description: Players decide on the nature of some kind of box and on what types of things it might contain. They additionally decide who they are to each other and where they are. The box could be a Christmas box full of toys, a costume trunk, a thrift-shop storage box, a box of summer clothes, an old attic trunk, a treasure chest, a laundry bag, etc. Through dialogue, players explore the contents through give and take and discover by agreement what is in the box, one piece at a time. The players must discover together the qualities of each object before it is named. Once an object is given a name, it is put aside and others are explored. To end the improv, all the team members reach for one object, finding it together. The realization of the final object should be a surprise, if the players leave themselves open to all possibilities. For example, a trunk full of old costumes. Each player will find a costume (imaginary), use it to make it real, then share it with the group. Agreement by other players will heighten and explore the object's reality.
Calls: You can't name any object until you have realized it. Naming the object won't make it happen. You have to earn the right to name it. Use texture, color, smell. Don't worry about the audience. Detail what's inside the box. Explore and heighten that object. No preconceptions. No questions. Get into the object. Keep exploring. Trust. Help. Give and take.
Variation: Combine Three on a Box with Moving a Heavy Object by having the group carry the box into the space and open it together. Agreeing on the weight and other characteristics of the box will help the group get connected.
Source: Unknown.

To Gets/Opposing Needs

Principles: Play – Impulse, Transformation.
Point of concentration: To adjust tactics based on different relationships.
Optimal group size: Two players.
Description: Players are located in a Who, What, Where situation. Player 1 has the objective of getting Player 2 to do something (e.g. to make the other player leave, to make the other player stay). Player 2 has the counter-objective and is involved in an activity that gives her a good reason to resist. Each player must supply for herself an instant reason why her objective is important. The teacher will call different relationships between the two players, first saying, "Freeze" and then making the call. A transformation is to take place. Don't spend time elaborating. Avoid questions. The Where must remain constant throughout (activity too).

Sample objectives: Get the person to: close the window; leave; stay; forgive you; give you something; let you practice; go with you; do a heavy job; leave you alone; change in some way – clothes, habits; like you; share your agony.

Calls: Try all different ways to reach your objective. Try a new way. Don't reason it out logically. Try a spectrum of different ways. Change as the relationships change.

Commentary: Don't get married to one way. I'm interested in the whole spectrum of ways to reach the objective. Transformation is a focus of this game and is a translation of Stanislavski's work with objectives and conflicts: How do I get what I want? The importance of transformation is absolutely crucial. When a new relationship is called, don't drop everything, don't rethink. Trust that the adjustment will happen. In real life, we often have the obstacle of knowing we are going to be rejected with the negative. Why is one refusing? One way to counter is that the one who is negative must have an activity that is so important that he/she cannot leave it.

Stay with the activities – it is more concrete. This focus removes all of the obligation. Trust in the transformation. Don't justify it. Understand the transformation viscerally. Continue in mid-sentence, mid-action – the moment is continued. We are never in a vacuum relating to another person – we are in a place. Interpret the conflict not so much as absolutes, but in terms of play and give and take. It must be related to play, otherwise you think your way out.

Source: Uta Hagen – conflicts and objectives.

Sample Scenes

Situation A: Two people riding a train. It is very hot. Player 1 tries to get Player 2 to open the window/Player 2 is working a crossword puzzle/First relationship – mother and daughter

Transforming relationship calls: She's your grandmother, your employer, your teenage daughter, total stranger.

Situation B: Two people hanging clothes in the yard – Player 1 tries to get Player 2 to cut hair. First relationship – mother and teenage daughter.

Transforming relationship calls: She's your maid, grandmother, total stranger, 18-year-old daughter.

Situation C: Two people setting up a new restaurant opening at 5 p.m. – Player 1 tries to get Player 2 to change clothes, get more dressed up. First relationship – boss and hostess.

Transforming relationship calls: Mother and daughter, employee and boss, mother and teenage daughter, wife and husband's ex-wife, total strangers.

Situation D: Player 1 is rehearsing for a play while Player 2 is doing his income tax. First relationship – wife and husband.

Transforming relationship calls: She's your grandmother, daughter and father, employer and employee, fiancée, total strangers.

Situation E: Player 2 to get Player 1 to lend you some money. You provide your own Where and activities.

Situation F: Player 1 is practicing something – a speech, a poem, a dance – for something very important. Player 2 tries to get him to stop practicing.

Situation G: There is a big grand piano. Player 1 wants to move it from stage left to stage right and cannot do it alone. Get Player 2 to help you.

Situation H: Player 1 loves to clean. Player 2 must get her to stop. Player 2 find an activity.

Situation I: Player 1 wants Player 2 to give up a very bad habit – something active like rearranging furniture.

Examples of relationships called: Strangers, mother–child, best friends, most important professor–student, sisters/brothers, very old grandmother–granddaughter/son, very young niece–aunt, next-door neighbors, roommate, cleaning woman–member of household, interior decorator–homeowner, adult–child.

To Gets in groups – Who, What, Where Scenes

Principles: Play, Agreement.

Point of concentration: To pursue your objective.

Optimal group size: Three or four players.

Description: Each group of players is given a situation and an overall "to get." The players in each group decide on specific details of relationships and five objects to define place that all must use.

Example of a scene game used to explore the event in a Korean folk tale, "The Clever Thief," a story about bribery of public officials.

Situation: Architect and corporate executives, for example, company representative and semi-retired president. The architect is "to get" the company rep to accept a bribe.

Players first establish place in silence relating to the objects chosen until the leader tells them to speak.

Calls: When I say, "Freeze" and point to you, give voice to your thoughts. Normal; double-time speech and action; slow-motion speech and action; 1–2 Decroux; 1 minute – find an end.

Commentary: What did the calls do for this sample scene? 1–2 Decroux forced them to listen and watch others. Double time lent energy to the scene and got exposition out of the way (usually plot gets scene stuck). Slow motion gave players a rest period. "Interior Dialogue" can clarify the now and can go with what the actor is feeling.

Variation: Scene example 2

Situation: Medical malpractice lawyer and two bridge partners involved with a speeding ticket.

Calls: Give voice to your thoughts. Repeating game – repeat the last phrase or word of previous player's dialogue.

Commentary: The Repeating game got them into play – took the pressure off. Objects would have accomplished the same thing. The purpose of double focus/game calls is to help players pay attention, help them take from each other, and get them out of playing in their heads. The games get you out of your head and into play.

Two on an Object

Principle: Agreement.

Point of concentration: To work together to communicate the same physical qualities of the object.

Optimal group size: Two players.

Description: Players work in pairs in agreement on an activity with an object, such as folding a sheet, folding a heavy sleeping bag, putting a leaf in a dining-room table, untangling two threads of yarn, or winding a ball of yarn from a skein.
Calls: Players must take in order to succeed.
Source: General.

Unacknowledged Actions
Principle: Play.
Point of concentration: To keep the scene going no matter what happens, without acknowledging the unusual actions occurring.
Optimal group size: Two players.
Description: Two people are onstage. The teacher gives them a very formal situation, like a first date or a television interview or a job interview. They begin playing the scene. When the teacher calls, "Go" or "Unacknowledged actions," one player starts to do physical actions that the other person does not acknowledge seeing. The players continue to play the scene while these strange actions are happening, but the actions can never be acknowledged or commented on. That player is performing unacknowledged actions while the other player stays in normal.

You can go back and forth between playing the scene straight and playing the unacknowledged actions. When normal is called, the players can slowly return to the original sitting position if they are caught on the floor or in some other unusual position. The teacher can keep the players "off-balance" by switching back and forth between normal playing and playing the "unacknowledged actions."

Actions can range from tossing a pillow around, tapping a foot, throwing off shoes, lying on top of chairs, moving objects or furniture, taking off clothes, lying on top of your scene partner.
Calls: Go. Normal. Continue without acknowledging that anything unusual is going on.
Commentary: This is a very difficult game. The most important part is that you never comment, acknowledge, or notice the other person's actions. Ideally, it becomes a game of subtext. This usually happens only on an advanced level of playing. When the game is really working, the actions become a subtext for what's not being expressed in the actual scene. It's also a game of catching the players in an "off-balance moment," which can open up possibilities within the improvised scene or within a scripted scene in rehearsal.
Source: Shira Piven.

What Am I Seeing? Hearing? Eating?
Principles: Play, Agreement, Specificity.
Point of concentration: Sense memory and showing agreement by their bodies and point of focus.
Optimal group size: 3–5 players.
Description: Seeing: A small group of players decide on a spectator sport or event they will be watching together (e.g. tennis, basketball, football, hockey, soccer). They go into the space, face the audience, and place their focus above and beyond the audience. The group watches the event without speaking. The point of concentration is to find the event together; to explore and heighten what others in the group are seeing.

Calls: Just watch. Don't tell us. Take from others. Don't lead the group to watching. Don't tell each other so much. Focus on each other watching that event. Let it grow together and explore and heighten it together. Find each other in the space. Know what others are doing through peripheral vision.

Something important is going to happen, for example, someone made a basket, a touchdown, a home run. Respond to it. The event is ending. Find the end. Thirty seconds.

Variations: Hearing: Players decide what kind of music they are listening to or what kind of sound environment they are in. **Eating:** Players decide on what food they are eating or what kind of meal they are eating together. What kind of **weather** or atmosphere are we in? What kind of **vehicle** are we riding in? This last game is most often called Four on a Moving Vehicle.

Commentary: The goal is to show rather than tell us. Showing is a real human being watching something. Telling describes in action what someone looks like when watching something.

Source: Spolin.

What's Between?

Principles: Play, Specificity.

Point of concentration: To play the scene without commenting on the "what's between," while letting it subtly influence behavior.

Optimal group size: Two players.

Description: Two players start a scene with a physical activity. Something has happened between them before the start of the scene. Players are not allowed to refer to the "what's between" during the scene but it should inform the scene as they play. For example, a mother and daughter are making brunch. They have had a terrible fight the night before. They may not refer directly to the fight.

Calls: Begin without talking. Continue the activity without the need to talk. You have just had the "worst" fight of your life. Nothing more is to be said. Both of you feel as though you had lost. You may talk, but you may not refer to the fight.

Commentary: After the scene, the leader might ask the audience what they observed was communicated without telling.

Variation: A group of 3–5 players quickly decide on a physical activity in a Where and choose a "what's between."

Calls: Trust. We don't have to know as long as you do. Don't obligate yourselves to funerals. Freeze. Let the "what's between" become heavily dominant.

Commentary: A "what's between" creates an actor's relationship to her material so all that she does, see or touches is informed by the subtext. This game can be a "call" for any Who, What, Where Scene. This game is similar to Unacknowledged Actions but it is not as abstract. What's Between? is more directly related to the idea of subtext and is more clearly grounded in the reality of the scene.

Source: Method work.

What's Beyond?
Principles: Play, Specificity.
Point of concentration: To communicate where you've been and where you are going through your physical behavior.
Optimal group size: One player at a time.
Description: The stage space is designated as a corridor or passage of some kind from one room or space to another. The player decides where they are coming from and where they are going. The player makes an entrance into the passageway, crosses the space, and exits to somewhere else. While making this journey, the player tries to communicate through their movement where they are coming from and where they are going. The players may use objects (e.g. they may enter carrying something or stop and find something on their way). The audience gives the player feedback by identifying what they saw.
Commentary: This exercise has its roots in Method work.
Source: Spolin.

Where games and their variations
Principles: Play, Specificity, Agreement.
Point of concentration: See individual variants.
Optimal group size: Variable.
Description: "Where" games are basically improvisational scenes. Players decide where they are, who they are to each other, and what they are doing, but that is all the pre-planning they do. They discover the nature of the scene as they play.
Source: Spolin.

Variation: Add an Object Where
Player 1 has an idea for a Where, but does not verbally share it with the group. Instead, Player 1 goes into the space and establishes an object that defines that particular place and then exits. Player 2 enters the space and must use Player 1's object and add an object of her own. The goal is to create a particular Where.
Point of concentration: To respect the space of the objects in the Where being created, so that, when an object is defined by its activity, its space is respected by the next person.
Calls: Try to use each object in a different way each time.

Variation: Activity in a Where
One player begins an activity in a Where. Others can join in and add dialogue.
Point of concentration: On what you are doing in that Where.
Calls: Detail it. The game is help. Help out with the activity. The game is hinder.

Variation: Verbalizing the Who, What, Where
Two or more players. The players go through the scene, verbally detailing the Where and every object they handle. They narrate for themselves. When dialogue is necessary, they interrupt their narration to relate to the other characters. The narration is done out loud, give and take, one at a time. Example of a situation: a family eating breakfast.
Point of concentration: To detail the Where.
Calls: Detail the eggs. Detail the coffee pot.

Variation: Six-Sided Where

Players describe the six sides of a Where (e.g. an interior room of a house). Players would describe the ceiling space, the floor space, and the four sides of the room. You can play this game in small groups as a scene exercise and also as a Give and Take game. A variant of this game includes finding three things you hate and three things you love about this Where and including that feeling in your description.

Source: David Shepherd.

Who, What, Where improvisations with game calls

Players are in groups of three or four. The groups decide on a shared activity they could be doing in a place (e.g. playing pool in a recreation hall). The scenes will be Who, What, Where with the Who as the players themselves.

Point of concentration: To engage in the activity in the Where.

The game is **Entrances and Exits**. The object is to enter and exit as many times as possible. A player cannot enter or exit without everyone's attention onstage.

Calls: Play the game. You must earn the right to enter again. Find a new way to enter. Find a new way to exit.

The game is **Verbalizing the Where**. Detail any objects you handle or any action you do in the Where in third person.

The game is now **Contact**. Players must make physical contact before they may speak. Each time they speak, they must have made a new contact.

Calls: Hands are dead. Elbows are dead. Contact. Find a new part of your body to make contact with.

The game is **Soliloquy** or **Interior Monologue**. A player steps out of the scene and addresses the audience directly.

The game is **Close-up**. The soliloquy is taken as a close-up to the audience.

Calls: Make a connection across the distance that's really there.

The game is **Give and Take**. Only one player may talk or move at a time; even an eyelash takes. If you take, you must take strongly; you must give at any time.

Calls: Anything is a take. One at a time. Give and take.

Other calls commonly used: Slow motion/double time, melodrama, modern dance, opera, gibberish. No talking unless absolutely necessary. Repeating game, one word, 1–2 Decroux, contact, gibberish, slow motion/double time, whisper/hard of hearing, double scene, give and take, entrances and exits, camera (intensify your focus on whoever has stage) – close up, medium shot, long shot, melodrama/soap opera, sing/opera, freeze and voice your own thoughts as character/as actor, help/hinder, agreement, all must use any object, all must use one object, narrate in third person (describe where/action), what's beyond, what's between (subtext), explore and heighten a word/a relationship/an emotion, silence/no speaking, rock the boat, hook up and twist, scene transformation, hook up and extend, dance styles.

Where with Five Objects

Principle: Play-Impulse, Explore and Heighten, Agreement.

Points of concentration: To show where you are through objects. To make sure everyone in the scene uses all five objects.

Optimal group size: 3–5 players.

Description: Players decide on one place and five objects in that place. They are to show where they are by the way they handle the imaginary objects. They also decide who they are to one another. This game does not emphasize character work, but it is important to know who you are in a scene.

Calls: When you are ready, say, "Curtain." Help each other use all five objects. Two scenes going on – give and take. Fifteen seconds to end.

Commentary: In picking the Where, try to avoid the over-obvious or over-exotic. If you do decide on somewhere over-obvious, your burden is to know exactly what kind of place it is (e.g. a kitchen). What kind of kitchen? A restaurant kitchen? A tiny apartment kitchen? A state-of-the art kitchen?

Don't be afraid if we don't get it. No need to tell everything. Showing vs. telling takes time. As players, you must always be in agreement even if it is an argument. You can be out front about admitting mistakes – honest moment. Leave imaginary people out of improvisations as much as possible. Trusting the objects and really using them will bring the space to life! When not worried about personal obligations but when in the moment and connected to what you have to do (POC) – achieve the moment of play! Anchors allow play – objects, texture, color, detail, precision in the use of objects, a sense of where things are, etc. As actors our job is to perform marvelously and not to deny that we are players.

Where Relay

Points of concentration: To make contact with the object established by the new player before exiting the space. To establish the physical qualities of the object and its use.

Optimal group size: 8–16 players, playing two at a time.

Description: Players decide on a Where and the location of the entrance/exit. Some successful Wheres include backstage at a theatre, or a place from a story. Player 1 enters the space and establishes an object by using it. Player 2 enters the space, relates to Player 1's object, and establishes an object of her own. Player 1 must make contact with Player 2's object before he can leave the scene. Player 3 enters and establishes another object. Player 2 must make contact with Player 3's object before she can leave the scene. And so on through as many players as you want. In this way, a Where is created in a series of two-person scenes.

Calls: You must make contact with the new object before you leave. Make sure the other player can see what you are doing. Accomplish your task.

Commentary: In this game, the players essentially create a one-act play. In this game, focus on the other player is crucial. In order for a player to leave, they must see the new object so they can make contact with it. Keep the players focused on their tasks to maintain a forward movement for the scene. Players should not get bogged down in playwriting.

Source: Byrne Piven.

Who Am I? (Waiting for a Bus)
Principles: Play, Specificity.
Point of concentration: To communicate who you are.
Optimal group size: 4–5 players.
Description: A space is designated as a bus stop. Players enter the space one at a time to wait for the bus. As they wait, they focus on who they are and let that inform their movement.

Players may talk but it is not necessary. The scene should end in a freeze. The audience gives feedback as to what they have come to know about the characters as they watched the scene.
Calls: Who are you? Where are you going? What do you do for a living? How old are you? The bus is late. It may be your bus way down there. It's a block away now. End in a freeze.
Source: Spolin.

Who Started the Motion?
Principle: Agreement.
Point of concentration: To follow the leader without letting on who the leader is.
Optimal group size: Variable.
Description: Players stand in a circle. One player goes out of the room. The players left choose a leader who begins making movements that the rest follow. The player who left the room returns and must walk continuously around the inside of the circle of players and try to guess who is leading the changing motions. They get three guesses.
Variation: No one leads, all of inner circle are in mirror.
Calls: Trick the player in the middle. Keep walking. Change your movements quickly. See how much you can see (to the player in the middle).
Commentary: The movement (in mirror) flowed organically. That POC changed the game, changed the focus of the group, and moved the players into a different space. Each new movement came out of the one before. After three guesses, if the player is unsuccessful in finding the leader, reveal the leader and start a new game.
Source: Children's game.

Word Toss
Principle: Agreement.
Points of concentration: To make contact through the space by saying and throwing the word simultaneously. To express the feeling tone of the word through movement and sound.
Optimal group size: Variable.
Description: Players position themselves at various points within the playing area or in a circle. From those positions, Player 1 makes contact with another player across the space by throwing a word out into the space. Player 2 will catch that word and then throw one of her own across the space to Player 3 and so on. Leader can give themes for the words (e.g. spring).
Calls: Start with words for colors. Throw the word across the space. Make contact. Say the words in a full-body whisper. Slow-motion speech.

Commentary: Ball Toss can be the warm-up game leading into Word Toss. After using words for colors, the leader can call a theme (e.g. spring, circus, Halloween, or use words of dialogue from a story or scene being worked on that day). The point of the game is to fill the space of the word, giving it its unique value. How does "red" sound different from "purple"?
Source: General.

Yes game

Principle: Play-Impulse, Explore and Heighten, Agreement.
Points of concentration: To play the game. To send your energy out to others. To explore and heighten sound and movement given to you.
Optimal group size: Variable – can usually accommodate an entire class.
Description:
Stage 1: Players stand in a large circle. Player 1 says their own name as they point to another player across the circle. That player does the same thing – points to someone as they say their own name. Play continues this way until players feel comfortable that they are getting to know other players' names.
Stage 2: Now when a player points to someone else in the circle, they say that player's name instead of their own. Play continues along these lines until everyone has been included at least once and everyone appears to know at least a number of names.
Stage 3: Now the game gets a bit more complicated. Player 1 will point to another player (e.g. Player 2). Player 2 must say "Yes" to Player 1 before Player 1 can move out of the place they are standing in the circle. The "Yes" is essentially giving permission to the player to move. Player 1 starts to walk toward Player 2 to take Player 2's space. Player 2 must get permission from someone else to vacate their space and open it up for Player 1. Play continues with players pointing to others, getting permission to move (the other saying "yes"), and moving to the new space. It is very important that a player not move until given permission. This rule is the difficult part of the game. Once the players get into a rhythm and work out the kinks, clearly executing the rules, the teacher can start to "play" with the game.
Calls: You can't move until you get permission. Play faster. Think less.
Variation: At any stage in the game, the teacher can tell the players to begin to play with the sounds of the names or the yes – varying energy, intention, or rhythms – slow motion, double time. Calls like "full-body whisper" and "hard of hearing" can help the players start to experiment. The teacher can tell the players to take what they are given and build on that, thus moving the play into an "explore-and-heighten" situation. All these calls help the players get connected and keep them "off-balance."
Commentary: The Yes game is an excellent game for learning names in a first class, but it is also a good warm-up for any class, especially when the play moves into exploring and heightening the words and taking from each other.
Source: Unknown.

Index